Great Martial Arts Movies

Great Martial Arts Movies

From Bruce Lee to Jackie Chan...and More

Ric Meyers

Original research associates:
Amy Harlib
Bill Palmer
Karen Palmer

Citadel Press
Kensington Publishing Corp.
www.kensingtonbooks.com

Citadel Press books are published by

Kensington Publishing Corp.
850 Third Avenue
New York, NY 10022

All Kensington titles, imprints, and distributed lines are
available at special quantity discounts for bulk purchases
for sales promotions, premiums, fund raising, educational,
or intitutional use. Special book excerpts or customized
printings can also be created to fit specific needs, For
details, write or phone the office of the Kensington special
sales manager: Kensington Publishing Corp., 850 Third
Avenue, New York, NY 10022, attn: Special Sales
Department, phone 1-800-221-2647.

First printing April 2001

10 9 8 7 6 5 4 3 2 1

Printed in the United States of America

Library of Congress Cataloging-in-Publication Data

Meyers, Richard, 1953–
    Great martial arts movies : from Bruce Lee to
Jackie Chan and more / Richard Meyers.
        p.   cm.
    "A Citadel Press book."
    Rev. ed. of: Martial Arts movies / by Richard
Meyers . . . [et al.]. c1985.
    Filmography: p.
    ISBN 0–8065–2026–4 (pb.)
    1. Hand-to-hand fighting, Oriental, in motion
pictures.   I.   Martial arts movies.   II.   Title.
PN1995.9.H3M48   1999
791.43'655—dc21   99–30571
                                        CIP

As before, as always:
To our masters, mentors, and friends
(not necessarily in that order)

Contents

Preface

For readers of *Martial Arts Movies: From Bruce Lee to the Ninjas* (or, as the trade paperback was known, *From Bruce Lee to the Ninjas: Martial Arts Movies*), some of the following pages may seem familiar. That's because, although much has changed in the fifteen years since the original book was published, some things haven't.

Therefore, the China and Japan chapters are virtually the same because their countries' history and contributions to the genre remain unchanged. Also, the facts of Bruce Lee's life, the beginning of Jackie Chan's career, and the Shaw Brothers' kung-fu–film legacy are the same as they ever were. However, everything taking place after 1984 is either new or improved, or both.

Therefore, to better serve you, our valued reader (and to keep things consistent), I continue to differentiate between the original Asian titles and their American names, supply the movies' original release dates in their countries of origin, occidentalize the Japanese names (Toshiro Mifune in lieu of Mifune Toshiro), and simplify the Cantonese versions of all the Chinese characters (Liu Chia Liang instead of Liu-chia Liang, etc.).

Some assembly is required. Your mileage may vary. Void where prohibited by law. Reflected objects may be closer than they appear.

Acknowledgments

The kindness of friends and associates has been invaluable during the past twenty years of study—especially that of Amy Harlib, Bill Palmer, and Karen Palmer, whose research contributions helped fuel the original 1985 book *Martial Arts Movies: From Bruce Lee to the Ninjas.*

Great thanks, past, present, and future, also go to: Lou Israel and Zita Siegel of World Northal (a.k.a. WW Entertainment); Raymond Chow and Russell Cawthorne, of Golden Communications Ltd.; Jackie Chan, Willie Chan, and Solon So, of Jackie and Willie Productions; Sammo Hung and Bojon Productions; Tsui Hark and Nansun Shi, of Film Workshop; John Woo, Michele Yeoh, and Terence Chang; Peter Chow and Fannie Ng, at Peter Chow International; Curtis Wong, Dave Cater, Sandra Siegel, and all the fine folks at Curtis F. Wong Enterprises; Helen Soo, Frank Djeng, and Tai Seng Video Marketing; Jackson Hung and Matthew Tse, of Ocean Shores Video Ltd.; Jonathan Ross and Alan Marke, of Channel X Ltd.; Miss Choi Suk-kuen of the Hong Kong International Film Festival; Rudy De Blasio and Rick Sullivan, of Theater Management Associates; Bill Connolly and Martial Arts Movie Associates; Pak Chan and Superior Oriental; Robert Tam and the Sun Sing Cinema; Ronald Lee and NYUE; A&E's *Biography*; Alan Goldberg and ABC News Productions; CEL Productions; Asian Cinevision; New Line Cinema; Renée Witterstaetter; Caroline Vié and Jean-Marc Toussaint; Fact-checker supreme Lana Zukowski; David Owens and the Japan Society; Merlin David and Samurai Video; Greg Yokoyama and Video Action; Larry Bensky, Seaton Chang, Rolanda Chu, David Chute, Fredric Dannen, F. J. DeSanto, Clyde Gentry III, Gere Ladue, Victor Lim, Gine Lui, Bey Logan, Joe Ragus, Mark Schreiber, Van Washington, Tom Weisser, Laurine White, and Jeff Yang.

PHOTO CREDITS

Cannon Films, Circle Releasing Corp., Columbia Pictures, Eternal Films, National General Films, New Line Cinema, New World Pictures, Ocean Shores Ltd., Seasonal Films, Tai Seng Video Marketing, Warner Bros., Inc. and World Northal.

All photos from Shaw Brothers movies are © Shaw Brothers and used with the permission of WW Entertainment.

All photos from Golden Harvest movies are © Golden Harvest and used with the permission of the Golden Communications Company Ltd.

Introduction

The history of [Asia] and the martial arts movie is a grand one, and this volume is a tour of it. To consider every [martial art movie] would be impossible, not to mention pretty horrible. Instead, these pages will tell you what to look for as well as what to watch out for. We will trumpet the best and decry the worst. From Enter the Dragon *to* Kung-fu Zombies, *get ready. This is the martial-arts movie.*

—From the introduction to *From Bruce Lee to the Ninjas: Martial Arts Movies*

"The man who started it all now gets the last word."

That's what an advertising friend said when I told him about this—the new book that would follow up the groundbreaking *Martial Arts Movies: From Bruce Lee to the Ninjas.* At that time almost no American knew anything about Jackie Chan, Sammo Hung, John Woo, Michelle Yeoh, Chow Yun Fat, Maggie Cheung, Jet Li, and many others. And while millions enjoyed the Black Belt Theater and Drive-in Movie series of classic Shaw Brothers kung-fu films syndicated on television around the country, almost no one really understood what they were actually about. I was one of them. After writer, artist, and actor Larry Hama and photo stylist Linda Sampson brought me to Jackie Chan's

original *Drunken Master* (a.k.a. *Drunk Monkey in a Tiger's Eye* in Hong Kong) in 1978, I ran to libraries and bookstores to find out more about these "comic books come to life"—only there was nearly nothing. So, with the redoubtable research assistance of kung-fu film fan Amy Harlib and jiu-jitsu professors Bill and Karen Palmer, I wrote a book myself.

A lot has happened since then. WW Entertainment, who syndicated the Black Belt Theater series, sent out hundreds of the books to educate their television stations. Ocean Shores, then the largest distributor of Chinese kung-fu flicks in the world, did the same to inform their video outlets. After that, television stations and magazines started calling us directly. Billy and Karen became the movie reviewers on the Madison Square Garden cable channel's *Martial Arts World*, and I became the monthly movie columnist for *Inside Kung-Fu.*

All that was merely prelude to when Jonathan Ross of the *Incredibly Strange Film Show* called me from London. Our subsequent collaboration resulted in landmark Jackie Chan and Tsui Hark-John Woo television specials viewed by millions on Channel 4 in England and the Discovery cable channel in the United States. After that, word spread quickly, helped along, I've been told, by my continual screenings of these movies at movie studios, science-fiction conventions, comic-book companies, and film schools. (In fact, one of the most flattering moments of my professional life came when a group of influential American writers and producers played a game of "six degrees of me," tracing their initial discovery of these films, within six incidents, back to my efforts.)

Public demand eventually became so loud that even Hollywood couldn't ignore it. The floodgates started to open, with these films infiltrating film festivals, video stores, cable movie channels, bookshops, and then, ultimately, the studios themselves. But just as Hong Kong actors and directors were excelling in every area of the English-speaking cinema, the United Kingdom's lease ran out, and Hong Kong, that motherlode of martial arts movies, returned to Chinese rule in July 1997.

So we've come full circle. No longer is the genre the most misunderstood, underrated, and vilified ever screened (thanks, hopefully in no small way, to our efforts). American studios have seen to it that the entire world knows that the martial arts star is also the stuntperson, creating a verisimilitude other action stars can't approach. Now millions more know that the best martial arts movies are kinetic combinations of emotional opera and acrobatic ballet. They now know what we knew then: that these are great movies which dare to take their action seriously, emotionally, and straight.

In the following pages you will find martial arts movies at their exploitively thrilling lows, their exhilaratingly delirious highs, and everywhere in between. Happily, the fruits of our labors continue to blossom, and the talents of the aforementioned Asian filmmakers, and many others, will continue to delight an ever-growing group of fans. But make no mistake: the golden age of kung-fu films and the Hong Kong New Wave is over. Long live the platinum age of martial arts movies.

RIC MEYERS

Great Martial Arts Movies

Bruce Lee: The King of Kung-fu

To most of the world, the martial arts movie can be summed up in one name: Bruce Lee. It was he, more than anyone else, who established the power of the genre internationally. It was his superlative martial-arts ability and canny filmmaking knowledge which touched audiences everywhere, leaving a mark that cannot be erased.

But it is also Bruce Lee who, through a series of unfortunate occurrences, set a trap for the martial arts film that it is just beginning to escape from. Had Bruce Lee lived, perhaps this trap would never have been sprung. But he did not live and his mysterious, frustrating death marked both the beginning and the end of the martial arts movie genre.

The beginnings for the teacher and filmmaker started November 27, 1940, when Lee Jun Fan was born to Lee Hoi Chuen and his wife Grace in San Francisco. While Orientals always put their family names first, Americans do it the other way around. Since the lad was born in the United States, the hospital needed an Anglicized name. Reportedly, it was the supervising doctor, Mary Glover, who conceived the name Bruce Lee, for the record.

Bruce was born into a family of two older girls, Agnes and Phoebe, and an older brother, Peter. Not too long after he was born, they were joined by another brother, Robert. To them, Bruce was known as Lee Yuen Kam, an adaptation of his original name. They were a theatrical family, with Lee Hoi Chuen a renowned actor on both American coasts and in Hong Kong. Just three months after his birth, Bruce joined his father onstage, in a production of *Golden Gate Girl*. Although hardly a triumph, it was a start.

When the family returned to the Orient soon after, Bruce continued his thespian ways while starting a few new distressing ones. He was a thin, small, and somewhat sickly child, prone to nightmares and sleepwalking. Compensation came in the form of energy. He always seemed to be moving, never satisfied with being still. Friends and family remember Bruce as an extremely positive, assured youth, and his assurance became brazen as he matured.

His progress was marked by appearances in Hong Kong movies, starting in 1946, when he was six years old. The director of one of his father's films was impressed by Bruce's attitude and cast him in a small part for the picture *Birth of a Man*, which was also known by the title *The Beginning of a Boy*. Only a year later, Bruce was already starring in films such as *My Son A-Chang*, in which he played the title role of a street-smart kid trying to get ahead in the sweatshop world of Hong Kong. His name then was Lung or Siu Lung, which means "Dragon" or "Little Dragon."

Bruce Lee's first success in America: playing Kato in
The Green Hornet.

Even at the age of seven, Lee's screen persona was strong. He was a clever, capable, but short-tempered little ruffian who specialized in the scowl, the pout, the stare, and the slow burn. This character served him on the streets as well. Ignoring the lessons of his films and his family, Lee, in his own words, "went looking for fights."

By the time he hit his teens, he was already well equipped to handle those fights. He was a natural dancer, becoming quite proficient in the cha-cha, and his natural grace lent itself to wing chun, the physically economical but brutal martial art he decided to follow. Some nights he would dance; other nights he would scour the streets for a fight. Already he was showing signs of obsessive behavior.

He would read voraciously, which led to the need for glasses. He would play practical jokes, which only became serious if he were personally challenged by his victim. Oftentimes it was no fun playing with Bruce Lee; his desire to win at all costs was almost consuming. Even when he lost a street fight, he would find a way to make it seem as if he had won. And all the time he exercised and trained—wanting not only to convince himself he was the best, but to actually be the best.

The tragedy of his ultimate fate was to be played out on a minor scale in the Hong Kong of 1959. The more famous Bruce Lee became as a teenage movie actor, the more uncontrollable he became in real life. Things came to a head with the premiere of his most successful film of that time, *The Orphan*. Although Wu Chu Fan was the ostensible star, playing a teacher who lost his family in a Japanese air raid, Bruce all but stole the show as Ah Sam, an orphan who survived as a street thief. Again, all the acting skills which were to lead to his superstardom were well in evidence here. Lee's emotional inten-

sity was powerful. He portrayed frustration beautifully as on-screen schoolmates laughed at his lack of education and his peers were embarrassed by his bad manners. When he finally fights back, threatening his teachers and fellows with a knife during class, it is a cathartic scene which Lee plays to the hilt, taunting and laughing.

Ah Sam returns to his gang, which masterminds the kidnapping of a rich man's son, but he can't forget the kindness of his teachers. He returns when Wu Chu Fan, playing Ho See Kei, discovers that Ah Sam is his own long-lost son, separated from him in the aforementioned air raid. Repentant, Ah Sam leads the police to the gang's hideout and single-handedly saves the kidnapped boy. The film concludes with Lee tearfully begging forgiveness from his father, teachers, schoolmates, and ancestors.

On-screen, Bruce Lee begged forgiveness. Off-screen, he begged from no one and gave nothing. Things were getting so difficult for his family that Bruce went back to America. The story goes that the Shaw Brothers Studio—the most powerful movie company in Hong Kong—offered him a contract which his mother forbade him to take, all but banishing him to the United States, praying that education there would straighten him out.

GO WEST, YOUNG MAN

So, at the moment when Bruce Lee was to gain his greatest success, he was forced to retreat. The exile, self-imposed or not, had served its purpose. Bruce Lee was a stranger in a strange land at the age of eighteen, forced to work all the harder to excel. At first he enrolled at the Edison Technical High School in Seattle, but moved on to the University of Washington. His energy did not lessen with maturity, but it was directed.

7

Delving deeper and deeper into the martial arts, Lee worked in restaurants for a while, but soon began teaching kung-fu.

Kung-fu, which is also referred to as wushu (a Chinese version of the words *martial arts*) and gung-fu, is a method of combat developed in China by Shaolin Temple monks. It is a brilliant method of fighting based on the nature of humanity and the animals that inhabit the earth. It was so effective in its use—and equally effective in developing the student to his or her optimum mental and physical capabilities—that it spread throughout the Orient.

Legend has it being taught in Japan, where it developed into aikido, judo, and karate—the latter a two-stage development of Tang boxing, which came from the Ryukyu Islands. From there it spread south to become the vicious Thai boxing, and north to Korea where it became the impressive tae kwon do.

Bruce Lee had a foundation in tai chi chuan, which had been taught to him by his father, over which was the effective structure of *wing chun*, taught to him by his master, Yip Man. He thought deeply about his skills and developed them further while attending the University of Washington. Lee's exhaustive research into fighting and self-perfection led to his writing the book *Chinese Gung-Fu: The Philosophical Art of Self-Defense* in the early 1960s. By 1964, the demons that had led him to the streets were now pointing him toward Hollywood.

The year 1964 was an important one in Lee's life. He married Linda Emery, moved to California, and met Ed Parker, Chuck Norris, Bob Wall, and Mike Stone. They were all at the Ed Parker International Karate Championships and became fast friends.

"He did a demonstration there and I won the grand championship in the heavyweight division," Stone remembers. "Afterward we went out for a Chinese dinner. We became friends and would work out together one day a week. I would work out with him one day, Chuck Norris would work out with him another and so would Joe Lewis." All three men would become influential in the American martial arts movie market.

But it was Bruce Lee who created the market the other men would enter, and the man who put Lee's foot in the door was Ed Parker. He had filmed Bruce's performance at the internationals and showed them to his student, Jay Sebring, who, in turn, showed them to William Dozier, who needed a Kato for his *Green Hornet* television show in 1966.

Television producer Dozier was riding high that year with the success of *Batman*, a show that camped up Bob Kane's famous comic-book character. The ABC TV network wanted another superhero to follow on the "Caped Crusader's" heels, and Dozier chose George W. Trendle's popular radio character, the masked master crime fighter known as the Green Hornet. Behind the mask was Britt Reid, created by Trendle as the grandnephew of John Reid, better known as the Lone Ranger, who was also created by Trendle.

Fortunately for Bruce Lee, Dozier did not eliminate the character of Britt's Oriental manservant and chauffeur. In half-hour episodes which lasted less than a year, Kato piloted the Green Hornet's supercar, "the Black Beauty," through uninspiring battles against organized crime. Dozier eliminated the outlandish villains of the Batman show but kept its unrealistic approach. The only time the show took off was when Bruce Lee did.

More than the Green Hornet's guns, which shot gas and needles, and his armor-plated, gadget-laden car, what sold the show to its preteen audience was Lee's kung-fu. Whenever Kato got out from behind the wheel and started kicking, the show started clicking. But as Mike Stone noted, "They had to restrain Bruce as Kato, because there was a star."

That star was Van Williams, who, although he became a friend and student of Lee's, couldn't convince the powers that be to give

Bruce Lee in the climactic moment of his first film, Fists of Fury. *Notice the man-shaped hole in the wall behind him.*

Lee more to do. *The Green Hornet* died quickly, but Lee's reputation only grew. By that time he had developed his own form of martial arts, a form commonly referred to as *jeet kune do*—"the way of the intercepting fist."

Jeet kune do was only a name, a label which came to irritate Bruce Lee. At first it was known as *jun fan gung fu*. Then it became "Bruce Lee's Tao of Chinese Gung-Fu—Using No Way As Way; Having No

The incredible leap that ends The Chinese Connection, *Bruce Lee's second and, some say, finest film.*

Limitation As Limitation." It was Lee's unique, simple, effective method of fighting, which stressed continual improvement and the joy derived therefrom. "Practice seriously," he said, "but don't seriously practice." In other words, work for the love of it.

By the time *The Green Hornet*'s stinger was removed in 1967, Lee had experienced a variety of setbacks and breakthroughs. His father had died in 1965, but his son Brandon had been born the same year. He attended his father's funeral in Hong Kong, but returned to California to continue pursuing the goal of stardom. His method of direct, practical kung-fu attracted a notable following, including many actors, writers, producers, and directors. This led to his being continually tapped for guest-starring roles.

In the two years following his stint as Kato, he built up his school's reputation, and therefore his own. When the entertainment industry was again ready for him, he had three jeet kune do schools, one in Seattle, one in Oakland, and another in Los Angeles. He played a martial arts teacher on an episode of *Ironside*, starring Raymond Burr; he was a technical adviser for the 1969 Matt Helm movie *The Wrecking Crew*, starring Dean Martin; but his most impressive work came in the 1969 movie *Marlowe* and the 1971 TV series *Longstreet*.

The film starred James Garner as author Raymond Chandler's popular hard-boiled private eye, Philip Marlowe. Lee costarred as a martial arts enforcer of the villain. His is probably the most memorable scene in an otherwise merely decent translation of Chandler's novel *The Little Sister*. To prove his prowess, Lee trashes Marlowe's office with just his arms and legs, culminating in a stunning kick that breaks the ceiling's hanging lamp.

After that, Marlowe's simplistic handling of the deadly character is forced and unrealistic. After taunting Lee with attacks on his manhood while standing on a balcony ledge, Garner merely steps out of the way as Lee delivers a flying kick that takes him over the bannister and down to his death. After the precision of the office attack, this sequence didn't work at all. Many more scoffed at the stupidity of the scene than laughed at the supposed cleverness of the detective.

The two-part *Longstreet* episode showcased Lee to better effect. "The Way of the Fist" was written by the series creator, Sterling Silliphant, a fan of Lee's. He had Lee coaching the blind insurance investigator, Mike Longstreet (played by James Fran-

ciscus), in self-defense so the man could trash a bunch of bullies who had mugged him at the outset of the show. In this role, Lee spoke eloquently of the martial arts and the mental serenity necessary to master them.

The two portrayals were perfect bookends—one all flash and the other all substance. While few in the United States were overly impressed, the Orient was buzzing. *The Green Hornet* had premiered there three years after its premiere in the United States, and Lee took the opportunity to promote himself to the Chinese audience. Legend has it that a kung-fu display during a talk show so impressed Raymond Chow, head of Golden Communications Company Ltd.— otherwise known as Golden Harvest—that he signed Lee to a contract to do a movie called *The Big Boss*, directed by Lo Wei.

THE BIG TIME

The "legend" was a bit misleading. The truth is that almost every major Hong Kong film company bid for Bruce's participation, but after almost a year Raymond Chow secured the actor-teacher's services to make the movie, on location, in Thailand. To American eyes, this film seems like just another in a long line of cheaply made exploitation pictures featuring a poor man persecuted by the corrupt rich, but it was nearly revolutionary for the Hong Kong movie industry. Up until 1970, almost all of the movies being made there were grand tales of legendary heroes, all promoting the gentle philosophy of Confucius.

Then, seemingly quite suddenly, directors like Chang Cheh, writers like I Kuang, and stars like Wang Yu were tearing up theater screens with violent visions of vengeance. That opened the door for Lo Wei to write and direct *The Big Boss*. Whether Wei collaborated with Bruce Lee on the script or was simply influenced by the actor's intensity is a

Bruce Lee directs then unknown karate champion Chuck Norris for the American's entrance in Return of the Dragon.

moot point. *The Big Boss* turned out to reflect many Lee images which would recur throughout his painfully short career.

Lo Wei had started in the film industry as an actor in 1948 and became a director in 1957. He worked steadily through the sixties and joined Raymond Chow on the ground floor of Golden Harvest. By coincidence or not, for *The Big Boss* he penned a tale of a

troubled young man who was unable to avoid fighting. He must leave his family in Hong Kong to toil in Bangkok at an ice factory, and promises his parents not to fight. Therefore, he must hold his prodigious kung-fu talents in check while the bosses persecute him and his associates.

But *The Big Boss* is not only a story of class persecution. The "Big Boss" of the title, played by Han Ying Chieh (who was also the fight coordinator on the film—known in the Orient by the title martial arts instructor), is using the ice factory as a front for drug running. When Lee gets too close to the truth, the bosses first try to buy him off, then seduce him with women, and finally try to kill him. But they only succeed in killing all his friends, after which he explodes with a barely controlled rage that thrilled audiences.

The scene is now considered a classic. Lee finds the drugs embedded in ice, and then finds his friend the same way. He is surrounded by about twenty knife-, club-, and chain-wielding thugs in the eerie, red-lit ice house interior. With mounting anger clearly etched on his face, he takes the villains apart in a battle that combines dramatic action with nearly cartoonlike violence. Aside from Lee's strong screen presence, the most memorable feature is the moment when a man Lee has hurled through a wall leaves a hole in his exact "man-shape."

From that climactic and cathartic scene, Lee races to the Big Boss's palatial estate to take on the main bad guy and all his minions. It is on the lawn of the mansion where the two antagonists have a knife fight, showcasing two more Lee trademarks—the wounds that inspire Lee on to greater heights of heroism, and the tension-building pauses that add to Lee's acting style. When Lee is cut by the villian's blade, he stops, tastes the blood, and moves forward, always letting the tension build. *The Big Boss* represented the first time moviegoers heard Lee's now trademark animal screeches clearly.

All three main filmmakers—Chow, Wei, and Lee—were happy enough with the results to immediately start work on a follow-up, but none had an inkling as to the first's effect. The trio were already at work on the second movie when word came in. *The Big Boss* was a gigantic success. Made for only $100,000, it made five times that much in Hong Kong alone. Bruce Lee was now, officially, a star.

The next film was to improve on the first at least one hundred percent. The basic structure was still there: a consummate martial artist is persecuted by bigots and snobs who also happen to be insidious villains. The martial artist takes on the superior forces of the villains and wins, but at a terrible cost. In *The Big Boss*, it was his freedom; in the finale, Lee was arrested by Thai police. In *Fist of Fury*, he would pay with his life.

The Chinese made movies the way some people make cars—on an assembly line. With such a gigantic population to supply, Oriental filmmakers in the early 1970s could wrap up a normal production in seventy-two hours, a "big-budget extravaganza" in a week. *Fist of Fury* premiered in Hong Kong less than five months after *The Big Boss* but proved to be at least twice the picture.

The production values of the second film made the first look even tackier than it was. It cost twice as much, but made twice as much as well. Again, Lo Wei is credited as director and writer, although it is said that prolific screenwriter I Kuang had a hand in the script. Whoever the author was, this time everything was in place—the cinematography, the costumes, the choreography—all were impressive to any eyes, Occidental or Oriental.

Here, Lee seems to be more in control than ever; it is his performance and skill that holds the movie together. This was no easy task, considering that when the audience first sees him, he is so overcome by grief at the death of his martial-arts school master (*sifu*) that he leaps into his sifu's grave and onto the coffin, clawing and crying. From there on, Lee's body became an extension of his mind.

Set in the Shanghai of the late 1920s, the film depicts a society in which the Chinese are all but spit upon by Japanese rulers. The racism has become so manifest that a rival Japanese martial arts school has poisoned Lee's sifu. It appears that almost every wak-

John Saxon beats on Bolo (Yang Sze) during an important bout in Enter the Dragon.

ing moment of the Japanese rivals was used to persecute Lee's school and its students. Lee, playing a fighter named Chen, has a much shorter fuse this time. He has promised no one to hold back. Using a series of disguises, including that of a rickshaw puller and, in a delightful turn, of a grinning, mincing phone repairman, Lee discovers the murderers and takes them apart.

The mood of the picture is set by Lee smashing a "No Dogs or Chinese" sign outside a Shanghai park with a *Marlowe*-type kick. From there he wades through the Japanese school, taking out all the students, the sword master, a brawny Russian fighter (played by jeet kune do student Robert Baker), and finally the head of the school. It is this series of bouts that makes up the heart of the action.

Lee is nothing short of masterful in each. Although Han Ying Chieh is again credited as the martial arts instructor, Lee's approach is plainly evident throughout. When fighting the Russian, he is caught in a leg scissors but bites the man in order to escape. Then his arms swirl stroboscopically in front of the confused opponent. He finally faces his main adversary with the infamous nunchaku—the small clubs joined by a short length of chain which Lee made famous.

Lee supposedly learned the particular nunchaku skill with his star student Daniel Inosanto. However he learned it, he had chosen a particularly impressive, esoteric weapon with which to dazzle viewers. To see Lee swirl and spin the sticks with ridiculous

ease was to experience pure enchantment. The moment of the character Chen's greatest triumph was the moment of Lee's ascension to superstardom. He had gone from being a suprahuman fighter to being a superhero.

Lo Wei himself played the Chinese policeman caught between his loyalty to his people and his Japanese masters. It is his sad duty to bring Chen in for the murders of the Japanese-school fighters. Lee, bare-chested and brazen, gives himself up to the cop, but not to the mob of rifle-toting Japanese outside.

was as fast, as precise, and as good as he looked.

And Lee knew it. No more would he listen to either Chow or Wei. After creating his own Concord Productions, he struck a deal with Golden Harvest to coproduce his next film, which would star, be directed by, written by, and choreographed by Bruce Lee. He had said all he could say on the themes of his first two movies. He wanted to explore other directions, in waters Lo Wei did not want to navigate. As a result, *Way of the Dragon* opened in Hong Kong just nine months after *Fist of Fury*.

Essentially, this is Bruce Lee's last film. It is the only film he controlled completely and the only film in which his approach was primary. In it he played an unassuming but fiercely patriotic and surprisingly clever young martial artist, Tang Lung, who travels to Rome to help relatives run a Chinese restaurant. Although the first part of the movie chronicles largely humorous "stranger in a strange land" confrontations with the English and Italian languages and Western ways, Lee slowly strips his character of his surface naïveté to reveal a supremely capable hero beneath.

Fist of Fury ends by freeze-framing on a tremendous leap by Lee, seemingly right into his persecutors' bullets, defiant to the end.

To say the Oriental audience went crazy would be an understatement. Unlike the screen heroes before him, Lee did not turn the other cheek, did not remain humble and unassuming. He stood up and shouted, "I'm Chinese and I'm proud of it!" Not only that, he had much to be proud of. His acting and especially his fighting skill were supreme, leaving other action actors miles behind. Lee

It starts slowly. First Tang Lung shows the other restaurant employees the superiority of "Chinese boxing" over other styles in the alley behind the restaurant. But when racketeers arrive looking for protection money, the lessons become more pointed. Lee is taken back behind the bistro by the gangster's hoods to be "taught a lesson." Instead, he teaches them a lesson in a nicely structured fight which culminates with the appearance of the nunchaku.

The other side of Bruce Lee's mercurial personality: whimsical, mischievous, and clever. From Enter the Dragon.

Probably the sharpest moment here is when the hoods' leader manages to grab a nunchaku. At first he seems to think that he will be imbued with some sort of magical power simply by the possession of it, but winds up knocking himself out with it. All this is achieved silently, and is a mark of Lee's skill as an action director.

The next major step forward *Way of the Dragon* takes is in allowing the appearance of guns. Guns could sound the death knell of kung-fu movies because no matter how skill-ful one is, no martial artist can fight a bullet. Bruce Lee confronts that problem in this movie, set in modern times, by having his character make wooden darts which he hurls into his enemies' gun hands. It is the most unlikely technique in the picture, but at least Lee attempted to deal with this partic-ularly sticky genre drawback.

Tang Lung repeatedly puts down the gang boss's takeover attempts, so the boss decides to fight fire with fire—by calling in a Japanese and two American martial artists.

The two former enforcers, played by Wang Ing Sik and Bob Wall, pretty much take care of the restaurant employees. The final American is flown in especially for Tang Lung.

He is Chuck Norris, seven-time karate champion, who plays Tang's ultimate Anglo enemy. The two face each other in the Colosseum and fight with all the graciousness and solemnity of honor-bound samurai warriors. Lee, the director and writer, even manages to infuse this somber scene with small humorous touches, mostly supplied by a mute kitten which witnesses the fight. He also creates a high point when he comes away from a clinch with a handful of Norris's bushy chest hair—which Lee blows off his hand defiantly.

Norris's character is winning at first, bloodying Lee's face. But Lee tastes the blood, spits it out, and carries on. It is Lee who finally triumphs, but not before a subtle, magnificent silent exchange between the two fighters. Norris almost smiles. Lee shakes his head. The two have communicated, and the audience clearly sees it. Then Tang Lung breaks his enemy's neck.

The movie ends with a confusing union of images. First, Lung drapes his enemy's shirt and belt over the fallen man's corpse and kneels beside it in silence—a strong, effective moment. Then it turns out that the restaurant manager has betrayed his help by siding with the gangster and stabbing his own employees. The police arrive to take the villains away before Lee can rip them apart.

Another change in Lee's approach is in the ending—he is not arrested or killed. Instead, it looks as if he will settle down with the romantic lead, played in all three Lee films by Nora Miao, only to suddenly pack up and go.

"In this world of guns and knives, wherever Tang Lung may go, he will always travel on his own," is the last line.

And travel Bruce Lee did. All the way back to America.

ENTER THE DRAGON

There is a respected producer in Hollywood named Fred Weintraub who fell in love with Chinese movies. He loved the last ten minutes, when the hero would take on an army of crooks and defeat them all bare-handed. He was certain a hugely successful American movie could be made in this image.

"I went to Hong Kong and saw Bruce's films," he recalls, "and brought one back to show Ted Ashley [then chairman of the board at Warner Brothers]. If it wasn't for Ted Ashley, the movie would have never gotten made. I had half the money but everybody else had turned me down—including other executives at Warners. But Ted asked me what I needed, and then said, 'Go ahead.'"

What he went ahead with was a movie called *Enter the Dragon*—a movie many think is the greatest martial arts movie ever made. And, in a way, despite all its shortcomings, it is. More on that later, but first things first. Weintraub and coproducer Paul Heller cut a deal with Lee's Concord Productions, then worked with Lee and screenwriter Michael Allin on the script. Robert Clouse was chosen as director because, in Weintraub's words, "Nobody else wanted to direct the picture except him."

The story was simplicity itself. In fact, it was James Bond by way of Fu Manchu. An unnamed espionage agency asks a Shaolin Temple teacher named Lee to compete at a martial-arts tournament in order to infiltrate an island off Hong Kong lorded over by a Shaolin renegade named Mr. Han. Lee goes to the island in the company of Williams, a cocky black fighter, and Roper, a gambler—both of whom are in trouble with the law.

Once on the island, they face the evil Han, an Oriental with a fake, interchangeable hand, a small army of guards, and a combination inner sanctum and museum. All three men discover his drug-pushing and white slavery operation, Williams paying for the knowledge with his life. Roper and Lee fight

Does this Han minion from Enter the Dragon *look familiar? Well, he should, because this is the only official on-screen pairing of Bruce Lee and future superstar Jackie Chan.*

the minions with the help of freed slaves. Then Lee faces and defeats Han in the name of his family and the Shaolin Temple.

To put it mildly, the script was fairly lame. The dialogue and situations seemed second-hand—all borrowed from 007 adventures. Han is little more than Dr. No. He even has a white long-haired cat like Bond's main nemesis, Ernst Stavros Blofeld. The only place the movie excels—in fact, the only place the movie is unique—is in its martial arts. And that was the territory of Bruce Lee.

Getting the project started, however, was no easy task. John Saxon, an actor who had been toiling in unspectacular B pictures since the mid-1950s, shared equal billing with Lee by playing Roper. A man named Rockney Tarkinton was cast as Williams.

"Jim Kelly was a last-minute replacement," Weintraub explains. "He came on the night before the picture was to start. At the last minute Tarkinton said I was taking advantage of him. I disagreed, and that was the end of that. At two o'clock in the morning I went to see Kelly and said, 'You're hired.'"

Weintraub had Saxon, Kelly, Hong Kong film veteran character actor Shih Kien as Han, Bob Wall and Yang Sze as Han's most prominent bodyguards, and even Angela Mao

Bruce Lee at his animal best in Enter the Dragon.

as Lee's sister, who commits suicide rather than be raped by Han's minions. What he didn't have, at first, was Bruce Lee.

"For the first three weeks, we shot around him," Weintraub maintains. "Linda Lee, his wife, was the one who kept things going when he wouldn't show up on the set. He was nervous. It was his first big film. He was scared. And he was fighting with Raymond Chow at that time. He was fighting with me, too, but not as much. It was just that he was so nervous. On the first day, he had a facial twitch. We needed twenty-seven takes. Then he settled down and we made the film."

19

Lee's contribution was telling. What the film's detractors don't seem to realize is that if *Enter the Dragon*'s plot hadn't been so pedestrian, Bruce Lee's first major international appearance would not have had the impact it did. This was Lee's showcase, and its every fault only served to bolster Lee's participation. He was truly the best thing about the movie. In that respect, it could not have been a better vehicle for him.

Enter the Dragon is a fantasy, and every device used to make the fantasy palatable worked in the film's favor. When first given the assignment to infiltrate Han's island by a Mr. Braithwaite, Lee again brings up the sticky subject of guns. Why not just blow Han's head off, he asks. Braithwaite explains that Han is so fearful of assassination that he doesn't allow guns on the island—a neat way to eliminate a most pressing genre problem.

Michael Allin's dialogue seemed extremely aware of the plot's shortcomings. At one point Williams says to Han, "Man, you come right out of a comic book." It is touches like these, in addition to the rest of the semi-Confucian by way of Spider-Man conversations, that make the nonfight scenes palatable.

Bruce Lee starred essentially as himself, and supervised all the martial arts. However, he also gave the entire film a heart most aren't aware of. "I don't think anyone else knows this," Weintraub reveals, "but when *Enter the Dragon* was finished, I completely reedited it. When it was initially done, it was a linear story that started in the United States. But Bruce went back and did the Shaolin Temple sequence. That was his. He did that without me and I loved it. I took that and opened the film with it. Then I went onto the boat and did flashbacks, which everybody thought I was crazy to do."

Although at first it seems that Bruce Lee played little more than an Oriental James Bond in the picture, he finally faces Han with the line, "You have shamed my family and the Shaolin Temple." The martial arts influence has come full circle. He is not destroying Han in the name of espionage but in the name of his Chinese ancestors. It is only Bruce Lee's participation and contribution that makes *Enter the Dragon* successful. It served Lee beautifully, and will always be remembered as Lee's greatest and *the* greatest martial arts film.

LITTLE GRASSHOPPER

Countering the success of this movie, Lee suffered a major setback in the television arena. Its name was *Kung Fu*. "Once we started *Enter the Dragon*," the producer recollects, "everybody thought Bruce was going to be something and started sending me scripts in the middle of shooting. There was a man at Warner Brothers named Dick Moore who understood the market, so we worked up a script with Ed Spielman and Howard Friedlander and showed it to Bruce. We tried to do it as a movie first."

The movie *Kung Fu* took place in the Sierra Nevadas of 1868 and is concerned with the coolie laborers building the transcontinental railroad. Among them is Caine, a halfbreed Chinese. Almost immediately, the movie flashes back to Caine's training by Shaolin Temple monks, culminating in a final test that has him in a booby-trapped hall blocked by a red-hot cauldron. He escapes the corridor by lifting the cauldron with his forearms, which leaves tattoos of a dragon on one arm and a tiger on the other.

From there Caine travels to Peking, where his blind sifu, Po, stumbles into a royal guard. He's shot for his mistake, and Caine kills the guards and, of all people, the prince. Then he escapes to America and gets a job on the railroad. From there, the script degenerates into a western *The Big Boss*, but with one added twist. After Caine leads the

The famous nunchaku make their appearance in Enter the Dragon.

Enter the Dragon's *Mr. Han has a hand made of blades.*

coolies in a revolt against their corrupt masters, another Shaolin monk appears to challenge him. It seems the temple was destroyed as retribution for Caine's act, and the monk wants revenge. Caine kills him, bows farewell, and disappears down the road.

"Tom Kuhn, who was in charge of Warner Television at the time, said, 'Why don't we try this as a series?' " Weintraub relates. "I said, 'Great. Bruce would be perfect.' We designed the series for Bruce."

According to one story, Bruce Lee ultimately turned down the offer to star in the series, thinking he wasn't ready yet.

Weintraub doesn't remember it that way. "When he didn't get the part," the producer says, "I was stunned. Bruce was heartbroken, and I couldn't blame him."

The executive who actually turned Bruce Lee down doesn't remember it that way either. "Ted Ashley wanted Bruce," he says, "but the network wanted someone like William Smith [a brawny American actor known for villainous roles and totally wrong for the part]. We felt that casting David Carradine made for a good compromise. To tell you the truth, I didn't think Lee's English was strong enough yet."

This executive also remembers a personal visit during which Lee proved his kung-fu prowess by touching the television man's nose with the tip of his foot. It wasn't enough. Carradine got the part in the series, which ultimately succeeded because of *Enter the Dragon*.

It would seem that Bruce Lee had the last laugh. He returned to Hong Kong to a tumultuous reception. It was months before *Enter the Dragon* would premiere, but just the very fact that he had starred in an international film after having attained star status from his first three movies put him in the Oriental catbird seat. Weintraub and he were already discussing a second American movie, for which he would receive a million dollars. He supposedly was on the verge of signing a contract with the Shaw Brothers studio to do a period piece; photos to the effect were taken.

Bruce Lee takes care of Mr. Han's leg at the end of Enter the Dragon.

Kareem Abdul Jabbar, the famous basketball player, laughs with Lee on the set of the incomplete Game of Death.

But first he had to do a project that went under the title *Game of Death*. Initially it seemed to be a sequel to *Way of the Dragon*. Tang Lung was to travel to Korea, where he had to fight his way up a pagoda, facing a different type of martial artist at each level. Bruce Lee filmed three fight scenes, one with Daniel Inosanto, one with Kareem Abdul Jabbar, and one with a hapkido fighter, Chi Hon Joi. He was frightfully thin and wan in these scenes, and, except for a few instances, the sequences had a rough, unfinished look to the choreography.

THE KING IS DEAD

On July 20, 1973, Bruce Lee died. He was found in the apartment of Betty Ting Pei, an actress. His death was attributed to a cerebral hemorrhage or brain aneurism. None of his fans could believe it, and the hysteria that followed was equally hard to believe. Stories circulated that he was murdered by envious kung-fu masters using the "Death Touch," or poisoned by envious film studio personnel. There were tales of his involvement with gangsters and drug pushers. In

24

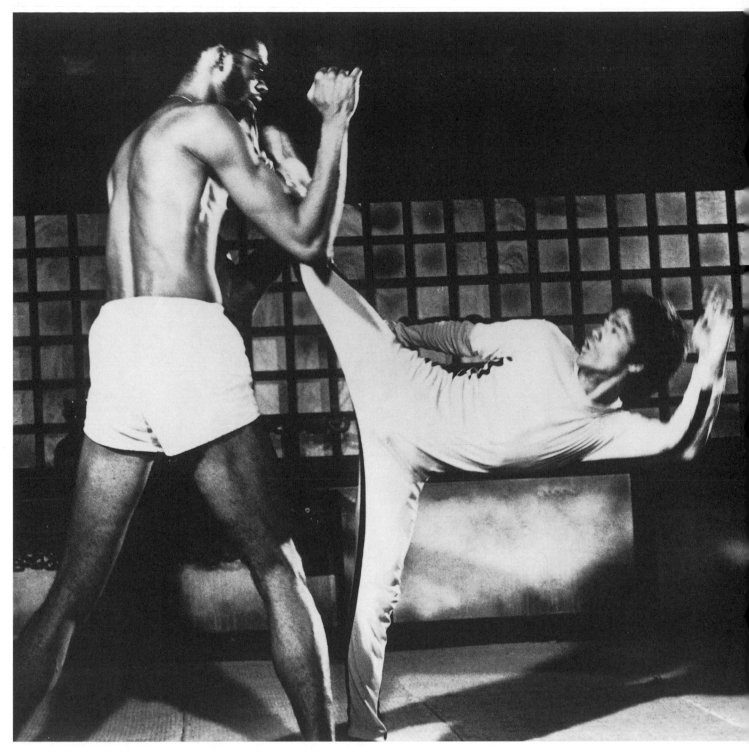

Kareem Abdul Jabbar on the Game of Death *set, with the diminutive Lee (5′7″) making up the difference.*

short, no one could believe that their super-hero had died naturally. He had to have been killed by a supervillain.

Enter the Dragon premiered in the United States in the summer of 1973 and opened in Hong Kong that October. In the meantime, a small distributing company called National General had secured the rights to present Lee's earlier films to the American public. Bruce Lee's voice was dubbed, and the

Chinese titles were translated. *The Big Boss* was to be called *The Chinese Connection* and *Fist of Fury* was to be called *Fists of Fury*.

But somehow, somewhere, the U.S. distributors switched the titles. Now *The Big Boss* was *Fists of Fury* and *Fist of Fury* was *The Chinese Connection*. That's how American audiences saw the features, and that's how

American audiences know them—by the wrong titles. But, like it or not, that's what they are to English-speaking Bruce Lee fans. Soon after, *Way of the Dragon* came to U.S. shores as *Return of the Dragon*—promoted as a sequel to *Enter the Dragon* although made before that film.

Bruce Lee was the most successful Chinese

into his body that would hurt him," he maintains. "I had him examined at UCLA the week before he died. He was in great shape. He had an aneurism. That happens to people under the age of thirty-five."

Mike Stone echoes Weintraub's sentiments. "I've met several people with Bruce's intensity and, interestingly enough, those people died quite young. But the unique thing about Bruce was that his belief in himself and the intensity with which he did things was always at a peak. He had a tremendous faith in himself and a belief in his ability."

Sadly, the Chinese film industry could not let their hero go. They chose to remember him by mounting literally dozens of quickie, rip-off productions that proportedly showed the king back in action or told his life story. Even the best of these films were dreadful. A Western equivalent would be to have Hollywood make a bunch of Dirty Larry movies starring Clint Westwood over the next decade.

Eastern filmmakers recruited Ho Tsung Tao, a tall young Oriental with good martial arts skills, to become "Bruce Li" in a series of forgettable adventures titled such things as *Bruce Lee Superdragon* (1974), *Goodbye Bruce Lee—His Last Game of Death* (1975), *Exit the Dragon, Enter the Tiger* (1976), *Fist of Fury II* (1976), *Bruce Lee the Invincible* (1977), and *Bruce Lee's Secret* (1977).

These movies are quite funny, both in terms of content and conception. One never knows when a Bruce Lee "clone" will appear behind trademark sunglasses (as in *Exit the Dragon*, when the "real" Bruce Lee asks Bruce Li to solve his murder if he just so happens to get killed in the near future) or when mountain gorillas will rise on their hind legs and fight kung-fu–style (as in *The Invincible*).

star in the world a month after he was already dead. But more than twenty years later, people disbelieve the "official" cause of his death. Many maintain that drugs had to be part of his downfall. While it is impossible to say for certain that Bruce Lee did not use drugs, Fred Weintraub is definite in his opinion: "Let me tell you that Bruce would never put anything

Ho Tsung Tao, otherwise known as Bruce Li, readies himself for yet another inferior exploitation, in this case, the movie Dynamo.

Following hot on Bruce Li's heels was Bruce Le, originally named Huang Kin Lung. At least Li is a decent performer, an actor who has been able to shake his Lee clone mantle in recent years to act in better, more honorable productions. Le is not the former and has not done the latter. Le is a decent martial artist, but not a decent actor. He is a wooden screen presence, sinking any scene in which he isn't swinging his fists. In addition, he seems intent on toiling in the exploitive garbage, trading on his vague physical resemblance to the original.

The directors and writers of these travesties manage to sink anything their star can't. Quite possibly the most interesting exploitation came with *I Love You, Bruce Lee*, known in America as *Bruce Lee: His Last Days, His*

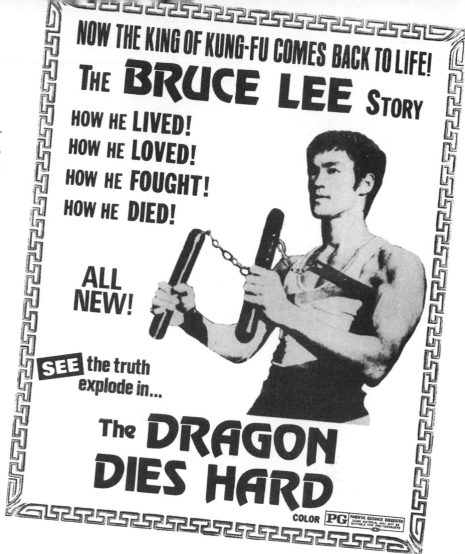

Last Nights (1975). This was reportedly Betty Ting Pei's own statement as to her alleged lover's fate. She was given credit as both star and cowriter of this trashy farce, which featured Li Hsiu Hsien as a Bruce Lee who gave forewarnings of his coming aneurism by gripping his head and collapsing in the middle of scenes. Ting Pei was constantly in the nude, and the movie portrayed Lee as an immature rapist.

This is the saddest pornography imaginable, made all the sadder by being a Shaw Brothers production. While the company can put out exceptional period pieces, their modern love, crime, and horror films were, until very recently, execrable. *I Love You, Bruce Lee* was no exception. For the record, Betty tells a sympathetic bartender her life story after the hate of Bruce Lee fans forces her to disguise herself and leave town. The bartender beats up some thugs at the finale and tells them to respect Bruce Lee's memory—which is far more than this film did.

However, the worst was yet to come. Word leaked out that Golden Harvest had in its possession 101 minutes of film Bruce Lee had completed before his death. Using that footage, they were going to complete *Game of Death*. They hired Robert Clouse to direct some "new" footage and set the premiere for 1978.

The result was probably the worst Bruce Lee exploitation of all, basically because it was the film with the most talent behind it. After a wonderful credit sequence designed by John Christopher Strong III, in which clips of Bruce Lee from his other films appeared in and on floating games of chance, the plot unfolded to disbelieving eyes. Rather than following Lee's original scenario, *Game of Death* was now about Bruce Lee himself, fighting off the corrupt desires of an insane actor's agent!

The 101 minutes of film turned out to be less than ten, which showed the real Bruce Lee fighting the aforementioned men, while the other ninety minutes featured snatches of film from his other movies, but mostly pathetically transparent doubling by Kim Tai Chung and Chen Yao Po, among others.

Viewing the picture is a schizophrenic experience, what with Kim in one shot, Chen in the next, and fading clips of Bruce Lee in a third. The single most unbelievable moment comes in a dressing room where director Clouse films a mirror on which a photo of Bruce Lee's head has been pasted and the stand-in positioned so his shoulders seem to come from the photo's neck!

Bruce Lee died in Betty Ting Pei's apartment. Sadly, the actress decided to tell her own cinematic story in the dreadful Bruce Lee: His Last Days, His Last Nights.

The stand-ins play a character named Billy Lo, who incurs the wrath of syndicate head and theatrical agent Dr. Rand, played by Dean Jagger. On Rand's side is bodyguard Steiner, played by Hugh O'Brian, and Stick the hit man, played by Mel Novak. On Billy's side is girlfriend Ann, played by Colleen Camp, and United Press International reporter Jim Marshall, played by Gig Young. Ann is kidnapped by the bad guys; Billy rescues her and then fights his way up the various levels of Rand's restaurant to kill all the villains.

This is one bad movie. Markedly better was 1981's *Tower of Death*, known in the United States as *Game of Death II*. Directed by Ng See-Yuen, who also directed *Bruce Lee, the True Story* (U.S. title: *Bruce Lee, the*

Man and the Myth, 1976), it now starred Kim Tai Chung in the leading role of Bobby Lo, the brother of Billy Lo, the lead of *Game of Death*. This time the actual Bruce Lee footage came from scenes edited out of *Enter the Dragon*, with all new dialogue dubbed in.

The real Bruce Lee appears in only the first half hour, playing Billy, who is mysteriously killed, allowing Bobby to investigate. Instead of trampling Lee's memory by trying to fool audiences, Kim is given a series of eight, increasingly more ambitious fights until he reaches the top of the pagoda, where he has an excellent battle with Huang Cheng Li.

In a bunch of dreadful movies, *Tower of Death*, also known as *Game of Death II*, reigns supreme, which, of course, isn't saying

Bruce Lee: His Last Days, His Last Nights was low on kung-fu and high on this sort of scene, as Betty Ting Pei fools around with Li Hsiu Hsien.

much. Many fans thought that *Game of Death* would be Lee's ultimate martial arts statement, had he lived. Given that Lee wanted to continue making movies, that theory is doubtful. For Lee to have shot his entire wad on his fifth movie would have been foolish. Besides, he had yet to realize his potential as a filmmaker. But there is little doubt that Bruce Lee's fully realized version of *Game of Death* would have been far superior to what we are left with.

At the present time there is Bruce Li, Bruce Le, Bruce Liang, Bruce Leong, Bruce Lei, Bruce Rhe, Dragon Lee, Rocky Lee, Bronson Lee, Conan Lee, and Jet Li (among others) to contend with. There are also scores of movies with the words *Enter*, *Fist*, *Fury*, *Dragon*, *Connection*, *Game*, and *Death* in their titles. Is this the legacy Bruce Lee has left us?

"Bruce Lee proved that someone from the ghetto or upstate New York, or Malibu, or wherever, would accept a Chinese as a hero," Mike Stone contends. "He proved that through his ability. Bruce set a standard of performance that hasn't been met. I don't think there's anyone who comes close to him in terms of ability or charisma yet. As a result, no U.S. filmmaker feels comfortable making martial arts films. In many cases,

we've taken a few paces back since his death."

That is probably the reason almost no Westerner outside the exploitation filmmakers have touched kung-fu films, despite the success of *Enter the Dragon*. In truth, English-speaking filmmakers just aren't that good at this kind of high-flying, highly emotional form of heroic moviemaking. The great majority of directors and writers seem to need to camp up their superheroes, to not take any of them seriously, be they

31

Jason Scott Lee, playing Bruce Lee, prepares to do battle with his personal demons for the last time in Dragon.

Superman, Flash Gordon, James Bond, or Bruce Lee. So what remains are people tearing at his legend with inferior product, misdirection, or outright deception.

Fred Weintraub puts the question of Bruce Lee in perspective. "I miss Bruce. I liked him. We fought, but it was never personal. It was for the film, for art's sake. He knew I cared and that was all that counted. He knew, in a funny kind of way, that I was the only one who cared enough to get him into the international market. Nobody wanted him. In the history of show business, there had never been an international Chinese star, especially not one who was five-foot-seven and not gorgeous.

"Bruce stood tall. Bruce is martial arts. He made the form work. No matter who you see doing martial arts, you always compare him to Bruce Lee. Say 'cowboy' and you think 'John Wayne.' Say 'martial arts' and the name that pops to mind is Bruce Lee. That makes him one of the few giants in show business. That's the mark of his influence and his genius."

LONG LIVE THE KING

Like any good icon, Bruce Lee would not stay down. Unlike Elvis, there were no afterlife "sightings," but then again, no true believer had to look very far to find their kung-fu idol. More than twenty years after his death, he remained a perennial bestseller in video stores and comic-book shops, on T-shirts and posters.

As yet another example of Lee's post-mortem fame, he set a record of sorts on the Arts and Entertainment cable channel's venerable *Biography* series. The program aired no fewer than three different biographies of the actor in a space of three years—one even being broadcast over a two-hour period. And each time, the ratings spiked noticeably.

The first and final programs were the best—both buoyed by the personal participation of Linda Lee, Bruce's widow. In fact, the final Bruce Lee *Biography* episode was only mounted after the first proved to be unreproduceable on video. (Apparently, not all the necessary film rights were secured prior to broadcast.) Nonetheless, each retelling of his life story proved to be memorable for both Lee veterans and novices.

In the first and final episodes, Linda contributed private home videos of Bruce working with James Coburn and Kareem Abdul-Jabbar in their backyard, in addition to heartwarming and heartbreaking childhood images of the Lee's two children. There were glimpses of the young Shannon, their daughter, romping in the garden, as well as images of Brandon, their son, even as a toddler, doing kung-fu kicks while learning to walk.

In addition, the hours were enlightened by footage from a supposedly lost interview Bruce did on Canadian television prior to the production of *Enter the Dragon*. This was Bruce at what his fans would call "his most intense," and his critics would call "his most arrogant." Obviously reveling in his newfound Hong Kong fame, Lee spoke passionately and pretentiously, under heavy lidded eyes, on the dubious nature of "superstardom," his accomplishments, and his beliefs. It was an illuminating performance, giving ample evidence of his state of mind at the time.

Hollywood finally went the way of Hong Kong—and executives started to figure out how they could take advantage of Bruce's

Jason Scott Lee (no relation) does his best to look like he can actually do kung-fu in Dragon: The Bruce Lee Story.

popularity even after death. There was only one easy way to do it: they would have to make a big-budget biopic. And there was only one thing they would call it: *Dragon— The Bruce Lee Story*.

The production started promisingly. Rob Cohen, an eclectic and enthusiastic director, and the producer of such popular projects as *The Legend of Billie Jean* (1985), *The Running Man* with Arnold Schwarzenegger (1987), and *Bird on a Wire* with Mel Gibson (1990), set about adapting Linda Lee's biography *Bruce Lee: The Man Only I Knew*, with the Lee family's cooperation. He even hired several top jeet kune do teachers to choreograph the film's many real and imagined fight scenes. Then the problems started.

Ironically, most of the people who created *Dragon* probably wouldn't think of them as problems. As far as they may have been concerned, *Dragon* was a critical and financial success, so what could possibly be the problem? There was really only one: finding the bite-size bits of truth amid the total fabrications, wild flights of fantasy, and totally inaccurate representation of the martial art Bruce Lee dedicated his life to creating.

Dilemma one: how to communicate the anger Lee reportedly felt throughout his life—the anger that made him win any confrontation at all costs. In the case of *Dragon*, the anger was visually manifested as a demon—a demon dressed in what appears to be Japanese, not Chinese, armor. Was this clever use of the Japanese villains who helped make *The Chinese Connection* so successful, or standard Hollywood racial apathy? You decide.

Dilemma two: the direct power of jeet kune do, like Chinese armor, is not very visual. Lee himself always did an exaggerated version of it for the cameras—but not so exaggerated that it would ever be mistaken for the acrobatics of the Ninja Turtles. Complicating matters further was that a non–martial artist was cast as Bruce. And while Jason Scott Lee (no relation) is an excellent actor, it was somewhat akin to hiring a nondancer to star in a Fred Astaire biopic.

So, although they had such jeet kune do notables as Jerry Poteet on the set, the decision was made: bring in the aerialists. Instead of showing the true power of jeet kune do, Lee was pictured flipping and cartwheeling all over the place like some sort of demented pinwheel. That way, the leading actor wouldn't be required to communicate the true artistry of Bruce Lee's martial art.

Not that many American audiences knew the difference. One critic even went so far as to review the movie's martial arts by saying, "Fittingly, fight coordinator John Cheung previously worked with Hong Kong martial arts star Jackie Chan." No, not fittingly. For Lee, this would have probably been infuriating, for Chan, as you will read later, purposely patterned himself as an anti–Bruce Lee. Their on-screen fighting styles were as different as Savion Glover's stunning tap dancing and Mikhail Barishnikov's powerful ballet.

Finally, how do you take the true drama of Bruce Lee's life and turn it into colorful Hollywood fantasy? Screenwriters Cohen, Edward Khmara, and John Raffo worked hard doing just that, and, despite the gross inaccuracies on the particulars of Lee's life and art, there is much to like in *Dragon*.

For instance, it is clever the way Cohen has Van Williams, the actor who portrayed the TV *Green Hornet*, play a *Green Hornet* episode director (guiding Bruce through a scene which incongruously showcases the lamp kick Lee did in the movie *Marlowe*, not in the superhero television series), or the way Cohen casts himself as Robert Clouse, the director of *Enter the Dragon*.

There was also the extremely effective way Cohen communicates Americans' casual racism by contrasting Linda's and Bruce's reactions to the egregious Asian stereotype Mickey Rooney played in the film *Breakfast at Tiffany's*, which the two are viewing while on a date. Of course Rooney was portraying a

Brandon Lee, Bruce's son, must be restrained from accepting his legacy in Rapid Fire.

Japanese in that film, but why start splitting hairs now? The final result was effective, and that was what the filmmakers were obviously shooting for throughout this fanciful endeavor.

If you want facts, watch any one of the Arts and Entertainment *Biography* episodes. You want fiction, fantasy, flipping, and fake fighting? Then *Dragon: The Bruce Lee Story* is for you. But, despite the aforementioned criticisms, the worst thing about it was its ending. The agonizing climax portrays Bruce Lee saving his son, Brandon, from the family demon.

Tragically, in real life, it didn't work out that way.

DEATH OF THE PRINCE

The first call came at about four o'clock in the morning. "Brandon Lee is dead," a crew member whispered to me. "He was shot."

I couldn't believe it. I had only recently met Brandon during the promotional campaign for *Rapid Fire*—the movie in which he had finally stopped trying to get out of his father's shadow. Instead, he had embraced it and come out, whole and happy, on the other side.

My colleagues and I had agreed: energetic, goodhearted, and talented, Brandon Lee was the next great hope for the American martial arts action film. But now he was dead— killed in a literally unbelievable accident on

35

the set of his breakthrough film, *The Crow.*

The crew member quickly and quietly gave me the particulars: they had been working all day and all night for weeks to get the movie done. The production's official "gun wrangler" had already left the production for another job when the film went overschedule. A prop gun, supposedly loaded with blank cartridges, had fired.

In the days to come, a more complete picture was supplied by the local police. According to press reports, a hunk of bullet wadding—usually used as a wall between the powder and the shell of a regulation cartridge—had lodged in the barrel of the prop gun. It was the wadding that was allegedly propelled, like a deadly bullet, by the powder of a newly loaded blank.

"If only the actor playing his killer had been off by just a few inches," I groaned some time later, after poor Brandon was buried. Only then did the friend I was with reveal that he knew the actor who had played the role. "He was a method actor," my friend told me with awful irony. "He had been practicing for days how to shoot to kill."

Brandon had died three months shy of the twentieth anniversary of his father's death, and just weeks before the release of *Dragon: The Bruce Lee Story*—mirroring his father's death, which occurred just weeks prior to the release of *Enter the Dragon.* No wonder the talk of a Lee family curse was so thick.

Brandon was born in 1965, and was only eight when his father died, but he had already appeared on Hong Kong television with him, successfully breaking a board. "Could you imagine what would have happened if I hadn't broken that board?" he asked later. But break it he had, and when Bruce passed away, it left a void in Brandon's life that would never be filled.

Although Brandon was already interested in following in his father's footsteps, Bruce

Death and cinematic rebirth: Brandon Lee in The Crow.

Lee's death pushed him in other directions. Just as Jackie Chan would struggle in Bruce's shadow, Brandon had an even greater fight on his hands. For years he was adamant in his refusal to mirror his father's moves and attitude, wanting to be accepted and applauded for himself, not for a happenstance of birth.

Finally, however, Brandon's need for cinematic exposure took priority over even his ego. Brandon went the way of his father, taking the leading role in a cunningly designed Hong Kong action film *Legacy of Rage* (1986), arguably the best movie of his truncated career. Here, Brandon played a kind-hearted, though supremely athletic, construction worker who is forced to slaughter his family's oppressors—but only after he is pushed way beyond endurance.

Although taking place in the modern day, *Legacy of Rage* was filmed in the overheated fashion of Bruce's first film, *The Big Boss* (U.S.: *Fists of Fury*). And while Brandon was clearly labeled a nice guy from the moment he was first glimpsed on-screen (running a lost child all the way across town without taking a rest), the explosion of violence his father was so good at riding was waiting just under an affable surface.

Only this was not kung-fu violence. Fight choreographer Mang Hoi had little to do here, as the filmmakers knowingly gave Brandon loads of firepower and showed him how to use it. In fact, in this movie the martial arts is essentially used as an in-joke, especially when the plot calls for a fight between Brandon and *Enter the Dragon* villain Bolo. Just as it seems Brandon would show some "family" moves, the battle is cut short and out come the guns again.

Director Ronnie Yu—later to be lauded for his helming one of the greatest fantasies ever, *Bride With White Hair* (1993), and then panned for his foolish first American film, *Warriors of Virtue* (originally titled *Five Kung-fu Kangaroos*, 1997)—knew what he was doing. He let the nasty machinations of slick villain Michael Wong grow and grow until, when the audience is close to the breaking point, Brandon finally explodes and the screen is riddled by thousands of bullets.

The bloody retribution at the end of the film seemed to purge Brandon of his paternal resentment as well. Having survived a Hong Kong production, he now seemed to know that he should no longer fight his father's celebrity. Instead, he should make use of it to create a legacy of fame. He also definitely knew that he should do anything to get out of Asia and into Hollywood. With its seat-of-the-pants production and unsophisticated special effects, Hong Kong could kill an actor.

The true sign of Brandon's acceptance of his destiny came with his next casting choice: to costar opposite the man whom racist executives had chosen instead of his father to star in the television series that had been created to showcase Bruce Lee. Brandon played a Shaolin assassin in *Kung Fu: The Movie* (1986) which should have been called *Kung Fu: The TV Movie*, since it played on network television.

Comedian Margaret Cho doesn't agree. She has always felt that the show should have yet another name. "I hated that show, because the lead actor, David Carradine, wasn't even Chinese," she said in her comedy act. "That show should not have been called *Kung Fu*. It should have been called *That Guy's Not Chinese.*"

Although the well-rated feature was really pretty boring—and proved once again that Carradine was about as good as Jason Scott Lee when it came to martial arts—Brandon used it to signal that he would be willing to do whatever had to be done to become as popular as his father. To accomplish that goal required a lot of courage and stamina—but it didn't always include pride.

Hence, Brandon's next starring role was in the cheap and tacky *Laser Mission* (1989), a U.S.–South African–German coproduction whose writing and direction reflected its fractured origins. Brandon plays an espionage operative who teams with a tough and resourceful female agent (Debi Monahan) to rescue a laser expert, amusingly played by the always game Ernest Borgnine. The oddly named director, Beau Davis, barely gets the job done, bringing in the proceedings at a trim eighty-three minutes—which still seem endless during viewing.

An under-ninety-minute running time is often a sign that a production was problematic, so you can imagine what was going on behind the scenes of Brandon's next starring vehicle, *Showdown in Little Tokyo* (1991), which blows by in seventy-six minutes. Here Brandon is a wisecracking supporting player to brooding beefcake Dolph Lundgren, as a cop who runs afoul of Japanese-American mobsters.

Obviously titled and released to exploit the nearly nonexistent success of *Big Trouble in Little China* (1986)—John Carpenter's inferior "homage" to such great Hong Kong fantasies as *Bastard Swordsman* (1980) and *Zu Warriors of the Magic Mountain* (1983)—*Showdown*, as directed by Mark L. Lester and costarring the comely Tia Carrera, was only fittingly entertaining. But once again, it showed anyone who cared to look that Brandon had charisma to spare and was only getting better with each scene.

The performance seemed to do the trick, because Brandon wouldn't have to wait as long before his next big break. It came with *Rapid Fire* (1992), the younger Lee's first major studio release, and a canny combination of the star's strengths. Here, for the first time, Brandon doesn't begrudgingly agree that he is Bruce Lee's son, he proudly proclaims it, happily acknowledging his father's influence but letting his own engaging personality carry the day.

Mixing equal parts of firepower and martial arts, Brandon struts his stuff with some clever action choreography, ironically reflecting the influence of Jackie Chan rather than Bruce Lee. Bruce is there in spirit with such labored dialogue as "Why don't you take your fists of fury and get out of here," as well as such power moves as a side kick through a stairway banister. But mostly Brandon borrows from Chan's acrobatics in sequences set in an apartment kitchen and an industrial laundry.

Under the generic direction of Dwight H. Little, Brandon plays a Los Angeles art student who, in the best traditions of martial arts movies, also happens to be a kick-butt warrior. He needs all his skills when he witnesses a murder and gets caught between warring drug smugglers. But he's more than up to the challenge, bouncing some thugs off a swinging door and spinning around on rolling clothes racks—among other, less memorable, moments of mayhem.

As before, it was the force of Brandon's personality, not his fists, which carried this otherwise predictable, unimaginative, and even occasionally dreary movie, and he was proclaimed a true rising star to watch. His next choice cemented his promise: He would star in the moody movie adaptation of James O'Barr's bleak black-and-white comic book, *The Crow.*

The story couldn't be simpler. A rock star is murdered and, a year later, with a crow as his harbinger, comes back to wreak vengeance on his killers. Ambitious director Alex Proyas, however, used the clothesline of a story to create elegant visuals, which stayed in the memory long after the rudimentary dialogue and muddled action choreography faded from the ear and eye. Basically,

Brandon's character lived in a fictional, futuristic, and seemingly postapocalyptic city of sleazeballs, where the only character who doesn't painfully posture and spout film noir clichés is a nice-guy cop played by the always able Ernie Hudson.

The excitement—and exhaustion—was palpable on *The Crow*'s North Carolina set, where everyone was inspired by Proyas's vision and Lee's appeal. They knew they had something special and exciting, but they also knew they had to slave to get it done in time for a pressing release date. The mocking "I survived *The Crow*" T-shirts, which were supposedly being planned, turned bitterly portentous on the night of March 31, 1993, when Brandon was shot—just days before his marriage was scheduled.

The allusions to his father's death continued in the tragedy's aftermath, but rather than being resurrected by stand-ins and tacky camera tricks à la *Game of Death*, Brandon's visage and power were reborn through multi-million-dollar computer special effects, which grafted the man's face to the body of a stunt double. The final mirthless mockery was that *The Crow*, unlike *Game of Death*, was arguably improved by the rewriting and refilming needed to complete the movie.

Brandon lies beside his father in a Seattle cemetery. In life, they created memorable entertainment. In death, they have forged a tragic dynasty that will never be forgotten.

China: The Source

"The problem with kung-fu," Fred Weintraub says, "is that it is fantasy. Once someone shoots someone else, everybody understands it. That's reality. But when somebody does fantastic martial arts, that's fantasy. You never see that in life. You never see that on the news. What you see is people shot and run over. When you're working in martial arts, you're working in fantasy. You're working with ballet."

Truer words were seldom spoken. And fewer people were better equipped to deal with the balletic fantasy of kung-fu than the Chinese. We're talking about a history that goes back to at least 2500 B.C. From that period to the present, the annals of the Chinese are rich in mythology, legend, and lore, and it is these legends that make up the bulk of the best martial-arts films. It is this rich tradition that Bruce Lee was planning to tap—and thereby introduce to an international audience—before he died.

Instead, money-hungry distributors invaded the Orient in the early 1970s, buying up the cheapest movies they could find to take advantage of the voracious Western martial arts market. Almost all of these films were chaotic garbage which hinted at almost nothing of China's fascinating culture. It is doubly unfortunate in that one of the very first kung-fu films seen in the United States, even before the bulk of Bruce Lee movies, was a 1972 classy Shaw Brothers production of director Cheng Chang Ho's *King Boxer*, known in America as *Five Fingers of Death*.

Lo Lieh played the naive lead in the picture, successfully shucking his reputation for playing villains. It was, again, about the struggle against the Japanese—using a martial arts tournament as background—but one done with richness, style, and pomp. It did extremely well in Western markets, which, again, made it all the more unfortunate that distributors chose to foist inferior product on American eyes in the post–Bruce Lee period.

But China is used to invasions of every kind, not to mention revolutions, insurrections, intrigue, and war. First, there was the ancient period, dating roughly from 2500 to 207 B.C. At the very beginnings of this Oriental civilization there were already great legends. Fu Hsi the Hunter, Shen Nung the Farmer, and, most importantly, Huang Ti, bringer of fire and music.

There were almost no kung-fu films made about this time period. In fact, there have been fewer than a dozen marital arts movies made about the entire ancient era, and most of those concerned the Chou and Ch'in dynasties, starting around 1100 B.C. Already Chinese history was full of complexities, complications, rivalries, and conflicts. There was much in this period to make movies about, but before the really juicy stuff could

Lo Lieh, a longtime Hong Kong screen villain, led the Chinese invasion of America with Five Fingers of Death.

occur, China had to settle in.

Most of this settling in took place in the Han dynasty, which stretched about four hundred years, from 200 B.C. to 200 A.D. By that time a certain ruling logic was in effect: a certain member of a family became emperor and other members of the same family succeeded that person when he died. It

sounds simple, but it was fraught with dangers. The Chinese had big families, and the infighting to become emperor was ornate and often deadly.

Also, craziness wasn't restricted to the royal family. Constant wars were being waged to take over China from both outside and inside. Different families wanted to cre-

ate different dynasties, and different Orientals wanted to create different Chinas. As it has been said—there was a lot to make movies about. Even so, one could count the number of kung-fu movies made about this period on the fingers of one hand (and have two digits left over).

However, these few films were extremely mystical. They were fantasies both in form and content, featuring gods, demigods, wizards, witches, devils, and demons. Thankfully, all these folk had swords and knew how to use them. Meanwhile, back in the real world, Chinese government was becoming more structured at the end of the Han dynasty. The central government was located at the capital, with a chancellor, an imperial chancellor, and a commander in chief advising the emperor.

Out in the field, as it were, were nine ministers of state, each supported by a staff of directors and minions. In addition, there was the Department of Agriculture and Revenue, and the Lesser Treasury. Throughout this organization were various officials, secretariats, and even eunuchs. None of these people were immune to the emotions that are the stuff of great motion pictures, such as lust, greed, pride, and envy.

As the population grew, the need for greater government controls became obvious. The emperor gave parts of the country to his relatives as kingdoms. Agencies and armies were everywhere, especially because warring nomads in central Asia, called the Hsiung-nu, kept attacking from the north. As 200 A.D. neared, things just got worse and worse. China was divided, and dynasties came and went with alarming frequency.

Because of this, the period from about 250 A.D. to 600 A.D. was known as the Six Dynasties. Now there was a mess. Almost no filmmakers touch that time period, but it

In the wake of Five Fingers of Death *came inferior works like this.*

The Sui dynasty reunited northern and southern China, but collapsed from overextending itself. The T'ang dynasty saw the creation of the Shaolin Temple, and, thereby, officially marked the start of kung-fu.

BLOOD FEUDS

Now we're talking. To make things even more interesting, outside the temple walls all sorts of court intrigues were going down, resulting in many lives being ruined or ended. Several of the emperors were truly perverse and depraved, creating all sorts of situations the Shaolin Temple monks could fight in (see the chart on page 48 for the kinds of kung-fu that were created).

Life went on as usual in the royal court, with everyone stabbing each other in the back. Everyone jockeyed for power, including the courtesans and concubines. One, Empress Wu, was so good at power games that she rose from being just one of the emperor's women to deposing the rightful heir to become empress herself. None of this happened—not the reunifications or deposings—without all manner of bloody confrontations.

Empress Wu managed to hold on until she was eighty years old, and then handed the empire over to a rightful heir, but he was poisoned by his wife, who tried to become Empress herself. She, however, was outclassed by Wu's daughter, who got her brother to the throne and tried to run the country

was an important one because both Taoism and Confucianism were weakening. Although the former promoted simplicity and the latter ethics and education, both were reinterpreted, like all religions, to fit the times. And the times were turbulent.

In their stead came Buddhism, an Indian religion founded on enlightenment and the elimination of suffering by eliminating desire. This led the way to the Sui and T'ang dynasties (approximately 600 to 1000 A.D.), which were the stuff of at least a dozen films.

through him. She, in turn, was foiled by her brother's rightful heir, who took over through a coup resulting in her "suicide."

Strangely, although Western filmmakers would no doubt make miniseries and soap operas out of this rich tapestry of intrigue, modern kung-fu moviemakers concentrated on the legends of the Monkey King—the most heroic and beloved character in the Peking Opera canon. Things improved noticeably (at least as depicted in modern cinema) with the coming of the following era, the Sung dynasty.

This lasted almost three hundred years, in which the battles came out of the back rooms and onto the battlefields. Two dozen corking-good martial arts epics were made concerning this turbulent period, featuring some spectacular meldings of the supernatural and Shaolin teachings. This dynasty started on an auspicious note.

The Sungs united a deeply fractured China, known as the Ten Kingdoms, into a Northern Sung and a Southern Sung. The Northern Sung consolidated and instituted reforms which didn't quite take. The Southern Sung had a sophisticated political structure which led to legal problems and clerical corruption. Overpopulation didn't help things either. Already the Chinese people numbered in the millions.

And then there was Genghis Khan. He led a horde of Mongolians who had decided to take over China. The Northern Sung made a deal with the Mongols, and for the next forty years waited until the time was right to take out the Southern Sung. Genghis Kahn's sons, Mangu and Khublai, marched down in 1250, and by 1268 Mangu was dead and Khublai was attacking. By 1280 the Mongols controlled the entire Chinese empire.

Thus began the Yuan dynasty, a less-than-one-hundred-year reign marked by resistance fighters and espionage. About half a dozen movies have been made about this period to date; it was not a happy time in Chinese history. Most Asians are deeply concerned about their pride—their "face"—and this era marked a great loss of face.

Fighting the Japanese is a greatly overworked theme in Chinese movies, and this movie overworks everything.

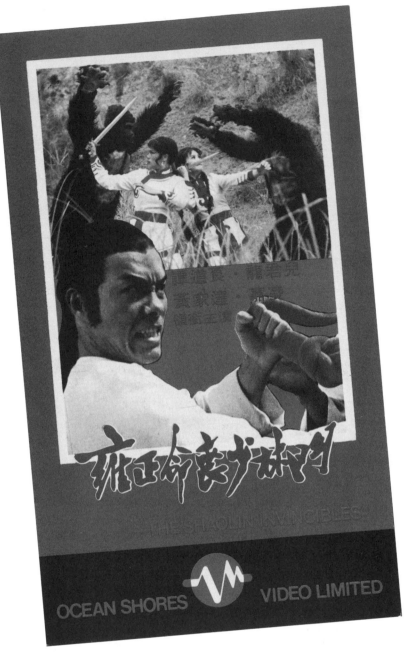

Chinese movies at their stupidest. Men in ape suits jump two knife-wielding girls and everybody does kung-fu.

Japanese, and internal warlord conspiracies. Things came to a head in the mid-1600s, when the Manchus combined with bandit leaders to take over China and institute the Ch'ing dynasty. This was yet another roughly three-hundred-year reign that made the stuff of another 150 films or so.

This period was of great change in which magnificent fighters were created to survive those changes. It marked the destruction of the Shaolin Temple, forcing the surviving monks to create new kung-fu forms so that they could take revenge. It was also a time of remarkable foreign contacts. The early Ch'ing emperors had relations with Russia, Tibet, Turkey, Nepal, Burma, Thailand, Vietnam, and Korea. They also had some trouble with Rome and Christianity.

Then drugs entered the scene. In the early 1800s, the British East India Company sent opium to China. Once introduced, it could not be gotten rid of. A booming smuggling trade sprang up, and the demand was so great that it even strained national silver supplies. The leaders in Peking and the walled city of Canton wanted opium out. England wanted the silver that opium brought. In 1841 the British attacked.

By 1846 China was open to the British, the French, and the Americans. Antiforeign feelings swelled in Chinese hearts, leading to some very nasty goings-on—what with British heads impaled on spikes and all. The central areas of anti-Anglo feelings were Kwangtung and Canton. Pirates and bandits were everywhere, taking white people's heads. In 1857 the British and French occupied Canton and started moving toward Peking. The Russians joined them.

By 1860, things had come to a boil. There were Taiping rebellions and Muslim rebellions, marking political and religious unrest.

All that changed in the mid-1300s. Bad government led to rebellion. The Mongols were pushed north and the Ming dynasty started in the south. Now here was a dynasty that modern Oriental movie producers could get their teeth into. Over 150 films are set in this roughly three-hundred-year period, dealing with all the ingredients that make history interesting.

There were clan intrigues, gang battles, threatening western Mongolians, threatening far eastern Manchurians, threatening

The more confusing things became, the more widespread was the corruption. All the outlying areas—Nepal, Burma, and the like—were falling under British control. Meanwhile, Japan was getting into the act, coming into conflict with China over the sovereignty of Korea.

Things got so bad between China and the foreigners that the government leased Hong Kong to the British for ninety-nine years to serve as an import-export way station. It was basically a liaison between the fractious powers.

KUNG-FU REVOLUTION

Things boiled over in 1900. This was the justly famous boxer rebellion, and an absolutely vital martial arts movie period, since this antiforeign movement consisted of zealous followers of the "Righteous and Harmonious Fists"—what they considered to be an invulnerable form of kung-fu.

According to their slogan, they fought for "support of the Ch'ing and extermination of foreigners." On June 20 it became full-scale declared war on all foreigners, Chinese boxing versus guns. Kung-fu lost. By 1901, China was no longer free and the populace was humiliated.

For the next decade China suffered under various foreign rule and had to be content with frothing at the mouth on the sidelines of international affairs. By 1911, it was all too much to take. Civil wars, Japanese invaders, and foreign influence all led to the development of the republic, starting in 1912. Although initially conceived as a democracy, China just didn't seem capable of sustaining it.

The National Assembly, another name for the parliament, was created, mostly populated by former revolutionaries. But just because they were revolutionaries didn't mean they were any less insidious than their royal predecessors. Dirty deeds and assassi-nations were the order of the day. One Yuan Shih-k'ai took over, making the parliament appoint him president, and then he disbanded the parliament. By the beginning of World War I, Yuan's government was a dictatorship.

Yuan died in 1916, and members of the government battled amongst themselves to see what sort of country China would become, imperial or democratic. When the smoke cleared there was the Nationalist party and the Communist party. By 1922, most of the influencing nations agreed to allow China to find its own way, and from there on in, it became a battle between Chinese regions—mostly north and south.

All this history was rich fodder for modern filmmakers. China's story was full of "no-win" scenarios. There were many times during its eras when both sides of an issue were "right," allowing producers to picture all kinds of heroes, Ming, Ching, Manchu, or Shaolin. The 1930s were equally rich in stories. The Nationalists had established a new order, which lasted from 1928 to 1937, even though they warred with the Communists most of the time.

What brought them both together was an outside enemy: the Japanese. For years the Japanese ravaged China, committing atrocities that the Chinese still can't quite get over. This is an absolutely vital aspect of Chinese kung-fu movies: hatred of the Japanese. It wasn't until very recently that a Japanese was pictured in a favorable light in a Chinese movie. For the most part, they are the worst kind of cowardly, arrogant, dishonest, and foul creatures imaginable.

By 1939, things had stalemated somewhat. The Allies threw in some $500 million to aid China in her fight. Sadly, the fight wasn't just with the Japanese; it also continued between the Communists and the Nationalists. On December 7, 1941, everything changed: Japan bombed Pearl Harbor. America was angry now, which didn't help the Nationalists. As World War II dragged on, bringing poverty and inflation with it, the reigning Nationalist government fell completely out of favor.

Once the war ended, Chinese civil war began and raged until 1949. It was Chiang Kai-shek versus Mao Tse-tung, and Mao won for the Communists. October 1, 1949 marked the establishment of the People's Republic of China.

In terms of martial arts movies, that's where it ends. Great Britain had acquired Hong Kong from China in 1898 with a ninety-nine year lease—the story of Chinese kung-fu movies actually becomes a story of Hong Kong kung-fu movies. The People's Republic didn't make a bona fide martial arts epic until 1981.

Kung-fu movies set in modern China reflect the concerns of the areas in which they are filmed. That means mostly Hong Kong, with a bit of Taiwan and the Philippines thrown in for good measure. All three areas are pretty depressed in terms of economy and quality of life, so modern martial arts movies are usually fairly squalid affairs filled with ugly pessimism.

Nevertheless, the period between 1912 and the present is the richest in terms of kung-fu material. At least two hundred kung-fu films are set during this era—everything from superheroic adventures to madcap comedies to sizzling crime tales. This is where we can begin. Now that we've established where all the martial arts movies' stories come from, we can get down to the history of the kung-fu films themselves.

CHINESE MARTIAL ARTS CHART

Different kinds of kung-fu are as varied as the characters who populate the martial arts film genre. To list them all would be impractical and, considering the way new "fictional" kinds of kung-fu are created in various movies, darn near impossible.

Listed below are the most prevalent forms of real kung-fu presented on the silver screen. All are extremely difficult to learn, so watching a master practitioner in a movie is almost always a delight.

Even more delightful is watching how two masters of two different forms fight each other and how the hero must adapt or adjust his style to defeat a seemingly invulnerable opponent. Such is the stuff of great kung-fu confrontations.

Choy Li-fut: Cantonese name for a popular southern style which relies on a strong stance. Its best known techniques are the back fist, downward scraping arm swings, and the knuckle fist. It is also a style that utilizes weapons. When you see someone using things such as the Eighteen Staff, the Baat Gwa Lance, or the Willow Leaf Double Swords, you'll know the fighters are proponents of choy li-fut.

Drunken style: An extremely popular, versatile, adaptable style which calls for astonishing ability, strength, and control because it seems to involve no strength or control. A student of the drunken style wobbles, weaves, and just generally imitates the actions of a drunkard. This student may even fall down, but watch it—it is just a ruse to draw an opponent into a lightning foot or hand. This style's popularity also rests on its adaptability to other styles; there can be a drunken version of almost any martial art. The art derives from legend, so listen for references to the Eight Immortals or The Eight Drunken Fairies.

Eagle Claw: A vicious but graceful art derived from the movements of the eagle. The emphasis here is on quick eyes and fingers twisted into a claw position to strike at an opponent's pressure points.

The Five Animal Styles of the Shaolin Temple:

1. Crane—The hands become beaks, and one-legged stances are standard. The crane fighter goes for the nerves and pressure points.
2. DRAGON—The most esoteric of the five animal styles; it needs the most power to perform. The object here is not to slash or break but to crush.
3. LEOPARD—Believe it or not, the foreknuckles of the hands are the primary striking area of this style.
4. SNAKE—A wonderfully cinematic "sneaky" style in which the arms and fingers turn into a snake, with all the dangerous "snake bites" that suggests.
5. TIGER—Rip and tear, rip and tear. A slashing, scratching style.

Hsing-I: One of the three "internal" systems. The other two are *tai chi* and *pa-kua.* The visible clues to these techniques involve soft, circular motions and regulated breathing patterns. But these three are actually methods of concentrating power. When a fighter pauses to do a strange sort of breathing, you can bet he's utilizing one of the three internal systems of China.

Hung Gar: One of the most popular southern styles because it combines the best from several other styles. One of the great kung-fu movies, *Executioners From Shaolin* (U.S.: *Executioners of Death*), was all about the development of this technique—the combination of the Shaolin tiger and Shaolin crane styles. Since this development took place in the eighteenth century, many films set in the time shortly after that period utilize hung gar extensively. No wonder, since it is a dazzling form to watch.

Monkey: Another extremely filmable style which imitates the movements and fighting strategy of the simians. Although a strong technique, it is most often unmis-

takably pictured as a mincing style, with the proponent screwing up his face in a monkey impression and making monkey sounds. The style has five main forms—lost monkey, which utilizes surprise attacks; tall monkey, which uses swinging arms for distance; stone monkey, which is the powerful attack; wood monkey, which is used to deceive the opponent; and drunken monkey, the monkey version of the aforementioned art.

Phoenix Eye: Another esoteric but popular cinematic style, since it uses the single or double foreknuckle. When the foreknuckles come up on-screen, the Phoenix eye is unmistakable.

Praying Mantis: A great-sounding martial art which has a Southern style, but the Northern form is prevalent in films. Both forms are referred to in three ways, as seven star, eight steps, or six harmonies. Listen for one of those, and watch for the hooklike hand and its grasping, clawing, and sudden punches.

Shuai Chiao: Did someone on-screen just grab his opponent's arms, legs, shoulders, or other limbs to throw him, while also using indefinable kicks, blocks, and blows? Well, he's probably using this unusual form of wrestling.

Tan Tui: An exhausting but watchable form characterized by low-kicking techniques. A sure sign of tan tui is the swift transition of high and low stances.

White Crane: Not from the Shaolin Temple, but from Tibet, this is a style based on the movements not just of cranes, but of apes as well. It's tough to distinguish regular crane styles unless they are openly labeled white crane, Tibetan white crane, and even sometimes by white lama crane or lama crane.

Wing Chun: The most powerful-looking form of Chinese kung-fu besides jeet kune do (which isn't really a form). This is a direct Southern style that emphasizes simultaneous defense and attack with multiple straight punches at close range.

THE FIGHTING BEGINS

There seems to be a slight disagreement concerning which was the first Chinese martial arts movie. The Hong Kong International Film Festival lists it as *Thief in the Car* (1920). The late lamented *Martial Arts Movies* Magazine listed it as *Monkey Fights Golden Leopard* in an article by James Seetoo. This was a 1926 silent film about the "Monkey King," taken from a famous Chinese novel entitled *Journey to the West*.

However, most English-speaking fans of the genre consider it to be *The Burning of the Red Lotus Temple* (1929). It hardly makes any difference, really, since the 1930s and 1940s were rife with nebulous martial arts–influenced films made in Shanghai and Hong Kong.

These movies were little more than filmed stage plays, all sharing an artificiality that reduced the effect of whatever kung-fu was included. Usually this kung-fu was either faked by actors who were laboriously choreographed and then filmed move by move, or was shown as amazing feats accomplished with wires and pulleys.

Even so, the films from 1920 to 1949 are interesting in terms of how they relate to the later movies, and for how their colorful titles compare to their somewhat staid presentation. For instance, there was *How Wu Song Killed His Sister-in-Law* (1927), *Bloody Fights* (1933), *Hu Weiqian Smashes the Engine Room* (1939), and *How Fan Shiyu Took a Ten Thousand-Mile Journey for Vengeance* (1948).

The reason movies were being made at all was that Hong Kong and Shanghai were westernized. That is, they were more modern and less restricted than their mainland Chinese comrades. These areas were also overpopulated and stricken with all manner of social ills that progress can create. Therefore, they were in far more need of mass media entertainment. Up until 1949, this entertainment was highly stylized theater and cinema, mostly based on ancient traditions.

But then a director named Hu Peng heard about a master of martial arts named Huang Fei Hong. Born in 1847 (d. 1924), Huang Fei Hong was the son of one of the famous Ten Tigers of Kwang-tung (a group around which several movies have been made). Other than the fact that he practiced medicine, was expert in many forms of kung-fu, and excelled at a sport-contest called lion dancing, not much is known about the fellow.

Hu Peng rectified all that by starting a marathon film series which comprised an incredible eighty-five feature films over a twenty-year period. *The Story of Huang Fei-Hong Parts One and Two* (1949) was only the beginning of a phenomenon which was to become the foundation of the modern kung-fu film. Up until then, most movie martial arts feats were totally ludicrous and completely inaccurate (a problem which still afflicts most bad kung-fu movies, namely, most of those that appeared in the United States immediately after Bruce Lee died). Men leaped higher than trees, women flew through the air for hundreds of yards, and fighters did endless somersaults.

The actors in the Huang Fei Hong movies insisted on realism in the all-important action scenes. For the first time, kung-fu was the heart of the film, not just a peripheral ingredient. So the need for accuracy became vital in order to honestly portray the leading character's life. It also didn't hurt that the lead actor was so similar to the character he played.

Kwan Tak Hing was the name of that

actor, and his similarities to the actual Huang are telling. Born in 1906 and still thriving when he made his movies, Kwan was an actor in Cantonese opera, but more importantly, he was an accomplished lion dancer and spectacular martial artist. He was initially well versed in Hung boxing, which goes several steps farther than hung gar. Instead of melding two forms, hung fist, as it is also called, melded all five Shaolin styles with the horse, elephant, lion, and monkey techniques. From there, Kwan became a master of the white crane style.

As the films progressed over the decades, he became skilled in almost all the areas Huang himself excelled at. Huang seemed dedicated to mastering the most esoteric, difficult skills, such as the iron wire, five forms, and tiger vanquishing fists, as well as the impressive shadowless kick, which actor Kwan seemed to delight in displaying throughout the film series. Kwan himself was the creator of what is now known as the omni-directional Gangrou fist.

So director Hu had the character and the actor. And while the honorable legend of Huang and the charming personality of Kwan were vital, it took more than those to make the film series a success. First, these were pictures about a beloved personage in fairly recent, happier times, so they became a nostalgic preserver of particular Cantonese pastimes, such as "vying for firecrackers."

This was another sport-contest in which fireworks shot a bunch of red sticks into the air which teams would fight for when they came down. Whichever team held the most firecrackers at the end was the winner. Being champion was a matter of great pride for many martial arts schools. Of even greater importance was being the winner of the various lion-dancing competitions.

This is a hallmark of Cantonese life. Beneath ornate costumes of the colorful Chinese lion, martial artists vie for what is called lucky money. Not only is the acquisition important, but how the prize is gained is equally telling. It is the skill of the dancers beneath the costume which imbues the rippling lion body and heavy, puppetlike head of the outfit with character. Maneuvering this lion in competition with other lion dancers can call for the greatest skill a martial artist possesses.

In this area Kwan was a master, making the many Huang movies that involved lion dancing a visual delight. But the nucleus of the Huang Fei Hong films was the martial arts. These pictures reintroduced China to the joys of watching realistic kung-fu exquisitely performed by masters. In this case, the real thing was far more impressive than the artificial, theatrical feats portrayed in years past.

For the record: there were five basic Kwangtung schools of kung-fu teaching—the Hong School, the Liu, Cai, Li, and Mo. They taught the ten major fist forms based on the movements of the crane, elephant, horse, monkey, leopard, lion, snake, tiger, and tiger cub. In addition, there was training utilizing the eighteen legendary weapons of China, which included staffs, spears, and swords. From there the possibilities become endless. The Huang Fei Hong movies made use of many of these possibilities, in addition to showcasing the subtler, but just as important, concept of *wu de*—which means "martial virtue."

Up until that time, Oriental action films concentrated on savage tales of vengeance, characterized by a plot that had rival martial arts schools in conflict with one another due to pride or greed. This tried-and-true plot is still being overused today, but the Huang Fei Hong movies introduced an expert martial artist who used kung-fu for health and self-defense only. He was a chivalrous, considerate saint of a man who was always patient, humble, and on the underdog's side.

Wu Yixiao, a Cantonese opera writer, scripted the first four films, but Wang Feng is generally credited as being the main influence on the series, since he wrote as well as direct-

51

ed many of the most popular. But this was truly a partnership between the actors and the crew. Kwan choreographed most of his own battles with his main opponent, Shih Kien (best known as the evil Han in *Enter the Dragon*). Together, they created stunning bouts which remain the series' high points.

Almost every major modern kung-fu director was influenced by or actually worked on these motion pictures. The best of them, like *Huang Fei Hong Vied for the Firecrackers at Huadi* (1955) and *How Huang Fei Hong Vanquished the Twelve Lions* (1956), not only displayed great martial arts but Huang's wisdom, courage, restraint, morality, and intelligence as well.

Although there were some other martial arts films during the 1950s and 1960s, the Huang Fei Hong movies practically monopolized the market. By 1956, twenty-five of the year's twenty-nine kung-fu pictures featured this hero. These films were in the cinemas practically every month, and there were some years when the only martial arts movies were the Huang Fei Hong ones.

About the only other film series that was any kind of competition at all concerned the character Fang Shih Yu, an eighteenth-century, fiery-tempered master swordsman and bare-handed fighter who was trained at the Shaolin Temple. There were about sixteen films concerning this legendary young man over the same two decades the Huang movies reigned, but his character was to flourish while Huang's languished once other moviemakers discovered the joys of the kung-fu film.

The reasons why the genre didn't explode sooner were many and varied. First, it is not easy to create good martial artists. It takes years of dedication to perform kung-fu well on-screen, no matter whether you are a martial arts student, a Peking Opera alumnus, a gymnast, an acrobat, or an actor. And if you don't perform kung-fu well it is painfully evident to the audience. A bad martial arts actor looks like a clumsy fool.

Second, the Hong Kong film industry wasn't sophisticated enough during the 1950s and 1960s to mount the extravaganzas which were soon to explode throughout the Orient. About the only man who seemed to know what to do with a camera was King Hu, a lush epic filmmaker who toiled in Taiwan. He is probably the best action filmmaker the East has so far seen, but far from the best moviemaker.

This is not as fine a distinction as it might first appear. The "film aspect" of entertainment is technical. The "movie aspect" is emotional. King Hu's films, which include the recently rereleased *A Touch of Zen* (1966), are sumptuous, grand affairs which concentrate far more on character interaction and cinematic technique than on martial arts. Certainly nothing wrong with that, but this is a martial arts movie book.

To Hu, kung-fu was a dance and was treated as such. There's hardly any action in *A Touch of Zen*, but plenty of mood and symbolism—not to mention three distinct endings—within its three-hour running time. King Hu showed what could be done cinematically with what Chinese movie industry people had to work with, but essentially his films were magnificent visual elaborations of legends and stage plays. By the 1970s, the audience was ready for action, and a few folk were ready to give it to them—with a vengeance.

Hong Kong: Wushu Warriors

The first hint of things to come was in 1967. There had been years of Huang Fei Hong films, but also other movies like *The Young Swordsman* (1964). Swordplay movies had been a regular staple in Chinese cinema since the beginning, ranging in quality from predictable to awful. They were also marked by a ponderous artificiality, so audiences weren't expecting anything special when the lights went down and the screen lit up with *The One-Armed Swordsman.*

No one was prepared for what they saw. People stared in amazement as a supreme swordsman is saved from a murderous attack by his servant, who dies in his master's place. The swordsman takes the servant's son, Fong Kong, as his own, teaching him everything he knows. Years later, the swordsman is ready to retire and plans to turn his martial arts school over to Fong. All the attention Fong has received has turned the swordsman's daughter bitter and hateful. With two male students, she plans her revenge.

The trio confront the confused Fong, and, in the ensuing fight, the daughter herself hacks off Fong's right arm. Blood pouring out of his shoulder, Fong falls into the arms of a girl named Shiu Min, who slowly nurses him back to health. But by that time the situation has only grown worse. A rival martial arts school, led by the "Long-armed Devil,"

wants to destroy the elder swordsman's school utterly.

They find the one-armed man and the girl. He manages to fight them off but is again badly beaten in the process. Bloody, exhausted, and despondent, Fong is inspired by his woman's love; it is she who tells him to start again. Laboriously, he learns to master the one-armed sword.

But time stands still for no one, one-armed or not. The villain kills the two men who conspired with the evil daughter and holds the girl as captive. Fong rescues her, instigating a series of bloody retributions. Fong goes to join his master, but is confronted by the villain's henchmen. He wipes them out.

Fong returns to his master's school to find the elder swordsman wounded and his students killed. Completely alone, he marches into the Long-armed Devil's headquarters and massacres everyone. With the screen littered with bodies, Fong Kong sets off to settle down with his woman.

The audience was not the same when the lights came up. They had viewed a cathartic experience. After years of Confucian morality and bloodless, unconvincing, stagy fights, *The One-Armed Swordsman* showed them a tortured antihero who thought nothing of slaughtering his enemies. And after all the abuse he had taken, the viewers went along with the slaughter—in fact, they cheered it.

tants, demanding an arm from each. As if that nastiness weren't enough, they kidnap Fong's wife. That was a mistake. It gets the One-armed Swordsman angry, and from there on, it is slaughter time.

The filmmakers had found a formula: take a quiet, unassuming hero, heap incredible abuse on him, and then have him fight back with equally incredible rage and bloodlust. But more than that, Cheh and Kuang liberally littered the film with sensitive touches and telling actor's moments—which build audience sympathy for the put-upon, otherwise noble hero. They also set striking backgrounds for the action, such as the snowy woods where Fong's arm is chopped off.

And the slaughter was realistic. None of this swinging a sword and having the opponent fall down. Here, limbs were chopped off, blood spurted, and victims fell writhing. Suddenly producer Runme Shaw, director Chang Cheh, writer I Kuang, and star Wang Yu had the first million-dollar-grossing movie in Hong Kong history.

A sequel was called for and made. Not surprisingly, it was called *The Return of the One-Armed Swordsman* and premiered in 1969. The production team was the same, as was the film's point of view. Fong Kong is living peacefully in the country with his wife. An invitation to a dueling contest arrives, which Fong declines. Then the Eight Demon Swordsmen capture all the contes-

Naturally, in a realistic movie, none of this could have been possible. The arm could not have been so easily and cleanly hacked off, and Fong would have fallen, screaming, to the ground instead of stumbling away, and would have died within minutes from the shock and loss of blood. But taken as a superhero film, it works, and works beautifully.

Not content with this extreme statement of their theme, the same team went even further with *Golden Swallow* (1968), which is a sequel to one of King Hu's films called *Come Drink with Me*. Both were about a swordswoman played by Cheng Pei Pei, but the Shaw Brothers production cast Wang Yu as the white-garbed swordsman Silver Roc, who is a walking, two-armed death machine.

Here the writer, director, and star went for broke, mounting riveting scenes of wholesale mayhem, marked by an extremism that bordered on the supernatural. Silver Roc takes on the Dragon Gang with sword, darts, traps, and weapons of all kinds, complicating matters until Silver Roc stands, mortally wounded, blood all over his white outfit, defiant to the end.

The name of the game here was hysteria. In all his films, Wang Yu, a small, unimpressive-looking actor, played an obsessed man, and the fans loved it. It was an image Yu himself promoted, and cemented in 1970 by writing, directing, and starring in *The Chinese Boxer* (U.S.: *The Hammer of God*). In this, Wang Yu added his own particular stamp: intense hatred of the Japanese.

Wang Yu plays Lei, the top martial artist in his school until a bunch of Japanese karate killers murder everyone. They would have killed Lei as well had they known he was not dead, but he was merely wounded, lying among the dead. So while the Japanese terrorize the town, Lei goes to a cave and tortuously learns the Iron Palm technique. He weights himself, burns his arms, and suffers mightily among the eerie confines of the macabrely decorated interior of the cave.

At the start of his career, audiences were curious as to how Wang Yu would top himself in succeeding films. The carnage of the last seemed insurmountable—that is, until Yu showed up again. In *The Chinese Boxer*, Lei builds up audience participation through his training as well as the astonishingly heinous violence of the occupying Japanese, until the two forces smash into each other.

Eyes are gouged out, knives are plunged into chests, and limbs are shattered until Lei is mortally wounded through trickery. Even so, he bounces around the room and wipes out the final Japanese martial arts fighter. Once again, Wang Yu,

the filmmaker, had exhausted and exhilarated his audience.

Curiously, Wang Yu's cinematic hatred of the Japanese began the year he completed his best film—a Japanese coproduction featuring the famous blind swordsman of Japan, Zatoichi. Directed by Kimiyoshi Yasuda, a master stylist of samurai movies, it had a poetic realism and sociological undercurrent that the Chinese couldn't get close to.

Zatoichi and the One-Armed Swordsman (Japanese title: *Zatoichi Meets His Equal*) was about blindness of all kinds, not just the

Kwan Tak Hing wasn't the only man to play the famous Huang Fei Hong character. Ku Feng, one of the great Chinese supporting actors, starred here as the beloved martial artist.

55

Although he's already wounded, Jimmy Wang Yu is about to lose an arm in order to become The One-Armed Boxer.

leading character's lack of sight. Fong is traveling through Japan and becomes the astonished witness to a mass murder during a funeral procession. He saves a single child and escapes, only to be accused of the killings and hunted down. Zatoichi, as always played by Shintaro Katsu, finds, and then allies himself with, Fong, to reveal the real killers and mete out justice.

This plot synopsis cannot convey the visual power of this nearly unique combination of Japanese and Chinese martial arts movies. The images and action of this ninety-four minute movie seem unsurpassable, and it also seems quite clear that Wang Yu learned much from it. Upon returning to Hong Kong, he left the Shaw Brothers Studio before his contract was up to pursue his own goals.

The immediate result of his departure were the last two films he made which could be called great. The first appeared to be a combination of two previous films; it was called *The One-Armed Boxer* (U.S.: *The Chinese Professionals*, 1971). Again, extremism was the watchword here. He does *The Chinese Boxer* several times better by having his character face not just the Japanese, but fighters from all over the Orient!

This is a wild tournament film that has Yu losing an arm in an early bout but learning the Iron Arm technique from a wise sifu so that he can return and do each of the other fighters one better with just one arm. He takes out a whole series of martial artists, who range from the barely plausible to the totally ridiculous. Of course, there's the trademark karate man, but also Koreans, twins from Thailand, Mongolian lamas who can actually pump themselves up, and an Indian mystic who walks on his hands.

The One-Armed Boxer marked the start of Yu's degeneration. Although still entertaining, this movie crossed the line from superheroism to ludicrous farce. The actor played his scenes straight, but the scenes were stupid. His last roaring shout was *Beach of the War Gods*, Wang Yu's ultimate statement. He plays Hsaio Feng, a legendary fighter intent on preventing Japanese pirates from destroying a small Chinese coastal village in the last days of the Ming dynasty.

The film is full of characters and fights, but Wang saves the best for last: an unrestrained twenty-minute battle in which Feng

Now, is this the face of a superstar? It's Jimmy Wang Yu, who was the biggest thing in the Orient before Bruce Lee, in The Tattooed Dragon.

57

lays low the whole crew of Japanese pirates. The second-to-final shot shows him standing amid the bodies on the beach as a slightly late group of Chinese soldiers approach. The

final shot shows him slowly dropping dead amidst the corpses as the army marches by.

It's hard for the action-film lover not to appreciate such grand visions and extreme

since he lived on to make a long list of uninspiring and, in some cases, dreadful movies, his contribution to the genre is tarnished.

In 1972, he made a series of mediocre films with Lo Wei as director, but Wei could not do with Yu what he had been able to do with Bruce Lee. Wang Yu was nowhere near the skilled stylist Lee was. His expertise was not in the martial arts, really; it was in the dramatic, cinematic use of his limited kung-fu ability. He could make fight scenes look good, that is, until a truly great martial artist, such as Bruce Lee, showed up.

These new films, made just months after Yu's greatest triumphs, were tacky-looking, small-scale adventures. He no longer seemed interested in, or even capable of, mounting a grand production. In *A Man Called Tiger*, Yu played a modern fighter who appears to join a crime boss until he can get some incriminating evidence for a cop played by Lo Wei. The ending had a bunch of thugs pulling axes on him. He gets his leg sliced up, but manages to hurl the bad guy off a Hong Kong skyscraper.

The Tattooed Dragon was more like the Wang Yu of old, but only in that he's persecuted, badly wounded, and taunted until the very end, when he wipes his enemies out. Still, the climax involved only a few people, and the battle took place in a claustrophobic tea house.

In 1974, an attempt was made to assure him an international following (he was one of the first to be declared "the New Bruce Lee!") with *The Man from Hong Kong*, an Australian-Chinese coproduction directed by Brian Trenchard Smith. For this film he was dubbed Jimmy Wang Yu, and the moniker stuck. He has been known by that name ever since.

Although well meaning, decently made, and featuring George Lazenby as the villain,

statements. However, it seemed as if Wang Yu had nothing else to say after those first few films. Had he died, like Bruce Lee, his reputation and fame would have grown. But this modern espionage-crime thriller did not impress audiences who had seen what Bruce Lee could do. It was back to the Orient for Jimmy Wang Yu, and to reams of pale copies of his past groundbreakers.

LET THE BLOOD FLOW

The same fate was not to befall Chang Cheh. He was too experienced to let youthful enthusiasm overwhelm him. He was almost fifty years old at the time, and had been toiling in the Oriental film industry since 1947, working for Shaw Brothers for ten years. When Wang Yu left the studio, the contract director seemed to realize that the day of the non–martial arts actor in action films was over. He started looking for stars who matched the charisma, attitude, and handsomeness of Bruce Lee. As it turned out, no one man could match Lee's popularity. In this case, it took two.

They were David Chiang and Ti Lung. Their first major effort came in the bleak, intense drama *Vengeance* (1970). Many consider it Cheh's best piece of "serious" kung-fu cinema. There is no doubt that his and scriptwriter I Kuang's juggling of images ancient (represented by the Ti Lung character's involvement with a Peking Opera troupe) and modern made for some of the director's most impressive relevant visual statements. As his career was to progress, his visuals would become more and more cartoonish.

But trying to pigeonhole Chang Cheh is difficult, considering he has made about one hundred movies in the last twenty-two years. His period of greatest fluctuation came in the years immediately after Wang Yu's departure. He made historical action films with Lung and Chiang as well as modern sagas featuring that duo and another young newcomer named Chen Kuan Tai. All three deserve attention.

David Chiang was born in 1947, the year Chang Cheh started in films. His parents were both actors, so he made his initial appearances in child roles. He grew to be a slight, short young man, but he was quick and accurate in the martial arts. In the movies, he started as a stuntman, but graduated to acting when Cheh discovered him.

In the early years he specialized in wily, con-artist characters—perfectly matched with Ti Lung's matinee-idol attitude and looks. He is sometimes known to U.S. fans as Rover, the street-thief character he played in *The Savage Five* (released in America in 1979). In the later years he played what parts he could, but was never completely convincing as a supreme kung-fu master because of his size and slight build.

Ti Lung, on the other hand, is probably the most majestic of all kung-fu movie stars. He has matured into a regal personage; a versatile actor with a staunch respect for, and a seemingly effortless ability at, the martial arts. This ability derived from studying karate, hung gar, tae kwon do, and Mantis Fist since 1961. His screen presence was honed by a year-long Shaw Brothers Studio course that sharpened his acting and fighting skills.

Both he and Chiang seemed to be naturals, and played off each other well. In the early films, Lung was often cast as the regulation hero with Chiang as the antihero. It was this sort of part which best suited Lung and has followed him throughout his continuing career, which includes over seventy martial arts movies. No one ever said the Shaw Brothers Studio didn't put their actors to work.

Chen Kuan Tai was the third wheel on this Chang Cheh bicycle, and didn't stay riding with the duo for long. Unlike the other two, he was known as a martial artist before his film career, winning the 1969 light-heavyweight championship at the East-Asian Tournament in Singapore. He started learning Monkey-style kung-fu when he was eight and in several films displayed how powerful the art could be. Unlike other screen

Angela Mao Ying herself, the first major female kung-fu star, as she appeared in the violent When Tae Kwon Do Strikes *(U.S.:* Sting of the Dragon Masters*).*

Monkey stylists, however, he never resorted to prancing monkey impersonations.

While Ti Lung was featured in Wang Yu's *Return of the One-Armed Swordsman*, Kuan Tai was in *The Chinese Boxer* as well as *Huang Fei Hong Bravely Crushing the Fire Formation*—the last Huang movie of the early 1970s. He achieved stardom with Chang Cheh's *Boxer from Shantung* (U.S.: *Killer from Shantung*, 1972) in which he played a naive martial artist in the corrupt, danger-fraught city of Shanghai on the eve of the Sino-Japanese war.

The most notable film the trio made together under Cheh's direction was *Blood Brothers* (U.S.: *Dynasty of Blood*, 1973), one of the director's more ambitious attempts at combining martial arts action with a meaningful story, about the dangers of power and friendship. It is set in the mid-nineteenth century during the Taiping Rebellion and is based on actual people and events.

Chiang and Kuan Tai are highwaymen until Lung convinces them to join the Imperial Army. As Lung excels, his absolute power begins to corrupt him completely. He has an affair with the Kuan Tai character's wife, then has Kuan Tai killed. Chiang takes revenge for his dead friend on his ex-friend, and then willingly gives himself up and is executed.

The film well represents the Shaw Brothers movies of the early seventies. The brothers, Run Run and Runme, own a gigantic studio with soundstages, standing exterior sets, and a costume warehouse. Sets and costumes are meticulously designed in intricate detail, covering a cross section of Chinese history. They have a school on the premises, complete with dormitories. In what is called Movietown, they are able to film massive productions with sweep and pageantry.

The Five Masters of Death: *(from left) Meng Fei, Alexander Fu Sheng, Ti Lung, David Chiang, and Chi Kuan Chun discuss their groundbreaking movie.*

They also have a waterfront, where Chang Cheh filmed *Deadly Duo*, another early seventies kung-fu adventure that represents a regular Chiang-Lung team-up. This featured the pair as noble heroes of the Yuan dynasty trying to save their prince from the Mongol hordes. Naturally, Lung is nobler than crafty Chiang, but it is Chiang who gives his life in the finale to save Lung and the prince.

Deadly Duo was also a good example of what was wrong and what was right about Cheh's early kung-fu output. Although the film was full of interesting characters and esoteric weapons—Lung had a battle-ax, Chiang a steel whip, and the villains were Fire, Earth, and Tree Men—time between fights crawled like a snail. In one particularly ludicrous scene, the main heroes' associates discuss at length crossing a treacherous drawbridge before each tries it in turn and falls to his death.

The ending, however, is worth the price of admission. Chiang and Lung chop away at the Mongol hordes until Lung is safely at sea with the prince on a raft while Chiang stands, dead, on the wharf, blocking the surviving Mongols. To paraphrase the final line by the Mongol general: "If the Chinese have other warriors of this quality, we're in deep trouble."

In 1972, David Chiang was given the distinction of playing in *The New One-Armed Swordsman*, whose title character must avenge Ti Lung's character's death inside the Tiger Fort. This one-armed swordsman was named Lei Li, and he supposedly chopped off his own arm when defeated in a fight, but no one was fooled. Chiang's intensity was not the alienated, obsessive kind that Wang Yu's was, and while Chang Cheh puts in some wonderfully clever visuals and handles the bloody battle scenes exceptionally, these proposed new adventures did not take off.

Where Chang Cheh distinguished himself from the directors who followed was in his use of blood. He has never shirked from its use while those around him sought a cleaner, less ugly format with which to display their martial arts expertise. He has also been fortunate in his ability to scout and promote talent in both his actors and martial arts instructors.

Chang broke the mold in 1972 with *The Water Margin* (U.S.: *Seven Blows of the Dragon*), in which he introduced a protracted-fight-scene filming style that has remained vital to this very day. Although crude at that time, this movie marked the end of the razzle-dazzle editing style which made non–martial artists look decent in fight scenes. Although the camera work can still be eye-straining, from this feature on the best kung-fu battles were filmed without technical "juice."

The Water Margin/Seven Blows of the

Dragon was based on the classic novel by Shi Nai-an called *Outlaws of the Marshes*, written in the fourteenth century. It concerned the 108 Mountain Brothers—a famous band of righteous mercenaries in the eleventh century (Sung dynasty) who fight bad guys where they find them. The movie and its sequel, *All Men Are Brothers*, gave Chang Cheh a chance to film kung-fu fights just for their own sake.

But he truly found his niche in 1975 with *Five Shaolin Masters* (U.S.: *Five Masters of Death*), the fourth in Cheh's Shaolin series. As far as critics were concerned, this movie marked the start of Cheh's decline. As far as this book is concerned, it marked the start of his finest martial arts movies. Indeed, he no longer seemed to be looking for relevant images. Now he seemed intent on producing one-hundred-percent superhero entertainment. He seemed to stop taking his movies' histrionics seriously and got down to some serious mayhem.

CHANG'S GANG

Five Masters of Death was based on the famous story of the Shaolin Temple's destruction and the survival and vengeance of its escaping students. It followed *Heroes Two* (U.S.: *Bloody Fists*), *Shaolin Martial Arts*, and *Men From the Monastery* (U.S.: *Disciples of Death*)—all in 1974. In these preceding films, Cheh introduced Chi Kuan Chun, a dark-skinned actor with high cheekbones and a ferret face, as well as Fu Sheng, a lively acrobat–martial artist who was in the first class of the studio's newly conceived project—the Shaw Training Center for Young Actors and Actresses.

The 1975 Shaolin movie teamed Ti Lung and David Chiang with Chun and Sheng, and then added a cute-looking fellow named Meng Fei to fill out the five. Together they take on early eighteenth-century enemies led by actor Wang Lung Wei—a brutish, mustached pres-

Ti Lung (right) shows what The Five Masters of Death *was all about: great fight scenes with esoteric weapons.*

ence who was to become one of the most versatile villains in the kung-fu genre.

Here is a telling distinction of martial arts movies. Wang Lung Wei is not a versatile actor; he is a versatile fighter. It is his particular skill that he can make defeats by everyone from Fu Sheng to David Chiang look believeable. When Wang Lung Wei is ultimately defeated, whether by a 150-pound lad or a hulking muscle man, the beaten fighter makes it work.

To beat him this time, Fu Sheng and Chi Kuan Chun learned the Shaolin animal styles, Meng Fei learned the "rolling" style (a form of wrestling that looks artificial on-screen—David Chiang did it in *Seven Blows of the Dragon*), Ti Lung became master of the staff pole, and Chiang used the steel whip with deadly accuracy (he hurls the sharpened point through two men at once during the climactic free-for-all).

Only Sheng, Chiang, and Lung survive at the fade-out, but this film's success was to lead to many other Shaolin movies made by Chang Cheh over the next two years. At this time he got the first of two brainstorms—that was to give Fu Sheng his due. In a very short time, this personable actor had won over audiences with his boyish and impish charm. Even when playing a serious character, he had a wit and prickly style unmatched by any other action star working.

Cheh secured Fu Sheng's future by starring him in *The Chinatown Kid* (1977) and the *Brave Archer* series (1978–79). The former film was probably one of the best modern martial arts movies made. In it Sheng plays an impoverished troublemaker who is forced to flee the Orient for San Francisco. There he slaves in a Chinese restaurant, meeting up with a quiet student (Sun Chien).

Because he is such a good martial artist, he runs afoul of two warring street gangs, led by muscular Lo Mang on one side and sophisticated Kuo Chui on the other. All Sheng's character wants to do is be good, so when Sun Chien's character becomes addicted to the drugs supplied by the gang, Sheng sees the error of his ways. Although a rich and successful member of the gang, he attacks, killing all his enemies, but dying himself.

The Chinatown Kid was more realistic than most modern chop-socky pictures, and the filmmakers pull off one of their cleverest symbols in the form of a digital watch. It represents the brave new American world to Sheng's character, and his actions all revolve around attaining and sustaining the watch. At the end, as he's dying, he offers it to Chien—who takes it. The whole business is obvious, but extremely effective.

Sheng proved his mettle in period pieces directly afterward with *The Brave Archer* (U.S.: *Kung Fu Warlords*), in which he played a Sung-dynasty hero named Kuo Tsing, who did precious little archery. But Chang Cheh dazzled audiences with his sunny, brightly colored scenes of astonishing mayhem. This stuff went far beyond the Bruce Lee style of hurling around grossly inferior martial artists. These were duels between fighters of at least equal ability, in sumptuous period costumes on exact, intricately detailed period sets.

Following quickly came *The Brave Archer Part II* (U.S.: *Kung Fu Warlords Part II*), *Brave Archer Part III* (U.S.: *Blast of the Iron Palm*), and *Brave Archer and His Mate*. All promoted Chang Cheh's interest in extremely complicated plots that involved liberal doses of stunning fight scenes in which characters routinely flipped, kicked, chopped, and leaped with the greatest of ease. His films required exceptional acrobats and athletes. Although all the actors did almost all their own stunts, these sequences can be literally unbelievable to Western eyes.

Eastern audiences loved it, which led to Chang Cheh's second brainstorm. Using the "team" concept from *Five Masters of Death*, why not film a series of lively kung-fu movies all starring the same actors in basically the same roles? This gave rise to Chang Cheh's teams. The first team was David Chiang, Ti Lung, Chen Kuan Tai, Fu Sheng,

Chen Kuan-Tai matured into one of the strongest of kung-fu actors. Here he's discovered the "umbrella skeleton of death"—his one hope against "The Flying Guillotine."

and Chi Kuan Chun—even though those five rarely all played in the same film.

He introduced his second team in the preceding Fu Sheng starring vehicles. The first team had split up to work with other directors and other studios, so the second team premiered on its own with *The Five Venoms* (U.S.: *Five Deadly Venoms*, 1978). In this film, set in the fifteenth century, a dying teacher taught five masked students the deadliest forms of kung-fu known—snake, centipede, lizard, toad, and scorpion. None of the students knew each other at the time, but now several had teamed to become criminals. The teacher tells his last student, who knows a bit of all five arts, to find the students and stop their crimes.

From this simple premise, Cheh extracted

Director Chang Cheh made his best modern kung-fu movie with Fu Sheng starring in The Chinatown Kid.

martial arts extremism. The villains practice esoteric, nasty killing styles. They defeat each other with a solid gold, knife-lined casket, pins in noses, knives in ears, as well as their own unbelievable skills. In the finale, when the venoms fight, the heroes literally walk up the walls and stand there. It is all done with bold, unapologetic style.

Thus the second team was introduced. Kuo Chui was always the main hero, and always played a street-smart supreme fighter who hid behind a guise of a beggar, transient, or criminal. Chiang Sheng was known by fans as cutie-pie, and indeed he is—just as small and thin as David Chiang, but almost always playing the acrobatic partner to Chui. Sun Chien was the kicker, sometimes hero, sometimes villain. Lo Mang is the thick-headed muscleman, and Lu Feng is almost always the insidious traitor who lures heroes into his traps.

Chang Cheh also used a variety of regular actors in secondary roles, but these five were the main unit for at least ten adventures that were unique in their extremism. The tone was set by their second movie, *Crippled Avengers* (U.S.: *Mortal Combat*, 1978). Chen Kuan Tai played a Ming Dynasty kung-fu master driven mad by his wife's death and son's disfigurement: some of his enemies chopped off the boy's forearms and the mother's legs.

Years later, Kuan Tai has taught his son (Lu Feng) the Tiger style and replaced his limbs with metal arms that can elongate and shoot darts. From then on, the wealthy man cripples whoever he doesn't like. He blinds a trinket salesman (Kuo Chui), deafens a blacksmith (Lo Mang), chops the feet off a passerby (Sun Chien), and makes retarded a hero who wants to avenge them (Chiang Sheng), by tightening a steel band around his skull.

The four unite, find the retarded hero's teacher, and learn new kung-fu techniques. The disfigured man is then given metal feet. The crippled masters return to town during a birthday party for their oppressor—which many of the country's great, but wicked,

70

kung-fu masters attend. The four wipe them all out, a climactic moment coming when Sun Chien puts his metal foot into the chest of one of them.

The Chiang Sheng character is killed by the metal arm's darts, but the others survive to take their vengeance on their insane tormentor. There is hardly a believable second in this adventure, but as a martial arts movie it works, as do such following adventures as

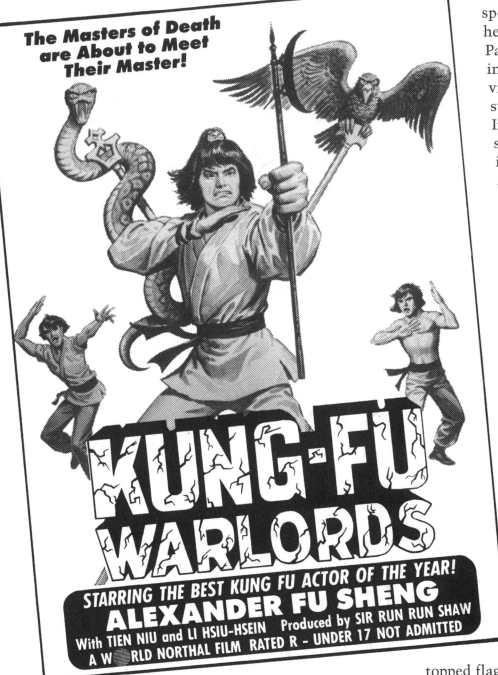

The Masters of Death are About to Meet Their Master!

KUNG-FU WARLORDS

STARRING THE BEST KUNG FU ACTOR OF THE YEAR!
ALEXANDER FU SHENG

With TIEN NIU and LI HSIU-HSEIN · Produced by SIR RUN RUN SHAW

A WORLD NORTHAL FILM · RATED R – UNDER 17 NOT ADMITTED

spear-, and wine-jug–carrying heroes face masters of the Iron Palm (which here leaves a black imprint that slowly kills the victim), the Iron Fan (a gigantic, sword-edged, steel war fan), the Iron Head (really, a man with a steel forehead shield), and the infamous Kid With the Golden Arm himself—a master of an art which makes him invulnerable to blades.

To see any of the Chang Cheh movies of this period is not to believe them, but to enjoy them for their kung-fu craziness and exuberant bloodiness. The director started searching out new talent while teaming his second team with Fu Sheng and Ti Lung for *Ten Tigers of Kwantung* (1979), a Cheh mess which juggled two stories through flashbacks, involved Huang Fei Hong's father and cousins, and had a man's head kicked off at the climax.

That out of his system, Cheh took the second team through *The Spearmen of Death* (1980) and *Masked Avengers* (1981). Kuo Chui fought spear-topped flags in the former and tridents in the latter, both about eight feet long. The two films were baroque and bloody.

The final complete second-team movie was *House of Traps* (1981), which pushed all Chang Cheh's concepts to the razor's edge. In the Sung dynasty, an evil man hides incriminating evidence in a death-filled pagoda and hires kung-fu criminals to guard it. Kuo Chui is the "Black Fox," a tarnished knight-errant who signs on as a guard but actually intends to secure the evidence for honorable Judge

The Daredevils (1978), an early Republic of China conflict in which street performers avenge themselves on a corrupt general (about the only second-team film in which the Kuo Chui character dies), and *The Kid With the Golden Arm* (1979).

Here Kuo Chui plays a drunken-style master who aids a hero-laden escort service trying to get a wagon of gold to a famine area during the Ming dynasty. The ax-, sword-,

Pao (an actual Sung dynasty lawman made famous in literature along with Judge Dee).

But first his associates must be slaughtered by the house of traps' spike-growing floors, spear-hurling walls, ax-swinging supports, arrow-shooting panels, and, most incredibly, razor-lined stairs which take off toes and parts of feet. The Black Fox masters them all, and at the fade-out is wondering about the evil that greed causes.

CHANG'S MASTERPIECE

The second team was no more. Kuo Chui, Chiang Sheng, and Lu Feng left the Shaw Brothers Studio. Sun Chien remained behind, but for some reason he was never given much to do in any of Cheh's pictures, even though he showed himself to be an accomplished leg fighter. Only Lo Mang, the strongman, remained, and he was the only second-unit "regular" who appeared in the director's most grandiose, and possibly best structured, but certainly bloodiest, superhero saga.

Five Element Ninja (U.S.: *Super Ninjas*, 1982) starred Chien Tien Chi as a virtuous member of a kung-fu clan attacked by the most insidious power for evil the martial arts world has ever known: the Japanese ninja. The film can be divided into four sections. Section one: The virtuous clan is challenged by an evil clan who have hired ninjas to do their dirty work. The good guys go to the five prearranged contest locations, only to be massacred by the ninjas who work within the five

elements.

The sun ninjas use golden shields to blind their victims; the wood ninjas use camouflage; the water ninjas come shooting out of a river; the fire ninjas deal fiery death; and the earth ninjas burrow underground. With all of their main fighters dead, the good clan rallies around their leader, expecting an attack at any moment. Unfortunately, a sympathetic clan member (Lo Mang) takes in a supposedly abused young woman (Chen Pei Hsi) who is actually a ninja spy.

Section two: The Ninjas attack, using

73

Ti Lung defeats all comers in
Seven Blows of the Dragon,
another breakthrough by
director Chang Cheh.

their spy for information. She also wounds Lo Mang, but it doesn't stop him from fighting like a man possessed, only to be speared to the smoking door of the locked house where the ninjas burn the clan leader alive. The ninjas then turn on their employers, killing the other clan, to become the masters of the martial arts world by themselves.

Section three: Chien's character, Hsaio, escapes to find an old sifu who knows all the ninja tricks. Hsaio joins this teacher's other three students to be laboriously taught new forms of kung-fu while voice-over narration traces the ninja arts (*Ninjutsu*) back to 200 A.D. After that they traveled to Japan during the Tang dynasty, which is where this sifu had to go to learn them.

Section four: Revenge! The four students, complete with metal axes that have more hidden weaponry than Batman's utility belt, face the five elemental ninja on the same sites where their Chinese associates were executed, and do the bad guys one better. They reflect the sun back at the golden-garbed ninjas and hurl the villains onto a cliff face. The wood and water ninjas are also dispatched, while the poles sprout flags which sweep away the flame and smoke of the fire ninjas.

Finally, the four take on the supreme ninja, who is the earth fighter. He erupts out of the

guy in half. The last shot in the film is a freeze-framed image of the surviving good guys smashing the ninja emblem, which had been carved into a boulder, to pieces.

After this elaborate phantasmagoria, Chang Cheh seemed to step back for awhile. Like Wang Yu before him, he seemed to have gone just as far as he could in one direction. His second team had dispersed, and the director really didn't have a third team. Although he had many young actors to choose from, most of them didn't want to be tied down to one director or one kind of film. By the early 1980s, the Hong Kong film industry had exploded with new concepts and new possibilities, both in the technical and creative areas.

Chang Cheh seemed to figure that since he had been essentially doing fantasies for the last few years, why not go all the way? His next few films were flat-out, old-fashioned supernatural kung-fu adventures with ghost children, avenging spirits, and demigods who could fight on water and in the air. *Attack of the God of Joy* (1983) and *The Nine Demons* (1984) were "anything goes" pictures, with explosions, colored lights, and horrors bursting in at any moment.

Interestingly, his second-team's first independent feature was *The Hero Defeating Japs*

ground time and again, slashing with his knife-covered boots until the hero forces the knives into his own chest to hold the villain still while his cofighters literally tear the bad

Ti Lung, after leaving his partnership with David Chiang, became the most majestic of kung-fu stars. Here he plays the leader of the Ten Tigers of Kwangtung.

(U.S. video title: *Ninja in the Deadly Trap*, 1983), a decent Ninja film that guest-starred Ti Lung and Shoji Kurata, a man who has made his living playing evil Japanese martial artists in Chinese films. Kuo Chui (who also directed), Chiang Sheng, and Lu Feng were in place as the heroes who fight Ming dynasty ninja invaders to protect a book called *Summary of Fighting Skills.* Although the movie had fine kung-fu and a workable plot, it was inferior to their previous master's wild, scarlet-soaked visions.

THE MASTER OF MARTIAL ARTS

"Forgive man and forebear. Never forget humility and kindness. That's the way real kung-fu should be."
—Challenge of the Masters

Once Bruce Lee, Wang Yu, and Chang Cheh started their early-seventies film careers, the basic stories of all kung-fu movies were established, as were their shortcomings. The difference between a good martial arts movie and a bad one was how carefully the film-

makers paid attention to details.

A sure death knell for these pictures was the appearance of a totally unrealistic kung-fu technique (such as shooting through the air like Superman), ridiculous plot developments, or such camera tricks as editing out individual frames to make a fight scene seem faster (which also makes it seem to lurch).

The challenge of the martial arts movie is to make the same tired plots seem fresh and important. The other trick is to make the well-worn kung-fu seem new and amazing. In the 1970s there were a few men who could do this, but there was only one man who did it strictly in the area of Chinese *wushu*. The others sought, wisely, to broaden the genre, to make it understandable to a worldwide audience.

But only Liu Chia Liang seeks to make the greatest movies about the ancient arts of China without dilution or distortion. He exaggerates, he certainly enlarges, but to him, kung-fu is the thing. And it shows. He is without doubt the finest pure martial arts moviemaker.

Liu Chia Liang has lived up to the promise that is inherent in his family. His father was Liu Chan, who learned kung-fu from Lin Shih Yung, who, in turn, learned it from the real Huang Fei Hong. As fate would have it, Liu Chan often played his own teacher in the Huang Fei Hong movies. Liu Chan also taught his small son kung-fu, starting him at the age of eight.

It wasn't long before Liu Chia Liang was featured in the Huang movies, learning as much about filmmaking as he did about martial arts. In 1965, when he was twenty-one years old, he joined the Shaw Brothers Studio after having served as martial arts instructor on two films (*South Dragon, North Phoenix*, 1963; and *The Jade Box*, 1965), along with a gentleman named Tang Chia. Chia was to start directing fine, traditional martial arts movies in the 1980s, but in the mid-sixties he remained teamed with Liang and assigned to the Chang Cheh unit.

The duo choreographed movies with Wang Yu (*Golden Swallow*), Ti Lung, David Chiang (*Deadly Duo*), and Fu Sheng (*Five Masters of Death*), among others. In some cases, the actors never looked better. While he advised them on the set, Liang also trained many of the actors off the set as their sifu. Finally, in 1975, he was given his chance to direct. Tang Chia went to other directors, and Kuo Chui, Chiang Sheng, and Lu Feng took over the choreography on Chang Cheh's pictures.

Liu Chia Liang's very first movie was a groundbreaker and a box-office success. *The Spiritual Boxer* (1975) was not only the first of what was to become Chinese "New Wave" kung-fu comedies, but a direct satire of martial arts films as well. Taking place before the Boxer Rebellion, it featured a drunken master and his student trying to convince a village that they are masters of spiritual kung-fu, which makes them invulnerable to any weapon.

But when the master is too drunk to convince the residents that they should hire him to protect the town from bandits, his student takes over, faking all the feats of strength and invulnerability—and neatly lampooning such feats in previous serious kung-fu films. The student is too successful: the townspeople hire him and the criminals attack. Although he isn't a spiritual boxer, he is versed enough in the martial arts that, when his master calls out different forms—Dragon, Tiger, and Snake among them—he is able to utilize each to vanquish his foes.

Not only was the subject matter special, but Liu Chia Liang's presentation was special as well. He had learned much on the Huang

Fei Hong and Chang Cheh sets. His filming of the elaborate, complex martial arts was clear, fluid, and concise. Somehow, through a unique combination of actor and camera choreography, the specific techniques of kung-fu were plainly displayed to the audience, even though the fighters were lightning quick.

In addition, his leading actor was personable. Rather than relying on an established Shaw star (both Ti Lung and Chen Kuan Tai are featured only in the prologue), Liang used Yung Wang Yu, one of his own students. The difference between Yung Wang Yu and Jimmy Wang Yu is the difference between day and night. If Jimmy could be considered the Chinese Bruce Willis, then Yung could be the Chinese Will Smith—a sprightly, clever, smiling survivor.

If *The Spiritual Boxer* made Liang a director to watch out for, his next film, *Challenge of the Masters* (1976), established his reputation for making a traditional concept seem brand new. In this case, it was the Huang Fei Hong movies. Liang had seen them all and figured it was about time that someone made movies about the character's youth—the all-important genesis of the ultimate Confucian hero. What made the man so saintly?

The film started on a striking note—one which would be repeated throughout the director's career. The credits played over a stark scene, obviously filmed on a huge soundstage. There had been no attempt to make the environment realistic. It was a huge white expanse with two towers of Chinese characters (lettering) around which two fighters practiced their moves. The fighters were Chen Kuan Tai, portraying Huang's teacher Lu Ah Tsai, and Liu Chia Hui, the adopted brother of the director, playing Huang Fei Hong.

This second film was a family affair, with all three brothers playing featured roles. In addition to Hui as the star, the director played the villain, and the third brother, Liu Chia Yung, played the policeman who dies trying to capture the crook. (Remember, the Chinese use their family name first. Liu Chia

is the family name; Hui, Liang, and Yung are first names.)

The director didn't falter. *Challenge of the Masters* was a well-paced, involving thriller. It starts with Huang's father's martial arts school being defeated in the "vying for fire-cracker" competition by a rival school, which cheated—thanks to the advice of a visiting kung-fu master, who also happens to be a wanted criminal. The Huang Chi Ying school (Huang Fei Hong's father) is badly abused and humiliated by the rival school's

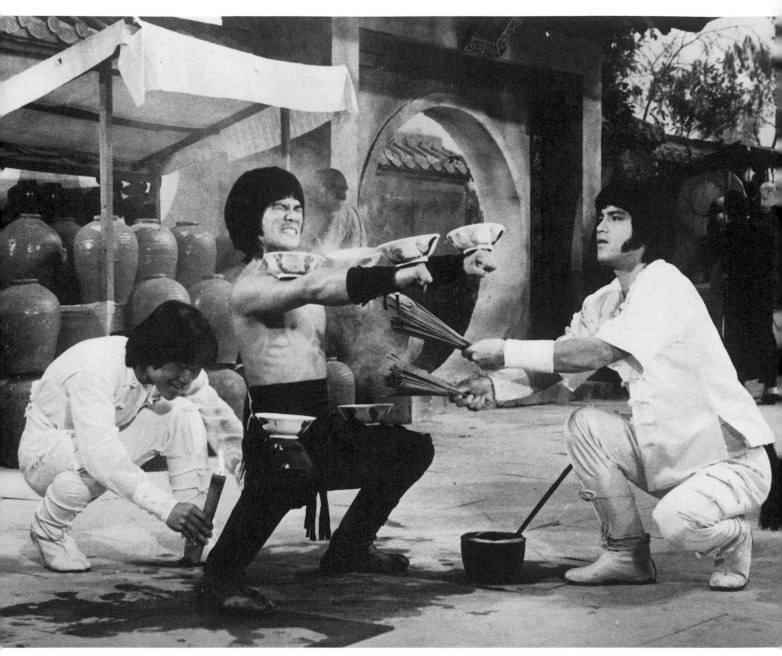

Ten Tigers of Kwangtung showcased the Shaw Brothers Studio's impressive sets and offered chances for young martial artists to be seen—not to mention torture each other.

vicious tactics, but the sifu still refuses to teach his son the martial arts.

Enter a traveling police officer who befriends Huang Fei Hong and introduces him to his father's sifu. After the boy goes off with his father's blessing to train for two years with the master, the cop corners the fugitive. In the ensuing fight within a bamboo forest, the killer uses steel shoe caps to weaken the policeman, and then finishes

him off with his deadly spear.

When Huang hears of his friend's death, he prevents the sifu from taking vengeance because he wants to do it himself. He throws himself into learning with even more dedication, and in the ensuing scenes a strong bond develops between teacher and student—a recurring theme in Liu Chia Liang's movies. In Chang Cheh's films, the sifu is a means to an end; he's just there to give Sun Chien metal feet. In Liang's movies, relationships, not violence, are important.

Huang spars with his teacher until he becomes skilled enough to take the smoking pipe from his sifu's hand. Then he returns to town on the eve of the vying-for-firecrackers contest. He faces the criminal in the same bamboo woods where the cop was killed, but remembers what his sifu taught him: "Forgiveness, forebearance, kindness, and humility."

He defeats the killer but refuses to finish him off, and then he almost singlehandedly prevents the rival school from using the metal slats they had secreted on themselves to unjustly win another firecracker contest. But when he and the other students refuse to beat them silly, the rival school realizes the error of their ways. Although this somewhat cloying ending would not have worked at all in another director's hands, Liang almost pulls it off.

Any audience doubts, however, were erased by his following feature, *Executioners From Shaolin* (U.S.: *Executioners of Death*, 1977). This starts where Chang Cheh's *Men From the Monastery* leaves off: the massacre of Shaolin students and the escape of one Hung Hsi Kuan, played in both films by Chen Kuan-Tai. Just to let viewers know he wasn't fooling around this time, Liang kills off his brother's, Hui's, character in the opening slaughter.

He wasn't kidding about other things, either. This new movie is a genuine Shaolin epic, but one in which the filmmaker is trying to make the audience understand why. In previous works, directors knew that the audience was already familiar with the Shaolin story. Therefore, they simply had the actors play staunch Shaolin heroes without texture or edges. In other words, they were representations, not real people. Liang was going for the real people here.

In terms of martial arts, the movie is about the creation of Hung Gar, otherwise known as Hung Fist or Hung Family boxing. It is the story of the Hung family. During his escape from Manchu persecuters, Hung Hsi Kuan meets Fang Yung Chun (played by Lily Li), who is a Crane fighter. They fall in love and marry as fugitives, constantly sparring. But unlike in Western movies, they don't fight verbally, they fight physically—testing each other's skill.

They have a son, and Hung spends ten years training for the fateful, inevitable revenge against Pai Mei, the White Browed Hermit (Lo Lieh), who killed the Shaolin sifu. Hung then fights up the steps to the Hermit's Temple and is soundly defeated by Pei Mei, just barely escaping with his life.

He returns home to train further, using a fascinating brass statue filled with moving metal balls which simulate the flow of Pai Mei's internal power. The dreaded hermit had developed a skill that allowed him to be impervious except for one single spot. Hung trains for seven additional years, until he hits the right ball at the right time in the right place. He goes back to face Pae Mai again, only to discover, to his horror, that "the Hermit" has also been studying. Now he can move his vulnerable spot *around.*

Hung hits what should have been the right spot and Pai just smiles, breaks Hung's legs, and kills him. By this time, Chinese audiences were reeling in their seats. They weren't used to this sort of thing. Sure, heroes had died before, but not this ignominiously—not after they had married and seen their son grow up.

That son had grown up to be Hung Wen Ting, played by Yung Wang Yu. Unlike his father, he listens to his mother's advice. She had begged her husband to learn her crane style in addition to his tiger style, but he would not. Wen Ting was raised with the crane style and now learns the tiger from his father's old manuals. It is he who almost casually enters Pai Mei's lair and kills him with the newly created Hung family fist.

Executioners From Shaolin was ambitious and audacious, and even though the white hermit's techniques were unrealistic and the reasons for Hung's failure and Wen Ting's success weren't that clear, the movie succeeded grandly on an emotional level. The scenes of the family practicing their skills on each other were very funny and combined well with the outlandish realism of the serious fight scenes.

But Liu Chia Liang wasn't about to let up. His next movie was the impressive milestone *The Thirty-Sixth Chamber of Shaolin*

MASTER KILLER

The American title for *The Thirty-Sixth Chamber* was *Master Killer* (1978), and it was the film that most impressed non-Oriental martial arts lovers since Bruce Lee's death. Up until then, most kung-fu movies forced the audience to accept the hero's mastery of his art at face value. Although there were training sequences in Chang Cheh and Wang Yu movies, they were terse setups showing the student at the very beginning and the very end of the process. What Liang had in mind was a movie about the process itself.

Master Killer starred Liu Chia Hui as Liu Yu Te, the reluctant revolutionary who was to become the famous real-life Shaolin monk, San Te. After Yu Te's family has been killed by Manchu assassins, the wounded, exhausted young man seeks shelter in the temple, vowing to learn kung-fu and take revenge.

What follows is a protracted set of training sequences, taking up almost a full hour of the film's 116-minute running time. Yu Te is taught the meaning of many things at the temple, having to discover much about himself before he even enters the first of thirty-five chambers. He learns balance, lightness, and intelligence before he is subjected to the tortures that pass for training.

To build up his arms, he carries water in heavy buckets, but knives are attached to his forearms so that if he lowers his limbs he will stab himself in his sides. He must hit a gigantic bell with a sledgehammer that has a twelve-foot-long handle—to strengthen his wrists. He must smash hanging weights with his head to build his skull strength. He must endure and master all of that and more before he actually starts to learn to fight.

Then he must become skilled with his hands, feet, and weapons. To the surprise of his teachers, he excels in all thirty-five chambers within five years and is offered the sifu-ship of any one of them, that is, until another high-ranking monk, played by Li Hai Sheng (another well-known genre villain), suggests that they fight. If the newly dubbed San Te can defeat his "Butterfly" double-swords–style, then he can choose his chamber.

In his first two tries, San Te is soundly defeated. Wandering in the bamboo forest nearby, he invents the three-sectional staff—three thin wooden poles approximately two feet long, each joined by a short length of chain. With this he defeats the two short swords of his opponent and is allowed to choose his chamber. Instead, he suggests instituting a thirty-sixth chamber, a place where other young men can be trained to resist Manchu treachery.

The remainder of the movie moves San Te out of the temple, where he takes revenge on his family's killers and recruits the first thirty-sixth-chamber students. Many Western viewers wonder why so much emphasis is placed on incidental characters during these climactic sequences, but Eastern audiences know that each of these men San Te comes across are actually famous historic characters—including some who had been portrayed in previous Liang films.

Master Killer was an amazing movie. It was the training sequences that made it fascinating and involving. It also secured Liu Chia Hui's stardom. Although wiry, baby-faced, and—when playing a Shaolin monk—bald, Hui had the internal power and acting

David Chiang returned to the Shaw Brothers Studio to shave his head, become a monk, and fight on the Shaolin poles for A Slice of Death.

talents to become famous. Presently he ranks as one of the Orient's top attractions (the first will be considered shortly).

After the power and influence of his first four films, Liu Chia Liang took something of a breather. Rather than take on another genre-shaking subject, he pulled an interesting switch with *Shaolin Mantis* (U.S.:

Deadly Mantis, 1978). It marked David Chiang's only appearance in a Liu Chia Liang film. His very presence marks this movie as a change of pace. In it, Chiang plays Wei Feng, a Ching dynasty official who investigates a suspected family of revolutionaries.

His presence there leads to a romance with the head of the household's granddaughter, played by Huang Hsing Hsiu, which results in marriage. Only then does he discover the proof of the family's treachery and fights his way out with the help of his newlywed wife. She dies during their escape, leading Feng to develop the mantis fist so that he can go back and practically disembowel the grandfather, played by Liu Chia Yung.

Although up until that moment the film is the usually entertaining Liang mix of character development and precise, dazzling martial arts, he distinguishes the film with its ending. Although soundly cheered by the imperial court, Feng is poisoned by his own father for helping the traitorous Chings suppress the Chinese people. Liang had neatly and surprisingly skewered another genre tradition by pointing out the yin-yang aspect of Chinese history. In this movie, David Chiang played a heroic *villain*.

The director did it again the following year with *Heroes of the East* (U.S.: *Challenge of the Ninja*). Here was a kung-fu movie in which no one was seriously hurt, let alone killed. Still, it is a thunderously good martial arts movie. Lui Chia Hui (with hair this time) played Ho Tao, a wealthy young modern man who marries a Japanese girl in an arranged ceremony. The couple's only problem is that they differ in terms of which country's martial arts are superior.

The wife, Kun Tse (Yuko Mizuno), is so stubborn that she won't accept her husband's continual martial arts superiority. She finally resorts to *ninjutsu* to win the contest. Tao firmly condemns what he considers this "art of cheating." Sadly, the woman can't accept the basic inferiority of the Japanese martial arts and runs back home to be consoled by

her teacher (Shoji Kurata).

When Tao writes a baiting letter which is suggested by his servant, the Japanese family misunderstands and sends their best fighters to challenge the Chinaman. From here on it's one long bout, with each of the Japanese confronting Tao on each successive day.

Initially he overcomes a samurai swordsman with a Chinese sword, and then he goes up against a spear man, a karate fighter, a *tonfa* pro (almost all TV cops use modified tonfas instead of nightsticks on their shows), a nunchaku user, and an Okinawan *sai* expert (the *sai* is a small trident with the center spike three times the length of the others) before facing Kurata's ninja skills.

Remember ninjutsu is an extension of Chinese arts. In the end, Tao has his wife back and defeats all the fighters—but also gains their respect through his adherence to the Confucian ways of Huang Fei Hong.

Audiences were delighted by Liu Chia Liang's ability to extend the kung-fu genre beyond its traditional limitations, but they didn't seem to realize that this was a Chinese movie which featured sympathetic, noninsidious Japanese. Although they were the bad guys of the piece, their villainy came from misunderstanding and a lack of communica-

84

tion—a problem they rectify at the picture's close. Under the guise of a kung-fu movie, Liu Chia Liang had made a very important film, one, no doubt, that was instrumental in making him and his brothers stars in Japan as well.

The director's next film was a step back in his progress, inasmuch as it was a sequel to his first film, which added nothing to his rep-

utation. Even so, *The Spiritual Boxer Part II* (1979) was an enjoyable martial arts comedy showcase for the star, Yung Wang Yu. Still, other directors had gone much further with the comedy concept Liang introduced in *The Spiritual Boxer*, so this follow-up was not the inspiration his past films had been.

Dirty Ho (1979), however, was. Although

Muscular Lo Mang (left) fights to keep out of the pointed torture device in The Five Deadly Venoms.

many Westerners were put off by the title that seemed borrowed from *Dirty Harry* (1971), this Ching dynasty period piece should have been called *The Eleventh Prince*, since it concerned Emperor Kang's eleventh son's attempts to keep from being killed by the fourth son, who thinks the favored man will be deemed heir. This eleventh son, Wang Ching Chin, is played by Liu Chia Hui, but he is not the Dirty Ho of the title. That

distinction belongs to Ho Chih, as played by Yung Wang Yu, a street thief and con artist who first comes upon the incognito prince in a brothel (many period Chinese brothels were on boats floating in a bay, as is this one). They compete with each other for the affection of the girls, revealing the disguised prince's desire to keep people from realizing what a master martial artist he is.

Throughout the first half of the movie he

keeps subtly using his skills so no one can tell that he is using them. He sees Ho as a perfect front, and cleverly manipulates things so that Ho might always be at his side, shielding him from the deadly machinations of General Liang (Lo Lieh), who has been hired by the fourth son to do away with Ching Chin.

Although at first glance this appears to be just another kung-fu movie, director Liang uses this almost sitcom situation to mount some of the most dazzling kung-fu scenes he has ever conceived—dazzling because they are so clever and subtle. The first of three high points comes when the supposedly cowering prince uses a female entertainer (Hui Ying Hung) as his "bodyguard" against an enraged Ho. He kicks, twists, and pushes the girl's limbs from behind to deflect Ho's blows, without Ho knowing they were his and not the girl's actions.

The second, and best of the martial arts sequences—ranking as one of the best ever—is Hui's "secret" bout with a wine connoisseur, played by the wonderful Wang Lung Wei. As the seemingly civil, polite gourmet serves the prince wine in a public place, he is actually trying to kill him. What makes the scene all the more wonderful is that the wines are named for different kung-fu styles, and the battlers—the prince, the connoisseur, and his waiter—use the style of the served wine as offense and defense. To cap it off, no one else in the place is aware that the pitched battle is going on. It is a marvelous display of subtle, masterful martial arts.

The finale is close in effect to that central scene. After fighting off the general's minions, the prince and Ho must face the general himself before Ching Chin can reach the royal court, his father, and thirteen brothers. Unfortunately, the general has two aides with him, and the eleventh prince has been wounded in the leg so bad that he can't stand. What follows is an amazing fight in which Ho becomes the prince's support as they frantically fight the evil trio, all of whom are using different weapons.

The sheer virtuosity of this scene is impossible to relate in words. The only sad note—and an interesting one—is the film's ending. After all they had been through together, the prince hurls Ho away as he enters the royal court, and the gigantic double regal doors slam closed as Ho falls backwards in a freeze frame. They were never truly partners after all—the prince had been using him all along.

Dirty Ho revealed another facet of Liang's achievement. It was in this picture that the director's ability to impart character and personality *simply through movement* became clear. Although Liang had already shown how interested he was in character and story development through images and dialogue, here he openly demonstrates his choreographic genius. A viewer can tell what a character is like simply by the way he does kung-fu. Liang adds and subtracts subtle flourishes of movement to achieve this effect. It is wonderful.

Liang put his own face on the line in *Mad Monkey Kung Fu* (1979). Although he had been featured in *Challenge of the Masters*, here he was playing a major role. It was that of a turn-of-the-(twentieth) century street performer, who, with his sister (Hui Ying Hung), travel from town to town performing monkey-style kung-fu. This film was another of Liang's "treading in place" movies, with a gimmicky story that only exists to showcase monkey stylings.

Lo Lieh plays a cliché—a lustful, evil rich man who frames Liang's character, Chen Po, for rape, and then breaks the man's hands and takes his sister as his concubine. The sister is killed when she discovers the frame-up, while Chen Po teams up with a pickpocket (Hsaio Ho) to take revenge. It was a good movie, far superior to the hundreds of poor kung-fu pictures that the majority of inferior Chinese filmmakers were doing, but somehow the audience had come to expect more from Liu Chia Liang.

He tried to give it to them with *Return to the Thirty-Sixth Chamber* (U.S.: *Return of the Master Killer*, 1980), but this sequel, which was not quite a sequel, didn't have the inspiration of the original. This time, bald brother Liu Chia Hui played a street con man who impersonates San Te (the character he played in the original) to punish the Manchu owners of a dye mill.

When they call his bluff, he travels to Shaolin to actually learn kung-fu. The switch here is that once the con man tricks his way into the Temple, he is put to work repairing the thirty-sixth chamber. Unbeknownst to the frustrated man, he is gaining strength and learning kung-fu techniques while building the bamboo scaffold around the chamber. He returns to his town, despondent and unknowing until he hurls a friend (Hsaio Ho) through the air with the greatest of ease. Then he returns to the mill and takes care of business.

Return to the Thirty-Sixth Chamber was just fine, but the audience wanted more. Liang gave it to them with *My Young Auntie* (1981),

the family's black sheep (Wang Lung Wei), he adds the commonplace conflict. Lung Wei wants the family's real estate titles, but others don't want him to have them. He gets them anyway and secures them in his high-security home (shades of *House of Traps*), where the son and auntie have to fight in and out to retrieve them.

Into this seemingly simple plot the director has mounted more wonderful scenes of "secret" martial arts—as in a ballroom sequence where everyone fights in costume—and added exquisite touches, such as the Westernized boy who constantly uses American slang and profanity incorrectly. The shining star of this movie, however, is Liang's protege, Hui Ying Hung. Although she was featured in his three previous films (as well as in *Clan of the White Lotus*; U.S.: *Fists of the White Lotus*, directed by Lo Lieh as a sequel to *Executioners From Shaolin* in 1980), this was her first starring role.

The story goes that the actress had been working the streets and dancing in clubs before a talent scout spotted her and Chang Cheh cast her in *The Brave Archer/Kung Fu Warlords*. But it was Liu Chia Liang who took her under his wing and taught her "everything she knows," as the saying goes. She did well by his training. Liang did a *"My Fair Lady"* on her here, transforming her from the prim girl in the film's first half to a stunner in a slit gown and high heels in the second. He also managed to surprise jaded viewers with this transformation; nothing like it had ever been seen in a kung-fu movie.

Liu Chia Liang was really on a roll now. His next movie was *Martial Club* (U.S.: *Instructors of Death*, 1981), another young Huang Fei Hong picture. Liu Chia Hui again played the youthful Huang, but not before Liang himself pops up during the credit sequence, lecturing the audience on the traditions and styles of the lion dance. The film then opens with a lion

a tradition-breaking kung-fu film about breaking tradition. Liu Chia Liang plays the father of a Westernized son (Hsaio Ho again) who takes a strictly brought up young Chinese woman, who married his brother, into the house upon the brother's death. At its heart, this is a movie about the conflict between ancient Chinese traditions and Western influences personified by the son and the aunt—who are roughly the same age.

But Liang is a martial arts movie director, and, through the cunning manipulations of

dance performed by Hui and his partner (Mai Te Lo, a young actor who has become the favorite of several directors).

It unfolds as a classic story of kung-fu school versus kung-fu school, complete with impressive battles and challenges, but the film is basically a setup for its final fight. The evil school has hired a northern Chinese stylist (Wang Lung Wei once again) to defeat Huang Fei Hong. Instead, the pair test each other's skills in an extended fight in a long alleyway that gets narrower and twists.

This is an amazing fight scene, displaying a range of styles, techniques, and subtle as well as grandstand plays. It is a testament to Liang's Hui's, and Wei's talents—which are prodigious. The Wei character winds up winning, but he never intended to kill the young man. He merely wanted to see what he could do, and was duly impressed. At the close he strongly suggests that the bad guys clean up their act. This was a special movie for Wang Lung Wei—he finally got to play a good guy.

THE GREATEST KUNG-FU FILM EVER MADE

Legendary Weapons of China (U.S.: *Legendary Weapons of Kung Fu*, 1982) is the quintessential martial arts movie. It is Liu Chia Liang's best movie and possibly the best genre film ever. We feel this way for several reasons. First, it is about kung-fu. It is not a western with kung-fu; it is not a love story with kung-fu thrown in; it is not a comedy with kung-fu. It is a movie about the martial arts. If kung-fu did not exist, this movie could not have been made. The martial arts here cannot be replaced with any other kind of fighting—which is not true of any other kung-fu movie.

Second, it is about kung-fu films. If the martial arts movie genre didn't exist, neither would this picture. It is about the strengths and the shortcomings of kung-fu motion pic-

tures. That is what the movie is about beneath the surface. On the surface it is about the end of the martial arts era in China. Outsiders—foreigners—have invaded, causing the various schools of kung-fu to band together to find a defense against their most dreaded, most powerful enemy: the gun.

This is the sort of thing that happens when you're a villain in a kung-fu movie. Lo Mang as "The Kid With the Golden Arm" becomes the kid with the hole in his stomach.

The opening sequence prepares audiences for the wonder to come. Four bare-chested students stand before four aimed rifles. Chinese mystics and a Shaolin monk dance and mouth incantations to protect these supreme fighters from the weapons. As the action and voices rise to a frenzy, the quartet is shot point blank in their chests. They remain standing. The monk prays even harder and slaps written incantations on their chests. The ritual climaxes. The men still stand. The collected school heads nod and smile at their success. Then the four men drop dead.

The glorious years of self-improvement have ended, perhaps even were for naught. Weaklings with guns can defeat the mightiest fighter, and only one sifu is willing to admit that. Lei Kung (Liu Chia Liang) refuses to force his students to commit suicide trying to find a nonexistent solution. He disbands his school and disappears. All the other schools want to kill him to prevent the foreigners from discovering his doubts. They send Tieh Hou (Hsaio Ho) and Ti Tan the Shaolin monk (Liu Chia Hui) after him.

The duo find their own trail dogged by the monk's niece (Hui Ying Hung), who wants to warn Lei Kung of the danger. Complicating things further is Lei Kung's brother Lei Yung (played by Liang's brother, Lui Chia Yung), who also wants to find the renegade fighter, but for reasons of his own. To do so, he hires a con man (Fu Sheng) to impersonate Lei Kung. To convince the townspeople he is Kung, Sheng fakes all manner of amazing kung-fu feats, cleverly lampooning the feats of past serious genre movies (as did *The Spiritual Boxer*).

Liang doesn't leave it there. He adds to this movie's mix a new ingredient: magic. The Chinese "magician-spies" are the original operatives who were to become ninjas in Japan years later. Here Liang takes the supernatural abilities of these fighters rather seriously, although using their talents mostly for humor, as in the memorable scene when Yung takes over Sheng's body with a voodoo doll. Whatever the doll does, Sheng does.

When Sheng's accomplices try to wrest the doll back from Yung beneath a house built over a narrow river, it is Fu Sheng's time to shine. This sequence was especially poignant to audiences in that Fu Sheng had just recuperated from an accident on another film which broke both his legs. There was some question whether he would ever work again.

Thankfully, his "official" comeback film, *The Treasure Hunters* (U.S.: *Master of Disaster*, 1982), directed by Liu Chia Yung (Liang's brother), laid that fear to rest. This was a film that was to establish Fu Sheng's screen persona for the rest of his career as a Chinese Bob Hope. *Master of Disaster* was essentially a kung-fu "road picture" with Sheng as "Hope" and his younger brother, Chang Chan Peng, as "Bing Crosby." Sheng's

performance in *Legendary Weapons* only reinforces this image.

The Hui Ying Hung character finally finds Lei Kung, who is disguised as an old woodcutter, and convinces him to start honing his rusting skills to confront the killers stalking him. In a few whirlwind confrontations, Lei Kung defeats both his pursuers, gaining their respect in the process. The monk returns to Shaolin Temple, and the young fighter sides with Kung.

Only then does the truth emerge. Kung's own brother had arranged the hunt simply to ingratiate himself with the government, the kung-fu schools, and the brothers' own clan. At the end, the two screen brothers, played by the two real-life brothers, face each other outside a temple at sundown to do battle with all eighteen legendary weapons of China.

It is no contest. Lei Kung's skill, combined with his honorable nature, defeats his evil brother every time. Although Lei Yung begs his brother to kill him rather than expose his plot or leave him with this dishonor, Lei Kung turns his back on his brother, letting him live with his guilt and shame.

Liu Chia Liang shot the works with this one. He threw in every kind of weapon except the Chinese kitchen sink. After this, there wasn't much more the man could say on-screen, and, indeed, his subsequent films have been well done reiterations of his previous works. *Cat vs. Rat* (1982) was a strange comedy, very Cantonese in presentation and form, taking place during the Sung dynasty.

In this one, taken from a tale of Judge Pao, Fu Sheng was once again a Bob Hope–type, terribly envious of a fellow martial artist—who served as the elegant Bing Crosby type. *Cat vs. Rat*'s only distinction is that it introduced Adam Cheng (Chinese name: Cheng Shao Chiu) to the masses. Cheng is the Chinese Cary Grant: athletic, sophisticated, fun loving, rakish, and, as was said before, elegant.

After this he became an extremely popular

movie star thanks to an impressive performance as both the good guy and bad guy in Golden Harvest's production of *Zu, Warriors From the Magic Mountain* (1982). This was one of the "New Wave" Chinese productions by young directors—in this case Tsui Hark, who had earlier made quite a splash with an impressionistic mystery thriller, *The Butterfly Murders* (1979). *Zu Warriors* is a Sung dynasty fantasy with demigods of good and evil fighting within the magic mountain for the fate of the earth. Although it completely loses control near the end, the first hour is a breathtaking stream of images and concepts that makes such American fantasies as *Conan the Barbarian* look ridiculous.

Cat vs. Rat looked just as ridiculous to Western eyes, and Liang compensated with *The Lady Is the Boss* (1983). This new film was a switch on *My Young Auntie*. This time Liang plays the traditionalist and Hui Ying Hung is the Westernized young lady who takes over his present-day martial arts

school. Leaving nothing to chance, Liang utilizes his whole crew of kung-fu actors—Yung Wang Yu, Liu Chia Hui, Hsaio Ho, Chang Chan Peng, and Mai Te Lo—as costarring school students.

They take to the streets on bicycles, battle in discos while dancing, and have a spectacular final bout in the gym with the bad real estate guys (once more led by Wang Lung Wei), before the girl decides to head back to

San Francisco and leave the school to Liang. As a neat turnaround, it is the girl who wears traditional dress and Liang who is wearing modern clothes in the final scene. The message is clear: if people meet halfway, things can always be worked out.

Tragedy struck the martial arts industry after this. Fu Sheng died in a car accident on July 7, 1983, at the age of twenty-nine. He had been in the middle of production on

94

Kuo Chui (left) fights trident to trident with the unmasked Masked Avengers.

the death of most of the loyalist Yang family, betrayed on the Tartar battlefield by a treacherous general. As the credits roll, Chang Chan Peng, Hsaio Ho, Liu Chia Yung, Yung Wang Yu, and Mai Te Lo's characters all graphically die beneath the invader's swords and spears on an artificial indoor set that gives the scene even more of a nightmarish quality.

Only Liu Chia Hui and Fu Sheng's character survive, but the latter is driven insane by his brothers' deaths and his father's suicide. He returns home to his mother and two sisters, screaming and contorting almost uncontrollably. His brother, Hui, is almost killed by the invaders, but a hermit (Liu Chia Liang) gives his own life to help him escape. He takes refuge in the Shaolin Temple, where his practical, killing ways conflict with the monk's peaceful leanings.

They practice pole fighting on wood and steel mockups of wolves—the actual counterparts of which often harass the temple. "Kill them," says the ex-soldier. "Defang them," suggests the sifu abbot. With the Fu Sheng character crazy, the mother (Lily Li) sends her eldest daughter (Hui Ying Hung) out for vengeance. At this point the Fu Sheng character completely disappears from the picture. Ying Hung runs afoul of the general (Ku Ming) and Tartar leader (Wang Lung Wei) at an inn

Liang's next movie, *The Eight Diagram Pole Fighter*. The actor had also just made the transition from straight kung-fu star to full-fledged comedy star in the box-office success *Hong Kong Playboys*.

The finished version of *The Eight Diagram Pole Fighter* (U.S.: *The Invincible Pole Fighter*), Liang's Sung dynasty tragedy, was his angriest and bleakest film. Instead of his usual instructional prologue, Liang portrayed

Kuo Chui (center) in a particularly uncomfortable spot during The Spearman of Death.

where they hold her hostage.

To rescue his sister, Hui pole-fights his sifu to a standstill using the eight diagram style (a technique which leaves an impression of an 8 on the floor), and then marches to the inn to take on all the villains simultaneously. The scene awaiting him is impressive. Coffins have been piled high. Inside one of them is his bound and gagged sister. All around them are the villains—with Wang Lung Wei at the very apex.

Hui is hopelessly outnumbered and is about to be killed when the Shaolin monks show up. Hui wonders in amazement if their attack doesn't go against their creed not to kill. "We will not kill," says the sifu, "mere-ly defang the wolves." Following is a weird, disconcerting, uncomfortable sequence in which the monks actually rip out all the Tartars' teeth. Then Hui personally hurls the two main villains head-first into the coffins. At the close he does not return to the temple—he marches to the sea.

After that, Liu Chia Liang completed a third Master Killer movie, *Disciples of the Thirty-Sixth Chamber*—an odd combination of kung-fu and *Animal House*. Following this was a period of semi-retirement, interrupted by the ascension of a filmmaker whose success was based, in large part, on lessons learned from Liu Chia Liang. That man? Read on . . .

THE SECOND BIG STAR

"One thing you must learn. Fighting and practicing are two different things."

—Dragon Lord

If Bruce Lee is the Chinese Clint Eastwood, then Jackie Chan is the Chinese Burt Reynolds. Lee was somber and serious; Chan is mischievous and clever. Lee was direct and vicious in his fighting; Chan is flamboyant and mutates the forms unmercifully. Lee made dramatic adventure movies; Chan makes comedy kung-fu. It was through Chan's personality and talents that the sub-genre of comedy kung-fu was concentrated and, perhaps, perfected.

Chan was born in 1954 in Hong Kong under the Chinese name Chen Gangsheng (Jackie Chan was always his American name). His parents placed him in a Peking Opera school called the China Drama Academy, where he studied gymnastics, acrobatics, and martial arts for ten years with sifu Yu Chan Yuan. He toiled in the academy from the age of seven to seventeen. His master remembers that he certainly wasn't the best in class, but when onstage he certainly gave it his all.

Like Bruce Lee and David Chiang before him, he appeared in movies as a child actor. The earlier comparison to Burt Reynolds is also apt here because both started adult careers as stuntmen and both had to toil in unexceptional, serious action films for years before someone gave their innate glib humor a chance to come out. The Oriental actor, now calling himself Chan Yuan Lung, was featured in 1971's *The Little Tiger of Canton*, which wasn't even released until he became a star. Then it showed up in the East as *Stranger in Hong Kong*, and in the West as *Snake Fist Fighter* or *Master With Cracked Fingers*.

By any name it was a cheap abomination, worked up by exploitive distributors eager to make money off the new star's fame by cheating the audience. The only interesting thing about this mess is seeing a seventeen-year-old Jackie Chan trying to do versions of Bruce Lee—before Chan had the cosmetic surgery to enlarge his eyelid openings.

Be that as it may, the young man's next major work was in *Hand of Death* (1975), retitled *Countdown in Kung Fu* and released in the Orient in 1976. It was a Golden Harvest film starring Tan Tao Liang, one of the genre's great leg fighters (a fighter who can kick like the dickens), and was choreographed by Jackie's classmate Hung Chin Pao—known by his nickname of Sammo Hung.

That seemed to be enough to bring Chan to the attention of Lo Wei, the director who was eager to find another Wang Yu or Bruce Lee. He cast Jackie as the star of *New Fist of Fury* (1976) and shortened his name to Cheng Lung. This film takes up where Bruce Lee's film (U.S.: *The Chinese Connection*) left off, with the survivors of the kung-fu school escaping Japanese soldiers to come across the Chan character.

Nora Miao, who was the female lead in the Lee picture, returns to her role and teaches Jackie what is essentially jeet kune do—here called Ching Wu. Then he goes back and takes vengeance on Lee's murderer. It's interesting to note that Jackie Chan really started his film career in a Bruce Lee exploitation picture, and, fittingly, he does mostly Lee moves, as he had in *Little Tiger From Canton*.

His performance fitted Lo Wei's bill, so he cast Chan in eight more movies over the next two years. But this was 1976, the American bicentennial year, the year Liu Chia Liang made his second film, Chang Cheh made three Shaolin movies with Fu Sheng and Ti Lung, and the year the redoubtable John Liu (perhaps the ultimate on-screen leg fighter) was introduced to a mass audience in director Ng Sze Yuen's *The Secret Rivals*. Jackie Chan's and Cheng

Lung's skills alone were not enough to make him an important star.

Nor was *Shaolin Wooden Man*, his second 1976 film for Wei's company, directed by Chen Chi Hwa. It was another straightforward kung-fu film with Jackie taking revenge for his father's death thanks to the coaching of a handy Shaolin monk. But this was the first film in which Chan was given a little freedom in the fight scenes. Slowly, he started to find his way.

There was little chance to improve in *Killer Meteor* (1977), since Chan was playing the villain and Jimmy Wang Yu was playing the hero. In this one, based on a novel by Ku Lung, Wang Yu and Chan spin swords mostly at each other, while Jackie bides his time—that is, until *Snake-Crane Art of Shaolin*, a Lo Wei produced–Chen Chi Hwa directed attempt to cut in on the Shaw Brothers' Shaolin profits. Here the best hope was Jackie, who proved himself in the fight scenes again. He was becoming more and more proficient, displaying more and more charisma.

To Kill With Intrigue was the last straw. Lo Wei's company didn't have the money or the materials to make great kung-fu films. Instead, they had to rely on Jackie Chan's skill as a fighter. But even a fighter of Chan's ability couldn't do much with terrible working conditions and mediocre scripts. When this film also failed at the box office, drastic methods were called for.

Instead of fighting against the inevitable restraints of bad martial arts filmmaking, Chan went with them. He "fooled around," helping to make what was, in effect, a kung-fu version of *Rocky and Bullwinkle*. This seminal cartoon show openly admitted it was inexpensive and utilized the fact. The animated squirrel and moose constantly jibed at their genre's limitations and clichés, as did *Half a Loaf of Kung Fu*, Chan's next Lo Wei production.

Bad kung-fu movies usually contain ridiculous overstatements, outrageous sound effects, music stolen from American successes, and various other indulgences. For this film, Chan and company pushed these weaknesses as far as they could. Chan plays a hapless bumbler who wants to be a great martial artist, and the movie chronicles his ultimate lack of success. He lampoons Chinese, Japanese, and American movies in this "Jackie Chan's Laugh-in" variation, which just barely manages to please.

After that, Chan made three final straight kung-fu movies for Lo Wei. The first was *Magnificent Bodyguard* (1978), a last-ditch effort to get viewers, since it was a period piece filmed in 3-D. Seeing Chan in any of these previous movies now is a lot like seeing Burt Reynolds in *Skullduggery* (1969), Roy Scheider in *Curse of the Living Corpse* (1964), or any well-known film star in a movie way below his or her talents.

On his last two Lo Wei films, *Spiritual Kung Fu* and *Dragon Fist* (both 1978), Chan is named martial arts instructor, therefore both films are closer to what most fans recognize as the actor's style. Curiously, both films feature concepts that were either borrowed from or inspired by Liu Chia Liang. The former film is similar in tone and title to Liang's *Spiritual Boxer*, while the latter has a climax similar to *Dirty Ho*, which the Shaws released the same year. In both, one fighter becomes the legs of another.

Finally, producer and director Ng Sze Yuen, maker of everything from *The Secret Rivals* to *Bruce Lee: The True Story*, became aware of both Jackie and martial arts instructor Yuen Woo Ping. Ng was assistant director on Wang Yu's *The Chinese Boxer* before going on to do a vital, but tacky, anti-Japanese movie of his own, *The Bloody Fists* (1972). In 1975, he gave both the Shaws and Raymond Chow's Golden Harvest a run for their money by creating Seasonal Film Corporation, better known as Seasonal Films. To everyone's surprise, he put out exceptional martial arts movies that made money.

The four last hopes for kung-fu fight the Sun ninjas in Super Ninjas.

Not only does he seek out new talent, but he seems unafraid to try new approaches and promote the "New Wave" of Chinese films—films that are inventive and don't depend on traditional techniques to tell their stories. So saying, he teamed Yuen Woo Ping as director and Jackie Chan as star with his own script entitled *Snake in the Eagle's Shadow* (U.S.: *Eagle's Shadow*, 1978).

The results were positive. The structure for Chan's next few films was also established by it. More often than not, the credits roll over Chan doing a kata—an exercise incorporating the techniques of the form he is showcasing. Immediately following is a fight between the main villain (in this case

the head of the eagle claw kung-fu school) and an expendable character (in this case supposedly the last of the Snake Fist school). The villains of these pieces, as with almost all period kung-fu movies, are easy to identify. They wear beautiful clothes and have long, flowing white moustaches, hair, and sometimes eyebrows. This is a theatrical tradition which displays their elder status, and in China, white is the color which signifies death.

Jackie is revealed as a well-meaning bumbler who is tortured by his friends, father, sifu, or all three. When things appear darkest, along comes a wizened old bum, sometimes with a handicap, who just so happens to be

99

the greatest teacher on two legs. Even so, Jackie is always defeated in his first fight with the bad guy. He goes off and makes a telling addition to his sifu's teaching, one of his own creation. Then, just as the villain is about to kill either the father or the sifu, the new, improved Chan arrives to save the day.

The variations that Ping, and then Chan, were to create through what was to become six hours of action is awe-inspiring. For the first film, however, Chan played what was supposed to be Huang Fei Hong in his very

early, formative years. In the actual case, Chan's character was named Chien Fu, a menial at a mediocre kung-fu school. He is rescued from his classmates' taunts by the arrival of an old man, who, unbeknownst to Fu, is the last of the snake fist fighters (Yuan Hsaio Tien, the director's father, better known as Simon Yuen).

Another classic Chan touch of his second era is the business of the student accidentally fingering the fugitive master by using his learned technique at the wrong time. This happens here. The eagle claw killer finds Yuen and the chase is on. Chan tries to prevent trouble but is mopped around the floor by the villain. Another common occurrence is the evil fighter letting the student live—thinking he'll never be good enough to beat him.

In this movie, Chan merely looks into the corner, where a cat is fighting a snake. Instantly he conceives "cat claw" kung-fu to beat the eagle claw man. Yuen is about to bite the dust when Chan fights through the murderer's minions and takes on the big boss himself. In this, and the succeeding three films, the climax often lasts as long as a half-hour as Chan fights the bad guy's bodyguards and the bad guy, one after another.

Snake in the Eagle's Shadow was a huge success, and the same team slaved to make the follow-up superior. They succeeded admirably. *Drunk Monkey in the Tiger's Eyes* (U.S.: *Drunken Master*, 1979) was essentially a remake of *Eagle's Shadow*, but the concepts were streamlined, and this new picture stands as one of the sleekest, flat-out, action-filled kung-fu comedies. But quantity of action is not enough. Quality of action was the object here, and while Chan's character, "Naughty Panther," simply moved from one fight to another, the imagination that went into creating the complex situations is staggering.

Although essentially one long action sequence (the outlandish training scenes can be considered part of the action), the movie manages to build until the battle between a tiger claw hired killer and the Naughty Panther.

Panther is such an incorrigible brawler that his father sends him to his sifu, a drunken old wino in the woods, again played by Simon Yuen.

Half the time Panther is being trained (tortured), while the other half he tries to escape but is always outwitted by the drunken master who teaches him the "eight drunken fairies"—a style that requires ample portions of alcohol. Chan "graduates" from the training part and moves into the kata sequence, where he shows the audience what he's learned. This is always the lead-in to the climax. Here, he must save his father from a hired killer, and does it by inventing a new amalgamation of the eight drunken fairies on the spot.

After this success, Chan seemed to feel that he knew enough to go out on his own. Making a deal with Lo Wei's wife's production company, he wrote and directed his next film himself. Meanwhile, Simon Yuen, at the tender age of sixty-six, achieved the stardom that had eluded him throughout his forty-five-year career. Before this, he had appeared in many Huang Fei Hong movies, usually as

Chen Kuan Tai and Lily Li spar on their wedding night, testing their Tiger and Crane skills, in The Executioners of Death.

villain Shih Kien's partner. He graduated to the role of elder sifu in Liu Chia Liang's *Heroes of the East/Challenge of the Ninja* and *The Thirty-Sixth Chamber/Master Killer.* He passed away in the mid-eighties, but his seven children continued to work in films, maintaining the level of excellence their father sustained.

Jackie Chan Superstar

Fearless Hyena followed the previous two Jackie Chan films in both form and effect. Here he plays Lung, the grandson of the last of the Hsin-yi fighters. Like the snake master before him, the head Hsin-yi man is being hunted down, this time by Ch'ing Dynasty General Yen and his trio of killers—all who carry a form of "switch spear," a spear that folds like a switchblade.

Crafty, opportunistic Lung sneaks away from his grandfather's forest shack to perform as a martial artist for money. He takes on all comers, disguising himself as a buffoon and a girl, until he inadvertantly leads Yen to his grandfather. The old man is killed, but Lung is prevented from interfering by a crippled old sifu. He takes Lung away to train him in "Emotional Kung-fu."

The effect of seeing Chan turn the Emotional Kung-fu on Yen during the final ten-minute fight is delightful. Chan, as director, has already shown how powerful Yen is—his method of killing is by gripping the fallen victim's neck and dragging him to his feet. With the new martial arts technique—based on laughing and crying and the body positions thereof—Lung defeats the general and saves his sifu.

Fearless Hyena was not as polished as *Drunken Master,* but its roughness was part of its charm. Audiences probably wanted to

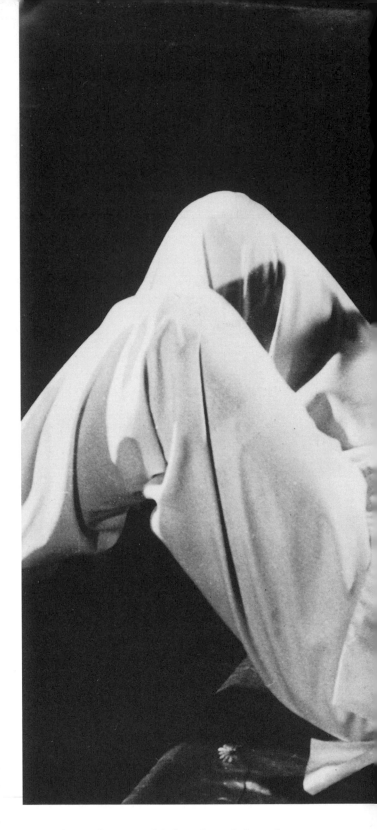

see what Chan could do when left to his own devices, and the result was ingratiating. Jackie Chan owes more to Stan Laurel, Buster Keaton, Charlie Chaplin, and the Three Stooges—not to mention Benny Hill— than to any renowned filmmaker.

His style is physical slapstick, utilizing every part of the body, every part of every other actor's body, and every part of the set. Furniture was to somersault, leap, climb, or flip over, to carry, throw, twist, or drop. The permutations of limbs and props seemed endlessly inventive.

With *The Young Master* (1980), his next film made for Golden Harvest, he came to the end of this particular line. *Drunken Master* was really as far as the subgenre could go in this direction. Both *Hyena* and

Young Master were variations on it. This was Chan's "kitchen sink" film, in which he throws in characters and conflicts at will. The plot, as it stands, has him trying to rescue a friend from a life of crime. As he attempts to bring the chief thief down, he keeps bumping into the sheriff and his two children—male and female martial artists.

There's a sword fight that becomes a complex juggling act, a lion dance, fights with elegant white fans, fights with furniture; and once more Chan dresses as a girl, this time to take out the main villain's cronies. The big switch this time is that Chan's character is not a good enough martial artist to defeat his enemy.

Throughout his last three films, Chan had made it quite clear that he likes torture-training scenes. The things he does to himself on-screen are scarcely believable. In the climactic fight of *The Young Master,* Chan is pummeled unmercifully but keeps coming back for more. He just keeps getting kicked and punched and hurled—sometimes in slow motion—until he beats the bad guy simply by surviving. The last shot shows every part of Chan's body bandaged except for two fingers of one hand. With those two fingers he waves to the audience, saying, "bye-bye."

From there, Chan headed to Hollywood. Fred Weintraub, the coproducer of *Enter the Dragon,* was coproducing *The Big Brawl* (a.k.a. *Battle Creek Brawl,* 1980) for Jackie as part of the deal with Raymond Chow and his Golden Harvest company. Chow, once the Shaws' second in command, was making up the distance that lay between the two companies for years. It started when he secured Bruce Lee's participation and continued through Jackie Chan's.

The Big Brawl was written and directed by Robert Clouse and starred Chan as a 1930s Chicago resident who runs afoul of a mobster who participates in bare-knuckled boxing competitions. It all starts when his father is muscled by some henchmen for protection money. Chan beats them up merely by dodging their blows in such a way that they hurt themselves. Throughout the film, Chan utilizes his acrobatics to get the better of the crooks; included are some energetic roller-skating scenes.

Even though the picture was directed too pedantically, Jackie Chan had, for all intents and purposes, become "the new Bruce Lee" by becoming the second international kung-fu star. If *The Big Brawl* didn't convince people, *The Cannonball Run* (1981) did. Chan, as a Suburu driver, was a high point in the otherwise dreary picture starring, of all people, Burt Reynolds. Both Reynolds and his Asian counterpart were in the even worse

1984 sequel, but that had no ill-effect on Chan's career. Between the two American films, he had made two groundbreaking Chinese movies.

The first was produced under the title *Young Master in Love*. Chan now had his own production company, with Golden Harvest as his distributor. He was given all the money and time he needed, and took full advantage of both. The movie's drawback was that it was an unfocused affair. Too much freedom was the culprit. The film's success is that it brought home a telling fact about martial arts movies: without growth they will stagnate and die. *Young Master in Love,* or, according to its final title, *Dragon Lord,* was a first sign of growth.

Chan purposefully downplays kung-fu for other kinds of action. In the movie, set in the nineteenth century, Chan plays the happy-go-lucky son of a wealthy man. The lad's main interests are in sports and women—actually, one particular woman, played by Hseuh Li. The film opens on a competition similar to vying for firecrackers, only the contestants have to climb up a bun-laden bamboo pyramid to grab the bun at the top. Reportedly, ninety actors were hurt during this sequence.

The film meanders on, leading to another competition, this time a form of soccer using a feathered shuttlecock as the ball. Finally the plot starts, with villains trying to steal art treasures. Chan gets wind of the plot when a kite with a message of love for Li goes awry and lands on the roof of the villains' headquarters. When Chan climbs to retrieve it, the guards try to perforate him with spears.

After he escapes, two henchmen try to rough him up at a temple, but Chan athletically foils them, even though he is not a consummate martial artist. He gets the inspiration he needs through the proximity of his love, Li. The film's strength is revealed when Chan's friend asks why the battle looked so haphazard. Chan tells him that learning kung-fu and actually utilizing it are two different things.

That message is underlined in the twenty-minute climax, which is really the only fight in the film. Huang Ing Sik, the veteran villain who had worked with Bruce Lee and Angela Mao as well as Jackie Chan in the past, appears as a kung-fu killer with one cataracted eye. He corners Chan and his friend in a barn and intends to tear them apart.

As always, Chan gets brutally beaten, but he shows that it takes more than martial artistry to win. Through luck and cleverness, he manages to defeat the expert fighter. This fight is the finest sustained realistic battle in the genre. Chan combines kung-fu with street-fighting at a dizzying pace, making a fight look real for the first time. While there are acrobatics and kung-fu, this is one of the few battles that doesn't look like ballet. It looks like a fight.

For this reason alone, Jackie Chan accomplished something very special in *Dragon Lord*. What he would go on to achieve in his next film, *Project A* (1984), was to drag the martial arts movie, kicking and screaming, into the twentieth century.

This next film, originally entitled *Pirate Patrol*, showed that Chan had a firmer grip on what he was trying to accomplish. The relatively poor box-office response to *Dragon Lord* helped. Although it made a tidy profit, it was not as much as expected, and critical reaction made clear that fans were disappointed. *Project A* put the director-writer-star back on track again.

No faltering steps here. Project A was the name of the plan that the Chinese Coast Guard had in 1903 to clean the harbor of pirates

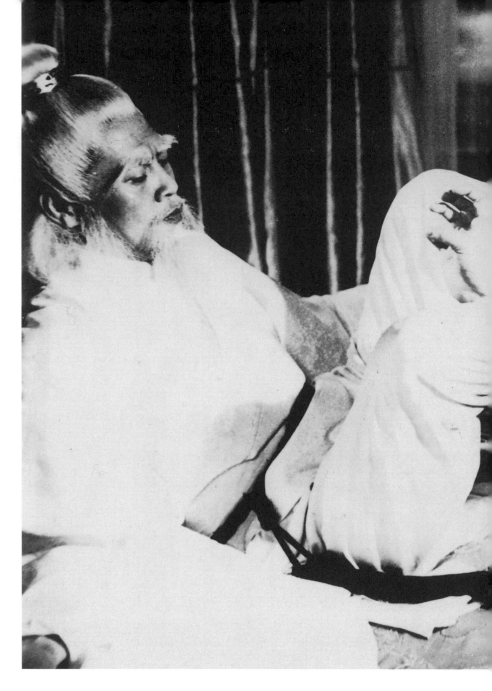

who preyed on foreign ships. Chan plays one of the sailors, who are constantly at odds with the young Chinese police over who should get the bulk of the government's budget.

A "discussion" of this turns into a barroom brawl where Chan shows off his sharpened physical skills as both actor and director. As a result of this fight, and the fact that their boats are sabotaged, the government assigns the sailors to the police force. After an initial conflict with the cops, Chan fits in with them, but then he finds his investiga-

tion into the sabotage and pirates is stymied.

It seems that the headquarters for illicit smuggling is in a swank nightclub, and the higher-ranked policemen don't want to make trouble there. Chan doesn't care and attacks the place straight on, again showcasing some literally breathtaking moments. Although he has uncovered the pirate's contacts, broken up the smuggling operation, and trashed the nightclub, he resigns his commission in disgust.

With the help of a con-man friend (Sammo Hung), he gets on the pirates' tail, and they

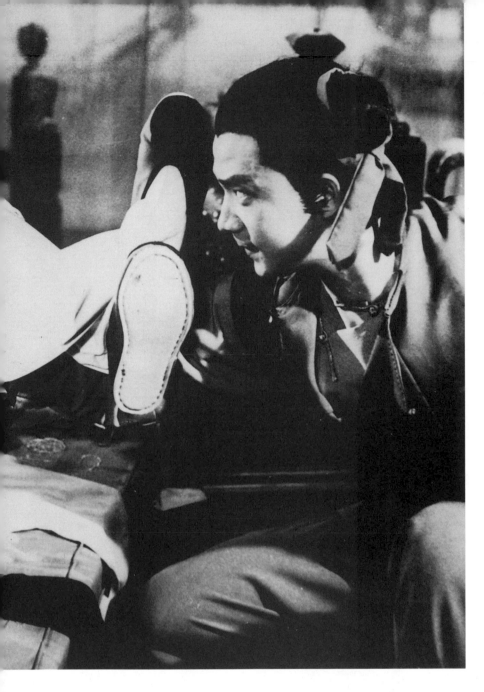

reinstates the Coast Guard. Chan disguises himself as the go-between for the ransom, Sammo disguises himself as a pirate, and both infiltrate the pirates' cave hideout—meeting the ferocious leader (Ti Wei). They are joined at the last minute by a young cop (Yuen Baio), and with kung-fu and bombs they destroy the place. The sheer frenetic activity of the final scene makes for a thunderously satisfying conclusion.

Even the end credits are entertaining. As they roll, Chan shows outtakes from the film—but not outtakes of flubbed lines, rather, outtakes of flubbed stunts, including some painful shots of the barroom brawl and clock-tower fall that go horribly wrong. Watching Chan bounce off the awnings that refuse to break and then smash into the ground is a humbling sight.

Jackie Chan does an excellent synthesis of his past work in this film, combining the best of all three of his phases. There's action that is more satisfying to martial-arts fans, kung-fu that has the edge of reality, and some physical stunts that defy gravity (as well as sanity). These ingredients make *Project A* not only one of the best kung-fu movies, but one of the great adventure movies, period.

However, Chan was not finished yet—not by a long shot.

on his. A mid-film chase has Chan doing amazing things on a bicycle, climbing a flagpole while handcuffed, then twisting around in a clock tower's mechanism to escape villain Li Hai Sheng (the tall bald swordfighter of *Master Killer*) before dropping off the high tower, ripping through two awnings, and hitting the ground (all filmed in one continuous take—ouch!).

Finally he overhears a high-ranking official give in to the pirates' demands for a recently captured British admiral's ransom. Chan demands justice, and the shamed official

107

This is the way the Shaolin Temple develops arm strength. Lower the arms and it's good-bye ribs. Liu Chia Hui gets closer to becoming the Master Killer.

SUPERSTAR ASCENDING

Jackie Chan had done it—he had revolutionized the Hong Kong film industry. And he had done this by consciously patterning his screen behavior to be opposite that of Bruce Lee. He ought to know, having served as a stuntman on *Fist of Fury* (U.S.: *The Chinese Connection*) and *Enter the Dragon*. (Study the mustached man Bruce is arm-locking in the photo from the *Enter the Dragon* underground battle on page 19 in this volume— look familiar?)

"While Bruce kicked high, I purposely kicked low," Chan explained. "When he strikes and looks tough, I strike, shake my hurt hand, and go 'Owwwww!'" That simple philosophy did the trick. There could never be another Bruce Lee. Instead, there had to be a new Jackie Chan, and, with

Project A, he paid off his promise in spades.

Following that landmark movie came a flurry of assured activity, with the triumphant trio of Jackie, Sammo Hung, and Yuen Baio at the top of their games. The three knew each other well. They were all part of "the Seven Little Fortunes"—members of the same Peking Opera school which had tortured and taught them in their youth. Sammo had been the eldest boy there, and Yuen the youngest, with Jackie in between. Thus, the three were truly brothers in every sense of the word, except for blood. In blood spilled, however, they had their relationship locked, because they were truly abused children.

"It said right on the contract my parents had with the school," Jackie remembered, "that if I was beaten to death, that was okay."

Thankfully, all three survived, and, thanks to *Project A*, all went on to become superstars. So, in the great tradition of the frenzied Hong Kong film world, the trio made five more movies together in the next few years. And what movies: flush with success and at the apex of their martial arts and moviemaking skills, the men stretched their physical and mental muscles to the limit—delighting and astonishing their audience.

First up was the quickly produced but very entertaining *Five Lucky Stars* (U.S.: *Winners and Sinners*, 1983), with Jackie guest-starring in the first of Sammo Hung's sophomoric slapstick series featuring many of Hong Kong's top comedians as hapless, immature thieves who try to go straight as house cleaners, only to constantly run afoul of criminals or get pressed into service by law enforcement agencies.

The highlight of this amusing little picture saw Jackie making use of the roller-skating skills he developed for *The Big Brawl*—only this time he did it right. In this amazing sequence, Jackie, as a never-say-die cop, "road-skis" behind a truck, jumps over a Volkswagen Beetle, and, most incredibly, roller-skates under a moving tractor-trailer truck on the highway before leaping onto a speeding motorcycle and, finally, causing a spectacular multi-car pileup. It remains one of Chan's most amazing series of stunts.

Wishing to escape from the Hong Kong–locked adventures of the past, the trio took advantage of their newfound financial freedom to film in Spain. In the seminal *Wheels on Meals* (1984), Sammo plays a private eye looking for a runaway heiress, while Jackie and Yuen run a motorized luncheonette (hence the title). They team up to help the beauty, whose stepbrother seeks to claim the family fortune himself.

As always, the plot is merely an excuse to create fabulous fights, loony comedy, and outlandish chase scenes. Sammo likes his kung-fu savage, and hired nine-time undefeated kickboxing champion Benny "the Jet" Urquidez to see to it. The movie is amusing and entertaining throughout, but the climactic attack on the villain's castle remains its pièce de résistance. Yuen fights Keith Vitale, another famed real-life martial artist, while Jackie takes on the Jet.

This, it turns out, would be the fitting successor to the "gladiator" sequence when Bruce Lee met Chuck Norris in *Return of the Dragon* (H.K.: *Way of the Dragon*). In fact, this battle reigns as the most realistic martial-arts fight in kung-fu film history. And little wonder. According to Urquidez, they filmed it in forty-eight hours straight, and his instructions were to connect. "There are times, on-screen, when you see the blows land," Benny said. "In the most obvious case, when Jackie is whaling on me in slow motion, I told Sammo, 'You only have one shot at this. I'll let him hit me for one take, but if you don't get it on film, too bad.'" The result is amazing, and painful, to watch.

More impressive, though, is Benny's spinning kick over Jackie's ducking head, done with such speed and power that the wind from the move blows out a nearby candelabra. "I got it on the first take," Benny reported. "But I thought I could do it better."

He could, and did, and that's the shot that's in the final film.

"I was very impressed with Jackie and Sammo's enthusiasm and skill," the Jet remembers. "In fact, my last line in the movie, 'Lift me up, let's go another round,' was true. That's the way I actually felt." To the fans' benefit, Urquidez would get his wish in just a few more years. But Sammo and Jackie, having stretched their kung-fu muscles to the breaking point, now wanted to stretch their acting muscles.

So deciding, they conceived *Heart of the Dragon* (U.S.: *Heart of Dragon*), also known as *First Mission* (1984) in Japan. This heartfelt drama of a young man (Chan) trying to escape the increasingly claustrophobic responsibilities of tending to a retarded older brother (Hung) was designed to show the world that Chan and Hung weren't just action slaves. Panic soon set in at the studio, however. "Why risk a sure thing?" was the constant litany from every quarter until even Sammo and Jackie began to doubt the movie's chances—despite passionate on-screen performances from them both. So the young man was made into a Hong Kong SWAT-team officer while more and more fight scenes were added (two of which only stayed in the Asian version).

Unfortunately for the boys' stretching of their acting skills (but fortunately for the picture as a whole) the climatic fight between Jackie, Dick Tei Wei, villainous thieves, a bunch of renegade cops, a half-dozen gunsels, and a mob of pick-ax-wielding construction workers remains the best filmed kung-fu battle in movie history. "I knew I wanted to do something special," said Sammo. "So I decided to challenge myself." The studio was screaming for a great final fight, so Hung designed it as dozens of individually filmed actions recorded by a constantly moving camera. A film school editing class could run an entire semester on this masterful ten-minute sequence alone.

Following that emotionally exhausting effort, the boys went to Tokyo—but brought a supporting cast and crew along. Actually, *Five Lucky Stars/Winners and Sinners* had been a big hit, and Golden Harvest wanted to revisit the well. *My Lucky Stars* (1985) took advantage of Chan's huge Japanese following by setting the action comedy in and around a Nippon amusement park in the shadow of Mount Fuji.

As before, most of the film's running time is taken up by the sniggering antics of five libido-challenged comics, but climaxes with a terrific fight scene in the park's wildly elaborate fun house. There Jackie battles in an upside-down room full of samurai-sword-swinging "ghosts," and in a snowy room filled with white ninja, before bursting into a multileveled gallery where Sammo and Yuen join in on the brilliantly realized mayhem.

By now, Sammo's camera skills and the men's martial arts abilities had become so sophisticated that there really wasn't much farther they could go. Even so, the studio was calling for more, and as fast as they could provide it. In an attempt to imbue fresh blood into the series—and looking forward to the time when either Jackie or Yuen would want out—Sammo discovered a young man named Andy Lau and introduced the handsome actor and singer as a fourth wheel in *Twinkle, Twinkle Lucky Stars* (1985). That time was soon coming, but, for the moment, Lau was quickly jettisoned from the disjointed plot, after appearing in only one fight sequence. He would later star in Sammo's ill-conceived and misbegotten combination of two of Hong Kong's most beloved comedy series, *Lucky Stars Go Places* (1986) (combining the *Aces Go Places* and *Lucky Stars* series), before going on to his own solo superstardom.

Meanwhile, back at *Twinkle, Twinkle Lucky Stars*, hapless thief Sammo and his girl-hungry crew join supercops Yuen and Jackie in tracking a trio of international assassins. The comedy is even sillier this time, with the comely Rosamund Kwan

110

David Chiang (left) never looked better than in director Liu Chia Liang's The Deadly Mantis.

playing a witness who pretends she's blind so the hit men won't whack her. Once again, however, the brilliantly choreographed and executed fights save the day.

Wisely, Hung always saved the best for last. For the first time ever, Jackie is wounded on-screen (shot in the shoulder), requiring Sammo to take on both Australian Richard Norton and Japanese Shoji Kurata in a virtuoso display of wit and wickedness. He matches Norton painful kick for painful kick, and then battles Kurata's "sais" (sword catchers) with tennis rackets in a scene that never fails to elicit cheers from the audience.

Jackie didn't really mind letting Sammo take center stage. He had realized that five

"Lucky Stars" were five too many. As great a director and choreographer as Sammo was, Chan had his own vision. Besides, while the Lucky Stars' movies were always entertaining, they weren't groundbreaking or ambitious. Actually, most of the films consisted of overage idiots trying to get a lecherous look at cute girls. It was time for another revolution. But first a lurch backward.

Jackie Chan had made Golden Harvest truly golden, and for that he deserved a rich reward. For the studio, who suffered Jackie's time-consuming perfectionism but also reaped the subsequent box-office gold rush, that reward meant a second solo shot at the international market. So, why not do for

Chan in America what he had done for them in Hong Kong? The logic was sound. If Jackie Chan had brought the Hong Kong kung-fu film kicking and screaming into the modern age, why not bring a Jackie movie, set in the United States, into the present day? Since the disappointing *Big Brawl* was a period piece, *The Protector* (1985) would not be. There was only one problem: the crew of this new effort made the exact same mistake as the "Battle Creek Brawlers": they refused to let Jackie be Jackie.

" 'I make you Clint Eastwood,' " Jackie quoted director James Glickenhaus—encapsulating *The Protector*'s fatal flaw in five words. To make the problem perfectly clear, Chan exclaimed, "But it's not me!" Complicating matters was Glickenhaus's generally patronizing attitude toward the audience, which came through in everything from the needlessly profane dialogue to the nonsensical plot to the illogically conceived action scenes.

The film starts with a perplexing sequence in which a truck is hijacked by a group of eccentric criminals. The purpose of this scene defies explanation, other than to start the film on a confusing downer simply to prepare the audience for the increasingly confusing downer the rest of the flick would become. Jackie is

only introduced later, basically as a somewhat thick-headed, not to mention thick-accented, New York cop who is not adverse to cold-bloodedly killing a profanity-spewing mad-dog murderer by ramming someone else's multi-million-dollar yacht into him. What exactly is "the Protector" supposed to be protecting anyway? Certainly not the hijacked truck or the cabin cruiser!

From there the plot stumbles on to Hong Kong, where Chan and his new hapless partner, played by Danny Aiello, trace the machinations of mob bosses. The one scene which vaguely reflects Chan's skills comes in a Japanese massage parlor where Jackie takes out a mob of thugs while running around in his underwear. But even there, the one decent martial arts move he makes—leaping onto a wall's molding and then spinning around to deliver a fine midair kick—was actually edited out of the American version because it was deemed "too fanciful."

Stupidity continued to reign until Chan was ready—not to go crazy—but to get even. Throughout the production, as Jackie watched Glickenhaus squander the contributions of lovely costar Moon Lee and, most painfully, the climatic battle between Chan and Bill "Superfoot" Wallace (one of the world's finest karate kickers), he would tell everyone who would listen how he, Jackie, would have done it.

Once the production was ruined (i.e., finished), Jackie put Golden Harvest's money where his mouth was. Unable to change the English-language version, he remade the Asian version in his image. *The Protector*

that ran in Hong Kong cinemas was considerably different than the American one. Back in went the wall-moulding jump, but also a whole new subplot featuring its own fight scenes and sexy Sally Yeh as a Hong Kong dancer Jackie needs to interrogate.

Chan then turned his attention to the climatic fight with Superfoot—a fight which should have rivaled his classic Benny the Jet duel, or at least the Bruce Lee-Chuck Norris *Return of the Dragon* confrontation. Chan and his Hong Kong crew added very clever footage which made the battle far more exciting and believable, but, much to Jackie's frustration, no amount of tinkering could really save the film from mediocrity.

What was a man with limitless studio support to do? Revolutionize the Hong Kong action film again, that's what. *The Protector* made Jackie look around at the modern kung-fu flick. Invariably, it was either an extremely cheap thriller in which traditional Peking Opera drama was given polyester trappings (à la Chang Cheh's *The Chinatown Kid*), or a campy adventure which ignored the high-calibre realities of modern weaponry (à la Liu Chia Liang's *The Lady Is the Boss*). Having remade the period martial arts movie in his (and Buster Keaton's) image with *Project A*, it was time to create a new kind of modern Hong Kong action film.

Chan's answer was *Police Story* (U.S.: *Jackie Chan's Police Force*, 1985), really the first film of the Hong Kong New Wave, and his testament as to how *The Protector* should have been done. It is also his most accomplished, complete, and personal film.

When *Project A* had gone wildly over-schedule, Golden Harvest had visions of *Dragon Lord* dancing in their heads and quietly asked Sammo Hung to see if he could help speed things along. "It had to be me," Sammo explained. "If it had been anyone else, Jackie would have been upset." But, given their history, Chan accepted the reality of the situation and welcomed the assistance, although never quite wholeheartedly.

This time, with *Police Story*, Chan intended to take everything he had learned about moviemaking and pour his heart and soul—and his alone—onto the screen. Jackie's story of an obsessed cop trying to bring down a drug kingpin had a sophistication of approach that was light-years ahead of anything else.

As with *Project A*, Jackie saw to it that much of the film's success came from characterization and plot, two vastly underused ingredients in the Hong Kong film mix. He balanced inventive comedy with emotional drama, making the audience care about the characters—something else which had been in short supply in Hong Kong cinema.

Then there's the action: one classic fight on film after another. First was the shantytown battle, ending with Jackie driving through a hillside village created especially for the film. Then, the double-decker-bus fight, starting with Jackie hanging off the back by an umbrella and ending with a scene Sylvester Stallone had stolen (using it badly) in the opening of *Tango and Cash* (1989). Finally, there's the greatest shopping-mall fight scene ever filmed. Jackie battles from one side to the other, imaginatively using all the store displays in a virtuoso performance that, like the central chase of *Project A*, rivaled anything that Chaplin or Keaton had done.

Seeing a man drop off a balcony and hit the floor in 1900s Hong Kong was one thing, but seeing someone flip backward onto a shopping-mall's steel escalator in the present day was another. The thrill of recognition seemed to shoot through Asian audiences, especially since everything was actually being done by the actors playing each role.

If Jackie Chan had been a superstar before, and the heir apparent of Bruce Lee, he was a screen deity now, with nothing "apparent" about his inheritance. In a word: incredible. In another word: universal. Despite there being three different cuts of the film—a basic

Chinese edition, a more emotionally rich Japanese version with character development scenes added to the beginning and the end, and a shortened American edit which was the hit of the 1988 New York Film Festival—*Police Story* works brilliantly in any language.

SUPERSTAR FALLEN

Now the question was: How to follow up a classic? Director Eric Tsang, who also played

tions where they were scheduled to film—starting with the action-packed prologue in Yugoslavia. "I had just flown in from a meeting," Chan remembered. "Maybe I hadn't had enough sleep."

The director was on another location (some say he was busy shopping), but that had never slowed Jackie down before. He and his handpicked team of stuntmen went to work realizing the sequence where the international mercenary known as the Asian Hawk saves a semi-naked sacrifice from bloodthirsty tribesmen.

The stunt was relatively easy: jump from a thirty-foot-high wall to a branch, hold on to the tall, thin tree as it bent over from his weight, and drop safely behind a second wall. The scene went well the first time they filmed it—and was, in fact, the version that is seen in the actual movie—but Jackie thought he could do better. The second time the branch broke.

"If the cameraman had tried to cushion my fall, or even just pushed me a little, I would have been okay," Jackie explained. "But he grabbed the camera and ran away"—leaving Jackie to hit his head on a rock. "At the time I didn't think it was that bad," Jackie remembered. "But when I looked up I saw my stunt guys crying, my father crying. . . . Later, when I looked at the film, I saw the blood coming from my ear."

In Hong Kong film it is customary that when someone gets hurt, even breaks a limb, they just go get it set, maybe have some Chinese herbs administered, and return to the set (as Liu Chia Liang did after breaking his leg while directing *Cat vs. Rat* in 1982). But this wound put Jackie in the hospital for weeks. After hours of operating to remove

one of the "Five Lucky Stars," had the answer. Jackie had shown the world how to make a modern *Police Story:* what about showing them how Hong Kongers would do Indiana Jones?

Thus *Armour of God* (1986) was conceived, and Jackie threw himself into this anxiously awaited effort. He was riding high, so the egomaniacal industry was waiting for him to fall, but no one thought he would do it—literally.

Jackie, in the meantime, ignored all the nay-sayers, reveling in the worldwide loca-

115

skull fragments from his brain, the doctors were amazed how quickly Jackie recovered.

Jackie was left with a coin-sized hole in his skull, covered with plastic, which vibrates when he hums. He was also left with a firm conviction that *Armour of God* must be finished. Many film industry leeches were waiting for him to fail, but he would not give them the satisfaction. Besides, Golden Harvest had a lot of money invested in the production, and Chan's work ethic would not let them down. After recollecting the cast many months later, Chan took over.

He restarted the production with a lot to prove—namely that he still "had it." Ironically, because the audience wondered how he would bounce back from such an injury, *Armour of God* became his most financially successful movie. It was also one of his most impressive, with a crackerjack opening (made all the more resonant by the accident), a French-farce-flavored middle using mistaken identities and slamming doors, and a tremendous action ending.

The only real victim of the accident—besides Tsang, who would not work very much in the next few years—was the plot, which all but disappears by the fade-out. It is written that if the Armour of God, five pieces of medieval weaponry, falls into evil hands or is destroyed, the world would be plunged into ruin. The money-loving Asian Hawk goes after the arsenal when blackmailed by a money- and sex-loving cult which has kidnapped his ex-girlfriend (who is abducted in a

At the end, Jackie must leap off a cliff and land atop a hot-air balloon, since he had blown up the villains' mountain lair, not to mention the armour. Despite the film's dire predictions of world destruction lest the armour be saved, the world, and, most especially, Jackie's career, seemed none the worse for wear.

Even so, Chan's accident had a chilling effect on his career. Much as the direction of the James Bond series had veered into farce as a result of Sean Connery's retirement from the role, Chan's injury caused him to reexamine his future—to the detriment of his films. Rather than continue to break new ground, Chan embarked on a series of sequels and "culmination" productions. It seemed as if the kung-fu film master had finally faced his mortality and wanted to get in as much sure-fire action as he still could.

Project A II (1987), the follow-up to *Pirate Patrol*, was first. This was Jackie's most obvious homage to the influence of Buster Keaton, and his last great attempt at a sophisticated story. Playing the same intrepid Coast Guard officer as he had in the original, Jackie is seconded to a corrupt police troop in a small city, where he must fight his own bribe-taking comrades as well as crime bosses, revolutionaries, sadistic mainland Chinese agents, and even the ax-wielding remnants of the pirates he defeated in the prequel.

Jackie took the opportunity to streamline and perfect the French-farce touches he had attempted in previous films, as well as mount a series of comic confrontations that take place in an exotic nightclub, a soy-milk factory, a fish hatchery, a chicken-plucking establishment, and, finally, throughout the entire town. In one sequence he is handcuffed to his corrupt superior—causing every move to be reflected in the painful reaction

sequence similar to one in *The Protector*, though, naturally, far superior).

Vying for the now-brainwashed girl with a clumsy rock star played winningly by Alan Tam, Jackie takes on a cavern full of cultists in a wonderful fight, choreographed with mostly circular movement, which explains how a lone kung-fu fighter can take on people who are all around him. Then he must battle four leather-studded, high-heeled Amazonian black women. Originally he was set to fight famed martial artist Cynthia Rothrock in this sequence, but after Jackie suffered his accident, the crew squeezed the new quartet into dominatrix costuming instead (created to fit Jackie's small stuntmen for doubling shots).

This is the climax of one of the greatest kung-fu sequences in cinema history. It's Liu Chia Hui versus Wang Lung Wei in Dirty Ho.

of the other. It is wonderful and impressive to watch.

Except for the odd ending, in which the villains are simply thrown or chased off-screen (rather than soundly defeated), *Project A II* is inspired stuff. There's so much great stuff here that it is hard to comprehend it all in a single viewing. After surviving with rep-

utation not only intact, but enhanced, Chan came up with *Police Story II* (1988), the first of his "two-part" pictures. That is, he embarked on a few two-hour movies, each with two one-hour plots.

The first part of *Police Story II* has the villain of the prequel being diagnosed with an illness that gives him three months to live.

Mai Te Lo (second from right) and Liu Chia Hui (second from left) clean up the streets of this Chinatown in Instructors of Death.

In those last twelve weeks, he promises to break every one of Jackie's bones. This sets the stage for two amazing fights, one in a restaurant and one in a playground—both of which set new standards for speed and complexity.

Plot number two features a group of demolition extortionists who plant bombs throughout the city, abduct Chan's girlfriend, wire a bomb to him that will explode if he attempts to remove it, and then face off in a fireworks factory. Here, Jackie continues the trait he had started in *Project A II*—of simply dumping characters off-screen rather than openly defeating them. Nonetheless, the final battle is wonderfully exhausting to watch. It ends with the entire factory exploding (with Jackie clearly running away from it in the foreground), and garnered Chan yet another Hong Kong "Oscar" for martial arts choreography.

Meanwhile, after eighty films as either fight choreographer, director, producer, or actor—including such classics as *A Touch of Zen* (1968), *Enter the Dragon* (1973), *Knockabouts* (1978), *The Magnificent*

120

Butcher (1980), *The Prodigal Son* (1981), and *Mr. Vampire* (1985)—Sammo Hung's remarkable and prolific Hong Kong career hit a rocky patch. The aforementioned *Lucky Stars Go Places* (1986), which combined characters from the *Lucky Stars* and the beloved *Aces Go Places* films, was deemed so arrogant, pandering, and patronizing that viewers stayed away from Hung's subsequent films in droves.

The box-office failure of his *Millionaire's Express* (1987), a charming homage to the spaghetti western, and *Eastern Condors* (1987), a thunderously exciting but wildly derivative war movie, seemed to give proof to that allegation. Sammo needed a sure-fire hit badly, and apparently the only way to insure that success was to have the name Jackie Chan above the title.

Meanwhile, at the age of thirty-four, Jackie was getting on in martial artist years. With all his injuries, legend had it that it took him forty-five minutes to straighten up in the morning. Sammo was getting even older, and was still smarting from Jackie's inability to appear in his last few films due to his own busy schedule. Some say they wouldn't have bombed had Jackie been in them. Wanting to appease and honor his "big brother," Jackie agreed to costar in what Golden Harvest was promoting as the Chan–Hung–Yuen Baio trio's farewell film.

So saying, they shot the works with *Dragons Forever* (1988), a literally fight-filled extravaganza featuring almost every kung-fu–film supporting player they could cram in. Curiously, each of the stars played anti-heroes, two of whom are redeemed by true love with sisters who are being persecuted by a drug pusher whose factory is poisoning their fishery.

Jackie plays the villain's initially amoral lawyer, Sammo is an illegal gun salesman, and Yuen enacts a benignly demented cat burglar. As the three struggle through the plot, the fights are fast, ample, and amazing. The trio fight each other and literally dozens of thugs in restaurants, nightclubs, parking lots, pleasure boats, and, finally, in a drug factory where each does some of his most impressive work. There Sammo stages a rematch between Jackie and Benny "the Jet" Urquidez, the villain's main cocaine taster. "This one took a little longer," Urquidez laughed. "We worked for weeks on this fight, and, yes, they [i.e. the action director, choreographer, and stuntmen] do pretty much make it up as they go along." The humor in this fight is more facile than in *Wheels on Meals*, and the brutality lessened, but they still get their kicks in, although, for the first time ever, Jackie is clearly doubled by a stuntman for the fight's penultimate kick.

"Jackie was on another set," an insider who did not wish to be identified maintained. "Sammo works so fast that Jackie didn't have time to be both places at once . . . and we needed that shot." It would not be the last time Sammo used stand-ins for Jackie in the midst of his frenetic fight sequences.

Despite an interesting story and many terrific fight scenes, it appeared as if the audience had not forgiven Sammo, or perhaps was a bit jaded by the trio's kung-fu skills. For whatever reason, *Dragons Forever* had a surprisingly soft box-office take in Japan, which had traditionally been a Chan stronghold. That, among other things, convinced Jackie that he had to follow his own heart— and his heart was saying—bigger, better, longer. Chan thought it was time to stop trying to join Buster Keaton and Bruce Lee and start following in the footsteps of his other idols: Gene Kelly and Steven Spielberg.

For the next year, Chan slaved on what was originally titled *Miracle*, but eventually became *Mr. Canton and Lady Rose* (1989). It was his combination of *Project A*, Francis Ford Coppola's *The Godfather* (1972), and, most especially, *Pocketful of Miracles* (1961). It was also Jackie's favorite directing job, featuring his most complex camera work, and highlighted by a sweeping crane shot that took seventeen hours to set up (and had to be done twice). Even so, this particular amalgam of a thirties' gangster movie, a romantic musical comedy, and a kung-fu flick leaps from genre to genre over its two-hour running time—and not always elegantly.

Wedged between an eye-filling musical montage and more French-farce sequences, are four brilliantly conceived fights, climaxed by one of Chan's finest. Having completed the rest of the filming, Chan and his stuntmen, now numbering seventeen, started to plan the finale. They set the crew to work building the interior of a rope factory from the ground up, and designed an intricate series of amusing and amazing battles amongst the many floor levels, stairs, elevators, and gigantic spools of hemp. The resulting choreography of flying bodies, wrapping cord, and rolling barrels is awesome. Some say, however, that it was too much, too late. The fights were only punctuation for long patches of somewhat desperate comedy. Although more impressive each time it is watched, *Miracle* was not enough of a miracle, so all involved looked across the globe to the single biggest box office in the world.

"No American movie theater will play a movie with an all-Chinese cast," Golden Harvest producer David Chan was told. "But what about Bruce Lee?" was his inevitable reply. "Oh . . ." came the equally inevitable answer. "He was the *exception*." So the seemingly *un*exceptional Jackie Chan, at least in American eyes, set about to create his most spectacular film—a world-hopping challenge to his skills as a director, producer, and star, featuring only two Asian actors in a large cast of Caucasions.

This was *Armour of God II: Operation Condor* (1991), and proved to be Jackie Chan's Waterloo. But Chan and company had no idea of that when they started. Taking an idea from famed Italian actor Aldo Sanbrell (seen in every Clint Eastwood "Man With No Name" spaghetti western) about Nazi gold buried beneath the Sahara, they developed a wonderfully exciting script to be filmed on location. But as soon as they left the comforts of Hong Kong, they discovered, to their dismay, that the weather and Middle Eastern film crews had no idea of who Jackie Chan was—and didn't care.

Operation Condor (reportedly named as an homage to Sammo Hung's *Eastern Condors*) was soon sunk in a sea of sandstorms. Since this effort eventually became a make-it-up-as-we-go-along work (like almost all of Chan's other films) it soon reflected Jackie's developing siege mentality. The entire film was like an overweighted plane which keeps gaining speed but never quite takes off.

"I think *Operation Condor* was Jackie's *Apocalypse Now*," said Vincent Lyn, the kickboxing champion, model, and actor who played Mark, the scarred villain. "Sets were being blown away and burned down. Equipment and film was actually melting in the Sahara heat. His entire crew was getting sick, and not just with the flu. The assistant director had a stroke. Jackie's production manager was arrested and kept in jail for months because extras were using the set 'play' money in town."

Lyn was brought in because one of the other Western actors accidentally kicked Jackie in the throat—a moment captured in the movie's end-credit outtakes. Originally it was this actor and his on-screen partner who were to fight Jackie in the film's climatic "Nazi wind-tunnel" sequence, but after that voice-and-life-threatening mistake, word went out to find two new villains. Kenneth Lo, Jackie's longtime friend and bodyguard, was one; Vincent Lyn was the other.

"Even though I had been in eighteen other Hong Kong martial arts movies, Jackie and his crew made me feel like I had two left feet," Lyn remembered. "They really were incredible, but Jackie had way too much to do. Even though the production was back in Hong Kong by this time, Jackie was writing, directing, starring, choreographing, and pro-

It's brother against brother at the climax of the greatest kung-fu movie, Legendary Weapons of China. *Director Liu Chia Liang (left) fights Liu Chia Yung. They may not be great looking, but they are great fighter-actors.*

ducing. It got so bad that Aldo Sanbrell used to joke around by calling, 'Hey, Jackie, I think I do the next scene with my finger up my nose, okay?' And Jackie, who would be deep in conference with the camera or stage crew, would just smile, wave, and say, 'Yeah, great!' He hadn't heard a word!"

Days became weeks, weeks became months, and months became years as Jackie slaved to finish *Operation Condor.* By the end of production, the characters had become unreasoning ciphers, and the three female costars—a Chinese, a Japanese, and an American (chosen to "please" the three movie markets Chan hoped to top)—seemed to be sharing the same semiretarded brain. But even a broken skull wouldn't deter Chan from finishing this cinematic albatross. Only this time, unlike the original *Armour of God,* it wasn't Jackie's head which got cracked, it was Vincent Lyn's.

"It was in the big wind-tunnel climax," he

An example of director Sun Chung's favorite shot, dwarfing his kung-fu fighters in their environment. In The Avenging Eagle *it makes their conflict small in comparison with the magnificence of China.*

said. "Since we were supposed to be buffeted by the winds created by two gigantic fans, the special-effects crew hung us by wires and hurled us around the set. You want to know what those wire harnesses were like? Imagine a giant grabbing you by the balls and throwing you into a wall. So, one time, the back of my skull hit one of the heavy, painted, wood slats that were made to look like the metal walls of the wind tunnel. They tell me it sounded like a gunshot. My head had broken it clean in two, and I'm hanging up there like a rag doll. Jackie asks if I'm all right and I open my mouth to reassure him . . . and the next thing I know I'm looking up at him, flat on my back on the set floor. I had been unconscious for half an hour."

"Take a rest," Jackie told him. "We'll try it again in fifteen minutes."

It would take Jackie more than fifteen minutes to recover from *Operation Condor;* it would take three years.

After that nightmare, Jackie Chan was probably at his lowest point, physically and mentally, of his entire life. So, naturally, the wolves who ran in the Hong Kong film business took that moment to nip at his heels. Chan needed to remind them that he was too important to the industry—not to mention to both the Hong Kong and Chinese governments.

That's how *Island of Fire* (1991)—Jackie's worst feature since his days with Lo Wei—came about. This sci-fi thriller was done as a favor to powerful producers, and cobbled together by old-time action filmmaker Jimmy Wang Yu from the plots of *The Wild Geese, The Dirty Dozen, Cool Hand Luke,* and *The Longest Yard.* Chan played a pool player in the corrupt Hong Kong of 1999, whose girlfriend is knifed by a vengeful gambler. Hospitals of the future demand cash before they operate, so in order to save her life, Jackie wins a pile of money in a card game, but must kill another angry gambler in order to leave the nightclub alive.

That sends Jackie to the jail from hell, where the dead man's brother, a gangster played by Andy Lau, challenges him to a duel. Between *Twinkle, Twinkle Lucky Stars* and this, Andy Lau had become a major singing star, but he was still no slouch in on-screen martial arts action, so their fight is the film's highlight. Eventually these two, as well as Sammo Hung, have their deaths faked by corrupt prison officials and are sent to the Philippines to serve as hit men. *Island of Fire*'s distinction is that it is the only film in which Jackie's character dies (and the fact that filming was interrupted by a short real war on location).

Upon his return to Hong Kong, Jackie was at a loss. As he himself put it: "I've done everything twice." So what was there left to do but a third sequel? To save Chan's sanity, Golden Harvest hired stunt coordinator Stanley Tong to direct *Police Story III: Supercop* (1992).

Up until this film, the women in Jackie Chan movies were set decoration at best. Although the marvelous Maggie Cheung was still playing Jackie's long-suffering girlfriend in this installment, she is portrayed as having something short of a full intellectual deck. Reportedly, it was Tong's idea to hire the magnificent Michelle Yeoh to play Jackie's mainland equal, and she matches Jackie kick for kick and stunt for stunt. It is here where Jackie, for the first time, really has to deal with both guns as well as his trademark kung-fu. The most memorable moments, however, come in the climax, when Jackie hangs from a helicopter ladder over Malaysia while Michelle jumps a motorcycle off a hill and onto the top of a moving train.

Having proven their worth, director Tong and costar Yeoh were pressed back into service for *Project S: Once a Cop* (1992) which promoted Michelle's character to the starring role but featured a strange cameo by Jackie in drag tracking a transvestite jewel thief (played by his *Armour of God* ex-director Eric Tsang!). This single scene mars an otherwise exciting and interesting tale, with Michelle's mainland cop tracking an ex-lover to a gang of thieves in Hong Kong.

Meanwhile, Jackie wanted to make a love story, but no one else wanted him to, so he took refuge in a charity production, *Twin Dragons* (1992), created to benefit the Hong Kong Director's Guild. It was codirected by Tsui Hark and Ringo Lam, and featured dozens of directors in bit parts. It starred Jackie in the dual role of twins separated at birth. One grew up to be a tough, hard-living Hong Kong car mechanic who's in with the local mob, while the other became an orchestra conductor in America.

When the latter returns to Hong Kong for a concert, he finds that the two share nerves and reflexes, à la Alexander Dumas's classic novel *The Corsican Brothers.* A merry mix-up of identities ensues, often placing the two Jackies on-screen together. It was Chan's first foray into the world of screen special effects, and was less than inspiring for him. "In special effects, you can do anything, and the audience knows it," Jackie mused. "Where's the excitement in that?"

Instead, Chan looked for excitement in *City Hunter* (1993), the Hong Kong version of a famous Japanese comic book (*manga*) character, directed by exploitation specialist Wong Jing. But, even though this is called

City Hunter, it is essentially yet another version of *Die Hard* (1988), only on a luxury ocean liner, making it also a knockoff of *Under Siege* (1992), but occasionally interrupted by a satirical musical number. It should have been called *Boat Hunter*, but even so, there are some memorable scenes, mostly the ones in which Jackie fights Australian Richard Norton and Englishman Gary Daniels.

There are also audaciously conceived, though not particularly well-executed, sequences in which Jackie is inspired by Bruce Lee, as when he fights villains in the ship's cinema, which is showing *Game of Death*. Even more audacious is when he plays the Japanese sumo wrestler and the female kung-fu fighter in a Street Fighter video game fantasy sequence. In any case, despite the participation of sexy costars Joey Wang and Chingmy Yau, *City Hunter* winds up as a crazy, campy, intermittingly amusing mess.

Coming off that "anything goes" satire, Jackie wanted to sink his teeth into something a little more substantial. He found it in *Crime Story* (1993), which was supposed to be New-Wave director Kirk Wong's first film in a projected modern crime trilogy starring real-life martial arts champion Jet Li. However, after Jet's manager was murdered in an underworld battle for control of the Hong Kong film industry, Li went to mainland China for awhile, and Jackie decided to take the role. After a much publicized tug-of-wills between the director and star, this movie became Chan's manifesto.

Although the script started as the tale of a conflicted cop trying to settle his psyche with the help of a sexy female psychiatrist while searching for a kidnapped millionaire, there's an amazing moment early on. Jackie has tried desperately to prevent the businessman's abduction when a motorcycle cop is hurt in the ensuing chase. Jackie carries him to the emergency room, where his gorgeous shrink waits. He takes one look at her sympathetic, caring, beautiful face—and then purposefully steps around her to share his frustration with the hospital wall.

He might as well have picked her up and hurled her off-screen, because from that moment on, *Crime Story* is for, by, and about Jackie Chan. In fact, the climatic scenes might serve as autobiographical sequences. As the bad guy lies under rubble in an exploding apartment block, he tells Jackie that everyone thinks Chan is crazy, that he tries too hard, and that he never gives up. Jackie replies that he can't help it, and continues trying to save the dying villain as well as an innocent child trapped in the blaze.

Aside from a confusing finale in which the kidnap victim is seemingly drowned only to turn up alive in the next scene, *Crime Story* is a landmark in the Chan filmography—as psychologically revealing as any Woody Allen film, and, as it turns out, more psychologically healing.

Following this film, Chan seemed rejuvenated. After many films in which he sought to separate himself from his kung-fu origins, he finally decided to embrace them with a movie that could be his final word on the subject. Elsewhere in the industry, Jet Li—the man Jackie had replaced in *Crime Story*—had made a hit in a series of movies featuring the venerable Huang Fei Hong, the character Chan satirized in the original *Drunken Master*. So now it was time for Jackie to reclaim the role.

Sixteen years after finishing the first film, Jackie made *Drunken Master II* (1994), hiring Liu Chia "Kung-fu" Liang to realize his ultimate martial arts vision as a director *and* costar. Incredibly, Chan is credible playing Huang Fei Hong where he last left him, the mischievous "twenty-something" (now really forty-year-old) son of a noble healer (played by the majestic Ti Lung).

The portion of the film Jackie allowed Liang to complete was impressive—filled

Athletic, gymnastic, buffoonish Jackie Chan shows what he's made of in Drunken Master.

Jackie Chan suffers under the feet of Simon Yuen in a scene that The Mask of Zorro *(1998) "borrowed" from the* Drunken Master.

with color, richness, imagination, and fights, fights, fights. Although the plot is of the hackneyed "evil foreigners smuggling Chinese treasures" variety, the director mounted many memorable battles, not the least of which is his own bout with Jackie beneath a steam train, under a wharf, and in a barn using fists, spears, and swords.

Liang continued to realize his vision with an impressive battle in a tea house with his character (a patriot), and Jackie taking on the "ax gang," hired by the villains to assassinate the pair. Using their fists, feet, and a shredded bamboo pole, the two wipe out literally dozens in this stunning sequence. By this time, Chan was fed up with taking orders.

"There can't be two tigers on the mountain," goes an old Chinese saying, and Chan was to quote it often after taking over the direction of *Drunken Master II*. Gutting a supporting role played by Andy Lau, Jackie called back Ti Lung and Anita Mui (who played his stepmother) to reshoot and design new sequences over a six-month period. He complained that Liang only wanted him to use "drunken boxing" during the last battle, and then to wipe out nearly hundreds with it. Instead, Jackie set about establishing the drunken style earlier in the film, and creating a spectacular one-on-one climatic battle with "superkicker" Kenneth Lo, directed in a clear, Americanized style of someone like Steven Spielberg.

Meanwhile, Liang took Lau and went off to complete what was to be called *Drunken Master III* (1994). Sadly, if the movie is any evidence, Jackie was right. Grievously disappointing, Liang's last completed film (as of this writing) has only a few sparks of the master's magic. In comparison to his many magnificent classics, it is much better forgotten.

Drunken Master II, happily, was another story. Chan was obviously inspired to live up to Liang's kung-fu skills, even in the scenes Jackie directed after forcing Liu off the movie. The final fight, in an audaciously designed metal foundry set, is among the very best things Chan has ever accomplished, mixing amazing martial arts and acrobatics with involving and emotional moments—culminating with Jackie as Huang Fei Hong being forced to drink poisonous industrial alcohol to achieve his ethereal, unbeatable Drunken-master status.

Incredibly, against all odds, *Drunken Master II* was a critical and financial bonanza, and clearly the best movie Jackie Chan had made since *Project A II*. Chan was back to full strength. It was time for him to conquer the one mountain that had always defeated this tiger. It was time to return to America.

THE BILLION-DOLLAR MAN

With *Drunken Master II*, Jackie Chan had accomplished something no other action star had ever done: he had gained entry to the mainland—only Jackie Chan films were allowed into Red China. Although ticket prices there were less than fifty cents, the cinemas have a potential audience of billions.

With voracious audiences in Japan and China, and a Hong Kong studio willing to give him almost all the time and money in the world, Chan was unique: clearly the most popular action star in the world, the only filmmaker with unquestioned authority, resources, and power, and the only movie star on the planet willing to die for his audience. "I'd much rather die on a movie set than in a car or plane crash," he has said. "I love making movies . . . and I don't want to die for nothing."

He didn't want to work for nothing, either. In 1995, he was forty years old. He knew that he couldn't keep up the kind of speed and power he displayed in *Drunken Master II*. To continue pleasing his insatiable Hong Kong audience, he decided to take the same road as American martial arts movie stars, and downplay kung-fu in favor of other kinds of action.

The time was right in America as well. Even though *Police Story* had been the hit of the New York Film Festival in the late 1980s, Hollywood was slow to accept Chinese-style action, but the underground video world was quick to pick up the slack. Intrigued by a book on the subject as well as television specials which were broadcast on the Arts and Entertainment and Discovery channels, thrill-seekers sought out Chan's films in Chinatowns and through vaguely legal specialty mail-order houses.

By the time New Line Cinema made a deal to distribute Chan's new films in America, and Dimension Films arranged to screen

Jackie Chan, a symbol of elegance, in an unusually still moment from the otherwise action-packed Young Master.

some of his older movies, the audience which had made *Star Trek* and *Star Wars* famous were already well aware of Jackie's talents. And therein lied the rub: to make these pictures true hits, the studios would have to reach those who hadn't seen them already—and those who saw them in their original, uncut format, too.

First up was *Rumble in the Bronx* (1995), fueled by an exceptional New Line promotional campaign. It made more than $30 million in the United States—despite the fact that the originally planned kung-fu fighting finale had to be scrapped because Jackie broke his ankle.

It was infuriating. While Chan was used to being injured on his sets in some spectacular way, his ankle was now snapping after a simple jump from a bridge to a hovercraft. This sort of piddling wound was to happen increasingly often in the future, irritating Jackie more and more. Even so, he had a film to finish, so he merely had a sock painted to look like a sneaker, put it on over his cast, and reworked the ending so it could be a car stunt instead of an extended kung-fu fight.

Then, much to his audience's dismay, Chan discovered that he liked replacing an extended, final fight scene with a car stunt. Somehow, it was a relief not to create a huge, complicated battle for his films' endings. So, from *Rumble* on, his movies were to end with a vehicular whimper rather than a martial arts bang. Until the late 1990s, each of Chan's subsequent films built up to an expected, hoped-for fight—that never happened. The effect of this tradition was insidious: it threw off the movies' structure and was one of the important reasons that his U.S. box-office clout diminished with each passing release.

This fact was not the case in Hong Kong, however. There, box-office returns were plummeting for an entirely different reason. With 1997 looming, and with it the return of Hong Kong to Chinese rule, the local gangsters were having a field day with the film industry, using intimidation and violence in lieu of good-faith negotiation. Coupled with the fact that most of these mobsters were just feeding their ego and couldn't care less about good movies, the Hong Kong film industry was going the way of the dodo bird.

In this small pond, however, Jackie Chan was the biggest fish, having already shown himself to be above this terrible fray. The majority of his audience came to his movies, however, not because they were better than what he did before, but because at least it was obvious that he cared about what he was doing. Such was the case with *Thunderbolt* (1995), a movie even New Line deemed too weak to release in America.

"Jackie Chan as Speed Racer!" the ads could have proclaimed for all the sense this makeshift racing drama made, stitched together by no less than five directors in order to finish it in time for Chinese New Year. In the danger-fraught world of Hong Kong cinema, the audience had come to depend on Chan's new movie being released at holiday time so there would be at least one decent movie the whole family could go to.

Where once there were many thrilling kung-fu fights in Chan's films, in this nonsensical tale of a psycho crime lord forcing a talented garage mechanic into "the big race" by destroying his home, injuring his father, and kidnapping his two sisters, there are only two. But these two are singular works of martial art by the great Sammo Hung; they also set records for speed of movement and editing.

In the first fight, against thugs who try to pay Chan off in his own garage, Sammo's camera follows Jackie's moving limbs and pumps up the sound-effect volume to create a riveting conflict. In the second and last fight of the film, he creates the ultimate athletic battle in a Japanese Pachinko pinball parlor, actually using the fighters like wildly bouncing pinballs. Any filmmaker would find his command of the camera and editing table incredible, but any true fan of Jackie would also notice that the superstar was doubled by stuntmen more in this sequence than in any other.

Thunderbolt did well at the box office, but Chan, himself, was disappointed by its disjointed storytelling. For his new film, he vowed to have only one director—and to make it coherent enough that New Line Cinema would release it in America.

In some places in Asia, *First Strike* (1996) was known as *Police Story IV: First Strike*; in others, it was known as *Police Story III Part 2: First Strike*; and elsewhere it was even known as *Piece of Cake*. By any name, it was Jackie Chan's homage to 007 movies, although directed by Stanley Tong. It was also one of Chan's weakest efforts, featuring only one kung-fu fight, which served to hurt the rest of the film because it reminded audiences of what they were missing.

In this fight, taking place all over an Australian-Chinese community center, Chan battles angry mourners who blame him for the death of a friend. He uses tables, chairs, doorways, a wheeled scaffold, and,

most impressively, a small ladder to keep them at bay. The rest of the globe-hopping effort is disappointing in comparison, as Chan and Tong replace involving characters and plot with feeble comedy and an endless underwater climax in an aquarium which mixes the absurdity of silly thugs with the impossibility of lame-looking, leg-chewing, obviously fake sharks who can stop and back up, unlike their real-life counterparts. And, of course, there was a lame climatic car stunt.

The year 1998 saw Jackie Chan's American hopes under siege. His U.S. box office had been hurt by the reediting, rescoring, and rereleasing of his older movies.

Jackie hangs on for dear life as he and his heavily disguised bodyguard, Ken Lo, are about to get blown off the screen during the Nazi wind-tunnel climax.

The many faces of Jackie Chan.

Dimension Films cut thirty minutes out of *Operation Condor*, and while it eliminated some of the rampant silliness of the female costars, it also removed several highlights from the exceptional wind-tunnel fight, including the highlight of the coming attraction trailer (when Vincent Lyn offers Jackie a deal, Jackie throws his head back, laughs, and then abruptly says, "No!").

It wasn't so much what was cut out of the U.S. version of *Supercop* that hurt, it was what was added: a new soundtrack that had Compton rap songs playing on a mainland Chinese radio, a reggae version of the disco hit "Staying Alive" playing in a mainland Chinese police station, and Tom Jones's cover of *Everybody Was Kungfu Fightin'* over the end credits. That ditty was tired twenty years ago, when American executives tried to subtly belittle Bruce Lee with it.

Finally, *Crime Story* was released directly to American video stores, and only in a dubbed version, and one that did not feature Jackie Chan doing his own voice—the first Americanized Chan feature to do this. These moves, and the generally lackluster films the studios chose to release, helped drop his American box-office take 66 percent since *Rumble in the Bronx*.

Even so, Chan's enthusiasm and workload had not diminished. *Mr. Nice Guy* (1997), the odd tale of a television chef running afoul of criminals in Australia, was conceived by New Line execs and director Sammo Hung as a compendium of many of Jackie's best moments from eight of his previous Hong Kong films. "[It] boasts more action than the last three Jackie Chan films combined," the studio proclaimed. And yes, while it has some nifty fights and stunts, it is hurt by a

Jackie Chan shows an impressed stunt double his own fist of fury during Rumble in the Bronx.

needlessly profane script, three more silly female costars, and a story which defies even movie logic. And, once again, there's that disappointing, albeit impressive, climatic car stunt.

Despite all of this, Chan carried on, with style. He was the recipient of the MTV Movie Awards' Lifetime Achievement honor, starred in a cleverly conceived, action-packed commercial for Mountain Dew soda (which urged him to "Feel the Dew . . . Be the Dew!"), had his hand, foot, and even nose imprints immortalized in cement in Grauman's Chinese Theater's sidewalk of fame, and then went to work on a new Hong Kong–produced film, aptly titled *Who Am I?* (1998).

Designed to please both Asian and American audiences, *Who Am I?* came at a time when Chan was seriously analyzing his future and testing the limits of his talents. The resulting film did not want for ambition. Globe-hopping from Africa to Holland, it tells of a special undercover agent on a secret mission to secure a superpowered meteorite, only to suffer amnesia and be pursued by gangsters, terrorists, and spies.

Unfortunately, rather than let the audience discover the truth at the same time as Chan's character, Jackie chose to reveal his identity to the viewer in an opening sequence—one that was virtually identical to an equally silly briefing scene at the beginning of *Supercop*—essentially robbing the film of any mystery or suspense.

Despite some interesting and amusing moments with an African tribe who saves him, a fight-filled forty-five minutes at the ending, and a terrific climatic stunt (sliding down twenty-five stories of a sloped Amsterdam skyscraper), the movie's fatal flaw is the inclusion of a ridiculously out-of-date and stereotyped gangster villain who looks like he wandered in from a third-rate

road show of *Guys and Dolls.* Even Jackie's American distributors couldn't bring themselves to release this one. *Who Am I?* had its American premiere on the Home Box Office cable television channel.

Following that, no pundit held out much hope for *Rush Hour* (1998), Jackie's first American-produced film since *The Protector.* The original script didn't even include Chan's character in its tale of a married cop couple who bicker their way to finding the abducted child of a Chinese diplomat. In the

rewritten version, Jackie is a special Asian agent sent from Hong Kong to help the local cops and Feds—who want nothing to do with him. Gone is the married couple. Now only an equally troublesome, fast-talking, ambitious cop is left, played by motormouthed actor and comedian Chris Tucker, who showed great talent with memorable supporting roles in *The Fifth Element* (1997) and *Jackie Brown* (1997).

Unfortunately, neither he nor director Brent Radnor showed particular promise with their first starring collaboration, *Money Talks* (1997), which only managed mediocre box-office returns. But that was when Tucker was teamed with Charlie Sheen. Now he was teamed with Jackie Chan, who knew a thing or two about holding his own on-screen. Cinematic karma seemed to be at work in that the pair were perfect opposites, and the marketing masters went to town with that fact.

"The fastest hands in the East meets the fastest mouth in the West," declared the ads,

Chan wraps up First Strike's *one and only fight scene, giving his stunt guy a first, and last, strike.*

but as the feature was quickly and efficiently put together, rumors of disquiet leaked from the set. It seemed that Jackie didn't like being just an actor, nor being at the mercy of Tucker's quick wit—especially in a language he was uncomfortable with. Despite Radnor's promises that his image was in good hands, Chan was concerned. After all, he had heard those promises several times before, only to find them hollow.

At first his worries seemed justified. Studio execs who viewed the footage and critics who attended the premiere gave the picture only a middling chance of success. Even the director himself was reported to have thought that the movie would probably gross only $30 million, tops. But those who went to the movie its opening weekend

knew different. In hundreds of cinemas across the country, something extremely unusual was happening. The seats were filling up with young and old, male and female, and black and white. Rarely had any movie attracted such a cross section of filmgoers—and rarely had any movie pleased every one of them.

Rush Hour turned out to be the movie that Jackie Chan had been promising for years—a fast, funny, action-filled entertainment with virtually no swearing and essentially no actual violence. The stars' real-life distrust of each other and their own career ambitions blended completely with their characters' motivations; neither gave an inch and both used every ounce of their skill and charisma. Tucker's mind and mouth worked perfectly in collaboration with Chan's brains and body, resulting in a film which made every audience member smile.

The director's cautious estimate was topped the very first weekend, with a take of $31 million in three days alone. *Rush Hour* went on to gross more than $150 million, a sum which required an immediate sequel for many a delirious studio executive. There were only two problems: neither Jackie Chan nor Chris Tucker seemed inclined to do it right away, each being anxious to prove their worth as a solo.

Chan returned to Hong Kong to make an oft-desired romantic comedy, originally titled *Bottle*, and then *Glass Bottle*. It appeared in 1999, on Chan's traditional opening date of the Chinese New Year, with the final title *Gorgeous*. Surprisingly to many (but not to those who knew the original titles), it was Chan's Asian take on the recently released Kevin Costner romantic drama *Message in a Bottle* (1999). There is no question that Jackie Chan has become a kung-fu film icon in America—now if only he'd continue *doing* great kung-fu films *for* America!

SUPERSONIC JET

Jackie Chan is clearly the crown prince of kung-fu. No one in the world is bigger, but someone in China just might be better—at martial arts, at any rate. His name is Li Lin Jei, and he had been a mainland Chinese champion martial artist since the age of eleven. Shortly after Bruce Lee died, Li was performing at the White House for Richard Nixon and Henry Kissinger. After being all-around winner of the National Martial Arts Championships five times, Li even received a backstage bouquet for his performance from Jackie Chan.

Little did either man know that, in a few years, they would be vying for the championship of the action-film box office. It all started in 1981, when Li was eighteen and already considered a kung-fu superstar in his homeland. After the death of Mao Tse Tung, filmmakers' freedoms were enormously extended. Greatly influenced by the work of Liu Chia Liang, the Hong Kong Cheung Yuen Film Production Company conceived *The Shaolin Temple*, a realistic martial arts epic featuring an all-champions cast, to be filmed on actual locations.

Despite having every Chinese kung-fu artist at their disposal, the filmmakers only thought of Li to play the leading role of Shiu Hwu, a young revolutionary who is out for vengeance against the emperor's evil nephew. The inexperienced actor threw himself into the production with the same energy he had brought to his martial arts. After three years of production and $10 million in expenditure, the movie exploded onto the international scene with the newly renamed Jet Li in front.

The film is a magnificent showcase for authentic martial arts, and is, in effect, a distillation of all the ingredients which made Hong Kong movies work for decades. In fact, it even used Shaw Brothers Studio space and Liu Chia Liang's expertise in certain sequences. Director Chang Hsin Yen was also able to utilize the studio's best equipment, resulting in a splendidly visual film, with impressive attention to detail, sumptuous cinematography, and truly great kung-fu.

With wit and imagination, *The Shaolin Temple* tells the tale of the conflict that ended the Sui dynasty and started the T'ang, but through the eyes of a boy seeking revenge for the murder of his father. The boy is rescued from his father's killer and then taught kung-fu by an unusual group of Shaolin Temple monks, outsiders who are not averse to drinking wine, eating meat, and even killing when they have to. And, as far as they are concerned, when it comes to Sui soldiers, they *have to.*

Yu Cheng Wei, the creator and master of the real-life "Shark Fin Broadswordplay,"

Jackie blocks one of hundreds of punches thrown at him in the always action-packed but occasionally silly Mr. Nice Guy.

played the villain, while mantis fist champion Yu Hai played Li's sifu, and National All-Around Champion Hu Chien Chiang played Li's temple "brother." The lovely Ding Lan played the sifu's niece and Li's love interest, who just barely loses him to the temple when the newly crowned T'ang emperor arrives a moment too late to prevent Li from taking the monk's "Thou Shalt Not Have Sex" oath. The monks celebrate as he eliminates the "Thou

Shalt Not Drink" rule by royal decree, leaving the niece to tearfully sneak away.

The movie was a greater success than anyone had anticipated. It was so popular in its home country that the government had to issue a request that students not leave school in order to go searching for the cinematic Shaolin Temple. Meanwhile, Jet Li was now a movie superstar in addition to being a martial arts champion. In fact, one of the bill-

boards greeting President Ronald Reagan when he visited China showed Jet hawking "Shaolin Wine."

Such success called for a sequel, and, surprisingly, *Shaolin Temple II: Kids From Shaolin* (1983) was as good as its predessessor, and, in some ways, better. The main cast and crew were the same, but everyone was a lot more comfortable with their new roles as actors. Taking place long after the destruction of the Shaolin Temple, the new film told of the Lung family of seven men, who lived across the Likiang River from the Pao family of seven girls, one tired mother, and one frustrated father (played by the villain of the last film, Yu Cheng Wei).

The dragons (boys) knew Shaolin kung-fu. The pheonixes (girls) knew *wu tang* swordsmanship. The father wanted a male heir, but no husbands for his daughters: He forbade them from fraternizing with the family on the wrong side of the river. Little did he know that his eldest daughters were already in love with the eldest Lungs, or that he was being set up for the kill—his main adviser was, in reality, a master robber who was preparing his gang of cutthroats to gut the town.

Upon this vaguely *Seven Brides for Seven Brothers*-style plot, the crew lavished heaps of eye-filling spectacle, from traditional musical numbers along the awe-inspiring river to astonishing swordfights inside gem-encrusted caves. It all finally comes together in the thieves' massive attack. By this time, the Lungs have been framed, exiled, and their home destroyed, while the Pao matriarch struggles mightily to protect his newborn male child.

Naturally, the Lungs come leaping, chop-ping, and kicking back just in the nick of time. The final fray, with all fourteen members of the family strutting their stuff, is a masterpiece of fight choreography, with Jet Li leading the way with fists, feet, a sword, rope darts, and three-sectional staff. The fade-out finds true love conquering all—with a little help from killer kung-fu.

The Asian audience was delighted, and the floodgates of cheap imitations opened. Even Jet Li was a bit stymied by the rush of junk which followed from both Hong Kong and mainland studios. There were almost as many mass-produced mediocre Shaolin Temple movies as there had been Bruce Lee rip-offs, the best of which being *Shaolin and Wu Tang*, costarring and directed by the

Jackie gets his kicks in First Strike, *but many fans felt there were too few kicks, too late, for the film to be an American success.*

"Master Killer" himself, Liu Chia Hui.

What was good for Lee was good for Li as well. Now proclaimed the biggest star in China, Jet used his fame to secure control of his next movie. At the tender age of twenty, he ambitiously decided to direct and star in *Born to Defence* (1985). The odd title was the first evidence that Li may have bitten off a little more than we could swallow. The plot was not at fault: Li played a young soldier coming back from World War II who is stunned to discover that his own village was proclaiming the Americans heroes while ignoring their own warriors. "Forget the atom bomb!" Li cries out in anguish at one point. "What about my fists?"

Tragically, the Americans start taking over the town, beating up the old rickshaw runners and raping the women with seeming impunity. Repeatedly maligned by his own people, Li is finally given the chance to fight back when the Americans arrange boxing matches in the local bar. Unmercifully pummeled as he slowly learns this new fighting art, Li finally explodes in a match that literally brings the house down during a typhoon. Once that scene is over, however, the whole film also goes to pieces, just barely holding on long enough for Li to kill the most corrupt American oppressors using a combination of boxing and kung-fu.

A good idea gone wrong, *Born to Defence*

made Jet realize that he had a lot to learn about filmmaking, not to mention American grammar. It was lucky, therefore, that the great Liu Chia Liang had just been given the chance to complete a lifelong dream. He was asked by a mainland Chinese studio to direct *Shaolin Temple III* (1986). Naturally, "Kung-fu" Liang subtitled it *Martial Arts of Shaolin* and just went crazy. Having spent his career training actors how to do decent kung-fu, he now had at his disposal literally hundreds of great kung-fu athletes whom he could help be decent actors.

If Busby Berkeley had learned kung-fu instead of dancing, this is what his great 1930s musicals might have looked like. Liang crammed dozens of Shaolin monks and evil Manchu warriors into every shot he could, all having them do the same intricate moves at the same time. Freed like he had never been before, Liang designed fight scenes of such complexity that they are occasionally eye-splitting to follow. And he filmed them on locations never before used, including the Forbidden City and the Great Wall of China.

The plot, as almost always, was simplicity itself. A myriad bunch of young revolutionaries want to assassinate a sadistic Manchu general (played by the villain of the original film, Yu Cheng Wei). Sure, there are some complicating factors, like Jet having been promised in marriage to the lead female revolutionary while his temple "brother" is in love with her, but that mushy stuff takes a back seat to the color and pageantry of Liang's martial arts tour de force. If there's any fault with his sweeping vision, it's that the actual finale in a fruit orchard is a bit subdued after the climax—a no-holds-barred battle on a huge war-boat on the Yangtze River.

Even so, Jet gets to show off his mantis fist just before the girl beheads the bad guy. All's well that ends well, with the two lovers getting together as Li heads back to the Shaolin Temple with his wise sifu. The actor Jet Li was not as lucky as his on-screen character. Following this final Shaolin Temple movie, he discovered that the rest of the film industry was just churning out product, and not that interested in quality.

Jackie 2000, Hollywood-style.

141

Yu Cheng Wei went on to star in the strangely sadistic, but beautifully filmed, *Yellow River* (U.S.: *The Yellow River Fighter*, 1987), playing a grief-stricken, blinded, poisoned warrior whose six-year-old daughter was delivered to him by an enemy at the end of a spear. But Jet was grounded, unable to find a quality project. When he finally returned to the screen, it was in a strange pair of movies set in America: *Dragon Fight* (1988) and *The Master* (1989).

The former was set in San Francisco and featured Jet as a recent immigrant who had to fight racism as well as Chinatown gangs. Its one distinction was Jet's costar, Stephen Chiao, who was soon to become the "Hong Kong Jim Carrey" in a string of delightful, hugely-successful, madcap comedies which satirized kung-fu as often as they depicted it. Chiao even had the gall to create *Fist of Fury 1991*, a surprisingly involving, often hilarious take-off on Bruce Lee's original, with Chiao playing a fighter with the strongest right arm in all of China—but the weakest left.

Meawnhile, Jet was left with the role of the student in *The Master*, the title character played by the great Yuen Wah, who had been raised in that brutal Peking Opera school along with Jackie Chan, Sammo Hung, and Yuen Baio. Wah had also done a remarkable job playing the unforgettable villains in *Eastern Condors* and *Dragons Forever*. Here, however, both he and Jet were at sea in a hoary miasma about evil Americans wanting to take over Yuen's kung-fu school in modern California. The single most important thing about this failure, however, is that it was directed by Tsui Hark.

Hark, often called the Steven Spielberg of Hong Kong, and the father of Hong Kong special effects, was the country's most politically daring filmmaker. Having graduated from film school in Texas, Hark returned to Hong Kong in 1977. There, he embarked on a series of challenging films in many genres. He gained his greatest fame, however, with the phantasmagorical action film *Zu Warriors of the Magic Mountain* (1983), an eye-popping fantasy adventure featuring Yuen Baio, Mang Hoi, and Moon Lee battling demons and demigods for the fate of the world.

He followed that with *Peking Opera Blues* (1986), a wonderful comedy action romance starring three of Hong Kong's most beautiful women (Bridget Lin, Sally Yeh, and Cherie Chung) as reluctant revolutionaries and eager acting hopefuls who run afoul of sadistic "sheriffs" and mad military men. Eager to explore burgeoning special effects technology further, Hark produced two groundbreaking classics at the same time: Ching Siu Tung's *A Chinese Ghost Story* (1987) and John Woo's *A Better Tomorrow* (1987).

Now, however, it was 1990, and Hark was rooting around for another genre to revolutionize. And, as Jackie Chan and Yuen Woo Ping had done before him, he set his sights on the Huang Fei Hong kung-fu film. And who better to play the young, serious, powerful Huang Fei Hong of politically unstable 1900s Hong Kong than Li Lin Jei?

As Liu Chia Liang had in his masterpiece *Legendary Weapons of China*, Tsui Hark turned his attention to the Chinese pugilists' vain attempts to defeat the gun with kung-fu, but he added layers of relevance by having the Hong Kong harbor filled with heavily-armed ships from Britain, the United States, and Germany. As the foreigners vied for political clout in the emporer's palace, Huang must rescue his lady love, Aunt Yee (Rosamund Kwan), from the clutches of evil English-speaking white slavers as well as a homicidally jealous tiger claw kung-fu master.

The climatic battle takes place on a series of precariously balanced ladders, and is a masterpiece of martial arts and special effects, during which Jet broke his shin. That wasn't nearly enough, however, to prevent the film from being a huge hit and Jet Li from cementing his superstardom.

In 1991, *Once Upon a Time in China*, named in honor of Italian director Sergio Leone's brilliant *Once Upon a Time in the*

Jet Li shows his high-flying authentic stuff in Fong Sai Yuk.

West (1969) and *Once Upon a Time in America* (1984), burst upon the scene, announcing to the kung-fu film world that Jet Li was back, and literally better than ever. Huang Fei Hong was the role he was born to play, and he played it with an assurance and command hithertofore unseen in his filmography. Then, as he had been for the Shaolin Temple movies, Li was back on the sequel treadmill, seeing *Once Upon a Time in China II* and *Once Upon a Time in China III* made and released by 1992.

It is the former of the two pictures which ranks the highest, because Tsui Hark beautifully balances action, romance, comedy, emotion, and politics in this tale of Huang Fei Hong meeting real-life revolutionary Dr. Sun Yat Sen while fighting the foreigner-hating White Lotus sect. Fittingly, it was the one-hundreth Huang Fei Hong movie made.

Veteran star David Chiang and relative newcomer Donnie Yen are standouts in this terrifically entertaining, exceptionally well-directed piece. Chiang plays Sun's assistant, who gives up his life for the cause, while Yen plays the violent and corrupt "sheriff" who is

143

a little too anxious to test his kung-fu skills against those of Huang. The action is plentiful and impressive throughout, but it is the three-part climax that stays locked in the memory. Huang decimates the White Lotus headquar-ters, and then battles Yen in a soybean factory before taking it outside into an alley.

From that dizzying height, there was no place to go but down, and Huang number 101 temporarily sounded the death knell of Jet's

144

Li felt he was as important to the Huang Fei Hong movies as Tsui Hark, but the director-producer apparently felt differently.

According to press reports, Hark's parting words were along the lines of "Without me, you're nothing," and the disjointed, overblown story line of *Once Upon a Time in China III* reflects the backstage conflict. Huang runs afoul of more corrupt foriegners and an insanely jealous rich man who wants to win the local lion-dance contest at any cost. The final lion dance is really pretty ridiculous, what with fire-belching entrants and way too much confusion.

With that, Jet Li turned his back on Tsui Hark, but not on Huang Fei Hong. With the director's harsh words ringing in his ears, he had a lot to prove, and he wanted to prove it fast. Jet Li made five movies in 1993, the first being the aptly titled *Last Hero in China* (one that Jet intended to be his last Huang Fei Hong movie). Adding insult to injury, he worked with the madman of Hong Kong cinema, Wong Jing, to put Huang and Tsui in their places.

Although Jet played his martial arts straight, the plot was the goofy tale of Huang being forced to move his kung-fu school and healing hospital next to a brothel. As is Jing's wont, there is even a musical number as the martial arts students drool over the semi-clothed girls next door. The climax also mixes straight kung-fu with satire as Huang defeats the villain in a martial arts contest using chicken-style kung-fu.

Ironically, the man Jet defeats is played by Zhao Wen Zhou, the actor Tsui Hark chose to replace Li in *Once Upon a Time in China IV* (1993) and *Once Upon a Time in China V* (1994). Although younger and a quite capable martial artist, Zhao did not have half of Jet's charisma, and, despite the fact that Hark used him in several subsequent Huang Fei Hong television series, the *Once Upon a Time* series

partnership with Tsui Hark. Having also starred in Hark's *Swordsman II* (1992)—the sequel to the troubled *Swordsman* (1990, which had to be completed by three directors after the original director, King Hu, fell ill)—

145

was considered over the moment Li left it.

Jet, in the meantime, continued to leave Huang and Tsui in his dust. He enrolled the help of the popular martial arts movie director Corey Yuen (U.K.: Yuen Kwai) and traveled to mainland China to take on the role of the firebrand title character of *Fong Sai Yuk* (1993), a famous, hot-headed Shaolin Temple survivor whose love for his mother is only exceeded by his kung-fu power. Former superstar Josephine Siao's career was revived by this film, which also rematched Li against Zhao Wen Zhou as Fong fights against the evil Qing dynasty.

This turned out to be one of Li's biggest hits, so out came *Fong Sai Yuk II* (1993), which is even more entertaining from a martial arts standpoint. Here, Li is reunited with Ji Chun Hua, who played villains in all three Shaolin Temple movies. His performance adds weight to the quickly produced film, in that he plays an insanely envious member of the initially chivalrous Red Lotus sect, who frames Fong and ultimately murders the sect's true leader, played by the charismatic Adam Cheung.

The climax has a blindfolded Fong chopping his once faithful sect brothers to bits (so he wouldn't have to see their betrayal) before rescuing his mother, who the bad guy has put in a hangman's noose atop a tall series of wooden workshop horses. It was another triumph for Li, Siao, and, especially, Corey Yuen, another student of the same Peking Opera school which produced Jackie Chan, who proved again what a fast and imaginative director he truly was. Yuen took the American name Corey (an asexual moniker which never failed to amuse his friend and "big brother," Sammo Hung) once he had directed a lion's share of successful kung-fu flicks. Even after those three successes, Li's year was not over. He continued to have fun with martial arts traditions with *Kung Fu Cult Master* (1993), another Wong Jing extravaganza which was supposed to be the first part of a series based on a famous martial arts novel. Perhaps he went a bit too far kidding the audience. The Asian audience wanted to see Jet Li do kung-fu, not make fun of it. So, despite some very amusing scenes, highlighted by one in which Jet learns a whole new martial art in a few minutes, this was his weakest film of 1993.

Fans hadn't turned their backs on him for good, though. His fifth film of the year was *The Tai Chi Master*, directed by the man who made Jackie Chan famous, Yuen Woo Ping. It also costarred Michelle Yeoh, the woman who had matched Jackie punch for punch. "Everyone had told me that Jet was so serious," Michelle reported. "But I found that far from the truth. We had a wonderful time on the set. In fact, we used to drive the director crazy with all our cutting up."

Yeoh also found Jet to be a very supportive costar as well. "Of course he was a better martial artist than me, but he never tried to show off," she explained. "In fact, he always made sure that I was okay, and he was always very supportive and helpful, both as an actor and as a martial artist."

Although Li spends too much of the story driven insane by the greedy betrayal of a Shaolin Temple "brother," the film ends in a flurry of activity, as he learns to harness nature's energy to create Tai Chi. It is in this self-learning sequence, not in the battles, that the film's most memorable moment comes. Standing in a windy clearing, Jet creates a spinning ball of fallen leaves without touching them, simply by the supreme movement of his arms. He then uses his new skill to defeat a superpowered eunuch as well as the aforementioned insanely corrupt betrayer.

By any criteria, 1993 was an amazing year for Jet Li. When it was over, it was clear to the entire film industry that he was still very much somebody, even without Tsui Hark (who had scored one 1993 kung-fu hit with the wonderful *Iron Monkey*, directed by Yuen Woo Ping and starring Donnie Yen, but also had several misses in *Green Snake* and *The Magic Crane*).

It was also a very frightening year—one,

Jet Li points the way as Hung Sze Kwan in The New Legend of Shaolin.

you will remember, when Jet Li's manager was gunned down in an underworld battle for control of the film industry. According to the Hong Kong press, Jet hastily returned to China to seek a divorce from his wife. According to insiders, however, he was waiting for the smoke to clear in Hong Kong before daring to return. Because of that, his output in 1994 was reduced: only three movies, but one of them remains a kung-fu classic, while the other two were the result of his newfound producing powers.

Borrowing a page from the traditional wedding ceremony, Jet gave his public something old, something new, something borrowed, but nothing blue. The "something new" was innocuously titled *New Legend of Shaolin*, in which Jet played Hung Shi Kwan, another legendary kung-fu character who took the road of vengeance after the Shaolin Temple was betrayed and destroyed. This new movie version, however, also showcased the pubescent martial arts prodigy Xie Miao, who played Jet's son.

147

The charismatic Adam Cheng marvels at what director Tsui Hark has wrought in Zu Warriors of the Magic Mountain.

Given that this effort was also directed by Wong Jing, things don't stay sane for long. Soon the Shaolin betrayer becomes superpowered, able to spit poison, and rides all over ancient China in a silver-spiked deathmobile. Besides that, Hung is eventually saddled with a whole bunch of Shaolin kids, all of whom must unite in the very confusing and, ultimately very silly, final battle.

A little more interesting was Jet's "something old" presentation, *The Bodyguard From Beijing,* director Corey Yuen's Chinese take on the Kevin Costner-Whitney Houston *Bodyguard* (1992). This Asian variation features the sultry Christy Cheung as a rich

man's wife who witnessed a horrible murder and now must be protected from a brutal kung-fu killer (powerfully played by Ngai Sing).

The beginning of the film is taken up with the mainland bodyguard getting used to Westernized Hong Kong ways. The middle is given over to silly comedy and gunplay, but the last half-hour is solid action, as Jet and Ngai go at it in Christy's darkened, gas-filled apartment.

Finally, there was Jet's "something borrowed." When it was revealed that Li was planning to remake what was arguably Bruce Lee's best movie, *Fist of Fury* (U.S.: *The*

Chinese Connection), the audience was in an uproar—sacrilege! And, indeed, when Jet's new version first came out the box-office returns were weak, but once people started to see it, the groundswell was impressive.

Jet maintained that his new *Fist of Fury*, now called *Fist of Legend* (1994), was more faithful to the famous martial-arts novel the film was based on, and that it was more relevant to the times. The differences in the movies were certainly telling. Unlike Bruce, Jet did not have to convince his audience that the Chinese were not the weaklings of Asia. Nor did he and director Gordan Chan think it wise to maintain the rampant hatred of the Japanese which drove the original. Instead, they created both good and evil Japanese, as well as good and evil Chinese. They even added an interracial love story—with Jet in love with a Japanese girl—showing how racism can cut both ways.

But it was the martial arts, directed by Yuen Woo Ping, which really made *Fist of Legend* a classic. Like Jackie Chan before him, Jet knew that he couldn't maintain his kung-fu strength and speed forever. It was more than ten years since he had starred in *The Shaolin Temple*, so, if he wanted to have his final word in kung-fu, he would have to have it now. So he did. *Fist of Legend* is filled with fights, each one better than the last.

The film opens with Li studying in Japan when a bunch of karate toughs try to force him out of school. He mops the classroom with them, sometimes literally. Then he hears that his sifu has been killed in a martial arts duel. Racing back to China, he confronts the winner's students and mops the place with them too (at one point flipping a person by his mouth, and then slowly wiping the student's saliva from his fingers).

He then tests the man who "defeated" his master, and when he immediately discovers that the victor is not nearly skilled enough to defeat his sifu, he responds by "getting in the man's face"—literally: Every time Jet brings the man down, he pushes his angry, accusing head an inch from the failing fighter.

By personally digging out his buried master's liver to test for poison, Jet runs afoul of both the enemy students and the racism of his own school's "brothers." He must finally confront his dead sifu's son, who is murderously envious of Li's skills. At first he goes easy on him, but Jet soon unleashes a new skill called "boxing" (shades of *Born to Defence!*). Emerging victorious, he is still exiled by his racist superiors in the company of his Japanese lady love. Jet must then face her uncle—Japan's finest martial artist, played wonderfully by Shoji Kurata. It is in that terrific scene, comparing and contrasting Asian styles, where the most telling dialogue is heard. After Shoji has called the confrontation a draw, Jet asks: "But isn't the whole idea to win?" To which Kurata replies: "If you want to win a fight, bring a gun. The martial arts is about balance and inner energy."

But it's not over yet. Jet must still face the school's true enemy and the poisoner of his sifu: the man known as the General of Death, powerfully portrayed by Billy Chow (U.K.: Chow Bey Lai). Chow also fought Sammo in *Eastern Condors*, Yuen in *Dragons Forever*, and Jackie in *Miracle*. Now it's Jet's turn, and, for fifteen beautifully orchestrated minutes, they go at it—until Billy grabs a samurai sword, forcing Jet to use his belt the way Bruce used his nunchaku. Although they can't bring themselves to kill Jet at the end, à la Bruce, *Fist of Legend* ranks with Li's Shaolin Temple movies as among the very best of the best. When *Fist of Legend* was first shown in New York, the audience was on its feet.

After that, it was time for Jet to slow down. The following year saw only two movies from the martial arts master, and both were odd, to say the least. *My Father Is a Hero* (1995) is Jet and Corey Yuen's low-rent version of James Cameron and Arnold Schwarzenegger's collaboration *True Lies* (1994, which was, in turn, based on a French film called *La Totale*).

This film reunites Jet with Xie Miao, the pubescent kung-fu prodigy from *New Legend of Shaolin*, and sorely uses the boy to wring pathos from its increasingly out-of-control plot. To push the audiences' buttons, they bring the kid back from the dead not once, but twice during the frenetic proceedings, and finish up the final fight with Jet using him as a living yo-yo—hurling him back and forth at the villains with a rope! Although the martial arts portrayed are occasionally impressive, the thing gets so silly by the end that it ranks as a disappointment.

Also disappointing, but for entirely different reasons, is *High Risk* (1995), which was reportedly Wong Jing's attempt to costar Jet Li and Jackie Chan in the same movie. Supposedly, when Jackie dropped out, the film became a vicious "satire" (read: attack) on Chan, featuring the talented Jackie Cheung as an action star who wears Bruce Lee's black-striped yellow outfit from *Game of Death* but has a father and manager who look just like Jackie's. To top it off, the character is a drunk, a skirt chaser, and a total fraud.

Responding to rumors that it was director Stanley Tong, not Jackie Chan, who did the famous jump between buildings in *Rumble in the Bronx*, Wong Jing sets up a similar stunt in *High Risk*, and then shows how Cheung's character fakes it—but takes credit for it anyway. From there, the movie paints Cheung as a coward to boot—an attribute that even the most negative of Jackie Chan critics can't ascribe to the superstar. They continue to mercilessly lampoon Willie Chan, Jackie's manager, and even go so far as to cruelly kill Jackie's cinematic father.

This cruelty really makes *High Risk* hit a sour note, despite Li's strong performance as a bodyguard who must save the star, *Die Hard*-style, from terrorists in a high rise. Despite its title, this mean-spirited effort marks a low point in Jet's filmography.

Thankfully, in *Black Mask* (1996), Jet tried for something different and stylish. He suc-ceeded in both, although the film was not particularly strong in the plot department. Touted as the most expensive non–Jackie Chan Hong Kong movie ($HK 65 million), this story of a top secret government plan to create supersoldiers has plenty of style, kink (the heroine and villainess spend a remarkable amount of time in bondage), and climatic action when our masked hero and the superpowered supersoldier supreme slug it out in a gas-filled catacomb.

Jet coasted the remainder of the year with the very odd *Dr. Wai in the Scripture With No Words* (1996), a movie within a movie, as Li plays both a frustrated author and the character in the writer's unraveling story. Suffice to say, neither part of the film is particularly riveting. So, just when Jet's career is threatening to go moribund at the end of the era, back comes Tsui Hark and Huang Fei Hong into his life.

"Okay, okay," Hark essentially admitted by his actions. "Without me, you're something." Given that they all needed something big to work on as Hong Kong was returned to mainland China, Jet agreed to star in *Once Upon a Time in China VI: The Lion Goes West*, also known as *Once Upon a Time in China and America* (1997). Having done *High Risk*, Jet again insulted Jackie by appearing in a movie which further stole Chan's thunder by "borrowing" an idea and title that the superstar had once wanted to use in a projected collaboration with Francis Ford Coppola.

Jackie had gone on record saying that he wanted to make a movie called *The Lion Goes West* about a Chinese amongst Native Americans, and here Jet was doing it, with Sammo Hung—fresh off helming *Mr. Nice Guy*—as director! Word has it that this was one insane shoot, with Sammo, Jet, and company traveling all over Texas, filming as they went along.

The finished film reflects the production chaos. Conflicts that are foreshadowed come to nothing. Main villains are changed mid-

Adam Cheng (center, in white) became a star because of his looks, his Chinese television experience, and an excellent performance in this film, Zu Warriors From the Magic Mountain.

stream. Huang Fei Hong jerks back and forth between fighting bloodthirsty Indians and protecting them. Characters and subplots are introduced, only to be summarily eliminated. There are some very exciting martial arts, but they are essentially over by the film's midpoint. Running out of time and money, Sammo and crew hastily patched together a painfully anticlimatic final battle that relies far more on photography than fine fighting.

Huang Fei Hong had returned from the living dead for little purpose. Jet Li might as

well have traveled back ten years. He was in America, just as he had been in 1988, doing uninspiring fare, not knowing what to do next.

Then superstar Mel Gibson, actor Danny Glover, and director Richard Donner came along. They wanted a powerful Chinese villain for *Lethal Weapon 4*, the latest in the team's series of "buddy cop" films. Reportedly, they first offered the role to Jackie Chan, but he supposedly turned it down because he didn't want to play a bad guy (choosing instead to do a riskier, lower-budgeted, action film titled *Rush Hour* with a rookie costar named Chris Tucker).

So Jackie's loss was Jet's gain, and he stepped into the role with his usual equanimity. When all was said and done, a reporter asked fellow costar Chris Rock if *Lethal Weapon 4* was Rock's breakthrough film. The talented comedian's reply was: "I don't know about that, but I do know it's Jet Li's breakthrough role."

Rock was right. After the original classic film's serious undertones about a grieving cop's suicidal desire to take greater and greater risks, *Lethal Weapon 2* was that rare animal: a sequel as good as the original, since the filmmakers chose to include a powerful racial equality statement in the action. *Lethal Weapon 3*, although not as effective as the first two, held its own through the stars' charisma and chemistry. But then, incredibly, the crew chose to play the fourth installment like a joke, imbuing every scene, even stunningly violent ones, with a "we're only kidding" approach.

Every scene, that is, except when the camera was on Jet Li. His intensity and refusal to take his role lightly made every eye in the theater focus on him. Despite the usual ham-fisted editing of his kung-fu skills and the inclusion of a superfluous garrote wire,

The glorious Michelle Yeoh shows her "everything nice" side in Supercop.

secreted in his prayer beads (which disappears midway into the film without explanation), Jet stole the show simply by being the powerful presence he had learned to be through years of Shaolin stardom.

With the end of the century looming, it's good to know that martial arts expertise and screen charisma can find a home in any great moviemaking country.

BATTLING BEAUTIES

It really all started with Angela Mao. There had been kung-fu heroines and slashing swordswomen before her, but never had a female action star taken center stage in world cinema, and held it, the way Angela Mao did. To many martial arts movie fans, she is, and will always be, "The" woman.

Mao, like Jackie Chan, was a graduate of a Peking Opera school. Luckily for her and her legion of fans, she was born late enough in the century (1952), when women were finally allowed to play the female roles in these fascinating Chinese mixes of grand opera and martial ballet. In fact, she became one of the most popular and famous *wu dans* ("female martial leads") of her time—known for being able to deflect twelve spears in succession with one foot (tantamount to Pavarotti hitting a high C three times in a row). She never failed to bring down the house, but the then prevalent Shaw Brothers Studio didn't recognize the value of a woman action star.

To directors like Chang Cheh, women were window dressing, and fighting women might as well be boys. They felt that in the eyes of the public a fighting girl lost her femininity. Upstart studio Golden Harvest, however, held no such sexism. Studio head Raymond Chow would do whatever he needed to get attention, and films starring this accomplished kicker might just do the trick.

Angela costarred in a few ensemble pieces, but it was in 1972, with her first major leading role, *Lady Whirlwind*, that she caught

Moon Lee (far left) gets ready for action with Yuen Baio (center) and Mang Hoi in Zu Warriors of the Magic Mountain.

the populace by surprise. Director Huang Feng perfectly understood her allure and showcased her in a series of increasingly frenetic and exciting films. With their subsequent *Hap-Ki-Do* (1972), she galvanized a generation.

Then came one of her most famous films, *When Tae Kwon Do Strikes* (1973), which is still a perennial favorite, regularly reappearing in this country under a variety of names. Under any name, however, Mao's potent screen presence and powerful kung-fu never fail to impress. Working with costars Jhoon Rhee, Hwang Jang Lee, and Sammo Hung, she fought her way into the hearts of millions. She was speedy, strong, and serious, and if she had only made these three films, she would still be fondly remembered.

But she did work in many other films. She was officially crowned "Queen of Kung-fu" by her inclusion in *Enter the Dragon* as Bruce Lee's sister, and then given further credibility with her appearance in the great King Hu's *The Fate of Lee Khan* (1973). From there,

sadly, there was no place to go but down. China is a paternalistic culture, and the desire to present her as more "ladylike" never died, despite the fact that she was now a third-dan hapkido black belt in real life. She was dressed as a boy through most of *Stoner* (1974), a fairly sad attempt to milk the nearly nonexistent fame of George Lazenby, who would be forever forgotten as the man who turned his back on James Bond after barely completing the otherwise excellent *On Her Majesty's Secret Service* (1969), dooming the 007 series to years of campy excess. She even tried to kickstart her stalled career by reteaming with Huang Feng for *The Himalayan* (1976), which also remains one of Korean kicker Tan Tao Liang's best films.

Finally, after such forgettable Taiwanese fare as *Snake Deadly Act* (1979), she married, and in the Asian male-dominated society, that meant she had to stop working, a fate which befell many great Hong Kong screen sirens, even as late as the 1990s. With her charming features and powerful presence no longer gracing the screen, there really wasn't anyone to take her place.

Other filmmakers used talented female martial artists, like Yang Pan Pan in *Story of the Drunken Master* and Hsia Kuang Li in *The Incredible Kung-fu Legs*, but even Hui Ying Hung didn't graduate to full-fledged singular star status in Angela's wake (in fact, Hui stopped appearing in Liu Chia Liang's movies because too many accused her of being the venerable director's mistress).

The only person who really came close was the wonderful Lily Li over at the Shaw Brothers Studio. Entering the Shaw's actors training course at the tender age of fourteen, Lily worked steadily, but first came to martial arts prominence as David Chiang's costar in *The Wandering Swordsman* (1969). Despite credible performances in romances and Cantonese comedies, a good female action star is rare, so Chang Cheh and Liu Chia Liang constantly put her to work.

Even with excellent performances in *The Heroic Ones* (1970), *Challenge of the Masters* (1976), and *Shaolin Mantis* (1978), she never got the kind of starring roles that Angela Mao essayed. The only time she got close was in *Executioners From Shaolin* (U.S.: *Executioners of Death*, 1977), highlighted by the wedding-night battles between her crane style and Chen Kwan Tai's tiger style. But even that didn't do the trick.

Eventually Li became a free agent, contin-

The beauteous Nina Li, who also dazzled audiences in Twin Dragons, *considers press-on nails in a romantic moment from* A Chinese Ghost Story III.

uing to give exceptional performances in every movie in which she appeared. Jackie Chan gave her a standout role in *The Young Master* as the woman he learned "skirt style" from, and she reunited with David Chiang for two cheap, but very entertaining, old-fashioned kung-fu adventures: *The Bloody Tattoo* and *The Deadly Challenger* (both 1987).

Meanwhile, the martial art movie business went back to what it had always been: a boy's club. Most actresses got their jobs in Hong Kong films by way of beauty pageants, and no one was going to risk their meal tickets by putting these beautiful faces and forms too close to flying fists or feet, that is, until 1985, when producer Dickson Poon got a really, really "bad" idea: Why not launch their fledgling D&B production studio with a movie about two butt-kicking babes?

Why, indeed. The resulting film, *Yes, Madam* (named for what police subordinates

156

say when replying to a superior female officer) was deemed unreleasable when director Yuen Kwai (U.S.: Corey Yuen) finished it. But then producer Dickson was attracted to one costarring actress and featured her in a present-day Japanese–Hong Kong coproduction called *Royal Warriors* (1986). This action-packed, ultimately agonizing tale of a female Hong Kong cop and a male Japanese detective foiling a jet hijacking, and then suffering the wrath of a crime boss as a result, caught the public's fancy. But the audience was especially impressed by the actress who played the Hong Kong cop. She was so beautiful, as well as so charming and capable, that they wanted to know more about the budding superstar that Dickson Poon had dubbed Michelle Khan.

The facts were simple: She had been a student at the Royal Academy of Dance in London before an injury sidelined her dance career. Falling back on her poise and beauty, she won the 1983 Miss Malaysia contest, which resulted in a trip to Hong Kong to film a TV commercial with Jackie Chan. Those few seconds on the small screen launched her movie career, and the groundswell following *Royal Warriors* did what she and Corey Yuen could not. *Yes, Madam* was finally released. And, naturally, it became a huge hit.

Looking at it now, it's hard to figure out what anyone would find unreleaseable about it. It starts fast, with an undercover Michelle slamming an open book on a pervert who exposes himself, before single-handedly foiling a violent daylight robbery. Shortly thereafter, a blond Interpol agent arrives and the two team up to attempt to take down a particularly venal drug lord.

"In the beginning, I substituted my lack of experience with guts and bravado," Michelle said, and that certainly was true. On the first day of filming the climactic fight in the villain's palatial house, Michelle was supposed to do what the action choreographer referred to as an "easy" stunt—which another stuntman was being taken to the hospital for. All she had to do was sit on a balcony banister, fall back, curl the back of her knees on the banister, swing headfirst through a pane of glass beneath the banister, grab the legs of two villains, and then pull them back the other way. "What did I know?" Michelle remembered. "I had dancing training. I just got up there and did it." And, by so doing, won the admiration of the entire crew.

The fervid story—featuring Michelle and her Interpol partner trying to save three hapless con men who inadvertently get their hands on incriminating evidence—is well suited to the many fights showcasing the talents of Michelle and Cynthia Rothrock, the first woman in history to win the weapons kata championship in mainland China.

"I think the crew was impressed," said Rothrock, "because here I was, a little foreign woman who they thought would be afraid to get hurt. But I did everything they asked"—including such terrific stunts as doing a split on the wall while fighting off thugs with a bamboo pole. All in a day's work for the real-life martial artist who was the number-one female kung-fu stylist in the world two years running.

Corey Yuen put them through their paces, making the kung-fu movie fan yearn for a director's cut which would include the no-holds-barred battle at a temple and the scene in which the two fight off the ferocious Dick Tei Wei, which was ultimately left on the cutting room floor. But what remains is the seminal Hong Kong woman-warrior epic.

While Michelle went on to *Royal Warriors*, Cynthia Rothrock moved on to an even more impressive follow-up. *Righting Wrongs* (a.k.a. *Above the Law*, 1986, not to be confused with Steven Seagal's *Above the Law*) is also considered one of Yuen Baio's best movies, an insane melange of *Death Wish* and *The Untouchables*. Yuen plays a law student whose professor is gunned down in front of him. After annihilating his prof's killers in a sizzling car chase and fight scene, Baio decides to go outside the law for justice.

Rothrock plays the well-meaning Interpol agent who tries to stop him, not realizing how deep police corruption goes or how far she's over her head. Incredibly brutal, with some amazing moments of kung-fu black comedy (as when Cynthia and Yuen do an acrobatic martial arts dance all around a seated murder victim), *Righting Wrongs* is not a happy movie, but it is consistently exciting, with some great martial arts. Not only does Rothrock fight Baio, but also fellow Caucasian martial artist Karen Shephard, who played a martial arts hit woman who murders a teenage witness to the villain's homicidal politics.

In the original version, everybody but everybody dies, but when that reality hurt the box office in certain countries, new scenes were shot which allowed either Yuen and Cynthia or both to live. There are literally four versions of *Righting Wrongs* floating around: one in which they both live, one in which they both die, and two in which only one lives.

Meanwhile, Michelle Khan was balancing her film work with a budding romance with the powerful Dickson Poon. She completed a nominal follow-up to *Royal Warriors* called *Magnificent Warriors* (1988), but it came out a full two years afterward. Although entertaining in its own right, it had nothing to do with its predecessor. Taking place during World War II, Michelle makes like a vengeful cross between Bruce Lee and Indiana Jones to save a small town from Japanese invaders.

Marred by a tone which fluctuates between honest emotion, insane action, and inopportune slapstick comedy, *Magnificent Warriors* is much better the second time it is viewed. Its faults couldn't slow Khan down, but marriage, by dint of Chinese tradition, could. Once she said "I do" to Dickson Poon, her movie career was all but over.

159

Enter the Lady Dragon

Cynthia Rothrock carried on. The only thing that slowed her down, ironically enough, was the color of her skin, not to mention hair. Just as American filmmakers had been slow to accept Asian action stars, Hong Kong looked upon the blonde, round-eyed Rothrock with skepticism.

It wasn't that they were racist (oh, no!), but the audience—would the *audience* accept her? Of course they would, but then there was the tricky question of what kind of role they could give her. Hong Kong was not exactly a melting pot, and a blonde white woman stood out like a marshmallow in chocolate pudding.

Sammo Hung eliminated the problem by making her just one in a mob of interracial robbers for his *Millionaire's Express* (a.k.a. *Noble Express*, 1987). There she fought alongside everyone from Richard Norton to Wang Lung Wai. Of course she got extra attention, because, first, she was the only woman villain, and second, she was the one who fought director and costar Sammo. While Yuen Baio fought Dick Tei Wai, and Japanese action actress Yukari Oshima beat off a gang of costars, Rothrock faced off against Hung in a memorable, nicely structured one-on-one battle in a hotel lobby.

She gives him far worse than she gets until Sammo is forced to take her seriously. He does his patented Bruce Lee impersonation to get in the proper mood, and then makes her spine sorry it ever ran into his knee. Although the film did poorly at the box office, both Rothrock and Oshima were the talk of the industry. Sammo's friends, Jackie Chan and Frankie Chan (no relation), took advantage of their skills next.

Although Jackie's *Armour of God* injury prevented an on-screen face-to-face with Cynthia, he tried to make it up to her by having her cast in *The Inspector Wears Skirts* (a.k.a. *Top Squad*, 1988), the slapstick action comedy he produced, inspired by the American *Police Academy* movies. As successful as that was (sprouting a fistful of inferior sequels sans Cynthia), it was Yukari who was thrust one step away from Angela Mao territory when Frankie cast her as his costar in the delightfully clever *Outlaw Brothers* (1987).

Frankie played one of two sibling car thieves who accidentally steals a crazy female drug lord's latest shipment. Yukari is not the villainess, rather the cunning cop assigned to crack the case. She ultimately teams up with Frankie, and they engage in both delightful banter as well as serious kung-fu. Frankie, despite his slangy name, is a classical martial artist who specializes in heavily traditional styles like southern Shaolin long fist, so it is always fun to watch him adapt these techniques to modern fights. This is clearly Frankie's best film and the apex of his career, which began promisingly but completely fell apart shortly after this.

Still, this movie is enough. It has many excellent martial arts sequences, climaxed by a battle royal in a warehouse filled with snakes, chickens, cigarettes, rice, and foreign bad guys who wield blade-encrusted fans and ringed swords as well as guns. It would have made a great series except for the sour fade-out, where Oshima reveals that she was playing Frankie for a sucker all along and never truly loved him. Instead, Oshima would have to be satisfied with playing the villain in the *Angel* series (1987), which was extremely difficult, because there was no unified brains behind this eminently commercial project. Of course, *Angel* (a.k.a. *Iron Angels*) was inspired by the *Charlie's Angels* television series, only the Chinese thought nothing of ladling whopping amounts of violence on the concept. Although there was more than one

With her award-winning performance in Actress, *Maggie Cheung proved she could be a lot more than Jackie Chan's flighty girlfriend in the* Police Story *series.*

160

Ferocious femme vs. fighting femme. Cynthia Rothrock (left) battles Karen Shephard in Righting Wrongs.

angel, the heroine who truly caught the audience's eye was the aptly named Moon Lee, a cute 'n' sweet powerhouse whom it was impossible not to root for.

She was also one fine little fighter, which made her attempts to defeat Oshima all the more involving. Which was a good thing, too, because otherwise the movie is a mess. Credited to no less than three directors—Ivan Lai, Raymond Leung, and Leung Siu Ming—the bad editing and gaping plot holes give ample evidence to the chaos behind the camera. Despite Teresa Woo, the single director of the sequels, and the continued presence of Moon Lee, *Angel II* (1988) and *Angel III* (1989) were even worse, but still loads of fun to watch.

In the meantime, Cynthia Rothrock fought on, finding that getting good parts in decent movies was almost as difficult as it was to defeat her on-screen foes. *Magic Crystal* (1988) was up next, an enjoyable kung-fu–sci-fi hybrid dreamed up by the extravagant Wong Jing. It had a strong supporting cast, which included Richard Norton and Andy Lau, and some great action (as well as some truly silly slapstick). Rothrock is back in Interpol, trying to save a kid from an alien assassin out to claim the title rock: a big magical gem which turns out to be a sentient being.

Then came *Blonde Fury* (a.k.a. *Lady Reporter*, 1989), the last time Rothrock took center stage in Hong Kong. At first it was directed by her friend Mang Hoi, but when rumor of a Rothrock film with Sylvester Stallone reached the producers (a film that never materialized), Yuen Kwai was brought in to bolster the B-movie origins. Kwai, in turn, brought in sixth-degree black sash Vincent Lyn. "That was a tough shoot, but Cynthia was a real trooper," Lyn reported. "She did everything they asked with no fuss.

I was the problem on that set. I couldn't get the timing right! Corey Yuen got so fed up he bounced a peanut shell off my head in frustration. Eventually, however, it all came together for a pretty exciting fight scene."

They completed the sequence of Lyn and Rothrock battling amongst stacks of corrugated metal containers, which included one of Rothrock's great screen kicks: three in midair. After that, things got a little factionalized. Rothrock was hopping back and forth from America to do *China O'Brien* with director Robert Clouse, and to Thailand to film *No Retreat, No Surrender II* (a.k.a. *Raging Thunder*, 1990) for producer Ng See Yuen. While the original *No Retreat, No Surrender* effectively launched Jean-Claude

couldn't contain myself."

With the ample assistance of voluptuous Amy Yip and the kung-fu prowess of Billy Chow, this tale of sex machines fighting a raping robot was laughed off the screen—by millions of fans who paid again and again to keep laughing. In America, these movies are known as erotic R-rated thrillers. In Hong Kong, they are called Category 3 films, and the floodgate was now officially open. Thankfully (or unfortunately, depending upon your point of view), martial arts and mammaries rarely mixed, but there were a few that snuck through. *Black Cat* (1991) was one, actually being the Asian version of *La Femme Nikita*, the French film which begot *Point of No Return* (1993) with Bridget Fonda and an authentically-named television series *La Femme Nikita* on the USA cable network.

The pouty Jade Leung starred as the street slime recruited as a top secret killer, and while she was able, she was far from experienced. The real star, aside from Leung's looks, was director Stephen Shin, whose stylish action made *Point of No Return* seem truly pointless. He was not so lucky with the 1992 sequel, subtitled *The Assassination of President Yeltsin*. Since there wasn't a *Femme Nikita* sequel to rip-off, the homegrown plot relied heavily on unbelievable intrigue and espionage nonsense.

But even this couldn't prepare audiences for what came next. Wong Jing had just been warming up. Seeing the audience grow slavish for exploitation, the producer-writer's fervid mind was more than up to the task. *Naked Killer* exploded into theaters in 1992, making jaded viewers' jaws drop heavily onto sticky cinema floors. The sexy, seemingly lascivious Chingmy Yau opened everybody's eyes to every imaginable screen perversion.

Okay. Chingmy kills her father's killer, which brings her to the attention of a nun–hit woman who throws her into her basement with a rapist. Passing that test

Van Damme, the in-name-only sequel did not do the same for Cynthia. It did, however, essentially put a cap on her Hong Kong career. Throughout most of the 1990s she would toil in American exploitation films—not risk life and limb in China.

It was just as well, for, at about that time, Hong Kong producers were asking actresses to thrust more than their arms and legs at the camera. With the release of *Robotrix* (1991), Hong Kong action cinema had unleashed its libido. "Now that was one wild shoot," costar Vincent Lyn recalled. "The cast and crew were all over the place and you were lucky to find out what you were doing before the cameras rolled. I spent more time laughing on the set than anything else. I just

with flying internal organs, Chingmy then runs afoul of her new teacher's former student, a lesbian assassin who has stopped trying to kill rapists and started trying to kill her mentor.

Got all that? Who cares. *Naked Killer* was about brilliant excess. It was so crazy and extreme that audiences could watch it without guilt, possibly because it was so well done. It had something for everyone to get excited

164

THE WRATH OF KHAN

The marriage was over. Michelle Khan was no longer Mrs. Dickson Poon; therefore she was no longer Michelle Khan, either. Her real name was Michelle Yeoh, and that was the name she was going by from then on. Khan had been forced on her by D&B (and, therefore, Dickson Poon), and when she left that union, she wanted to leave it all behind.

Poon, in the meantime, passed on the pseudonym Khan onto a Taiwanese actress who tried to borrow some of Michelle and Rothrock's thunder as "Cynthia Khan"—star of the *In the Line of Duty* series. While no Yeoh, the new "Khan" was cute and capable enough, especially during *In the Line of Duty 4* and *In the Line of Duty 5: Middle Man*, the best of the lot because they were directed by martial arts master Yuen Woo Ping and featured such other kung-fu greats as Donnie Yen and Vincent Lyn. After that, the fabricated Cynthia Khan kept sinking in cheaper and cheaper films while her namesake kept rising.

Police Story III: Supercop was Michelle Yeoh's comeback film, and, not for the last time, she was rescued by filmmakers hithertofore not known for their kindnesses toward actresses. It was a mark of Yeoh's talent and personality that such world-class superstars were willing to take a step aside to make room for her—not as pretty window dressing or a damsel-in-distress, but as a full-fledged costar of equal rank. And once Jackie Chan gave his approval, the line grew outside her offices. Yeoh followed *Supercop* with the greatest superheroine movie Marvel Comics never made: *The Heroic Trio* (1992).

about: It was the first major movie for feminists *and* perverts; and, to top it off, the action was good. Although many sick, depraved films would follow, *Naked Killer* was one of a kind. We would truly not see its like again.

165

Codirected by Johnny To and Ching Siu Tung, this was the movie that comic-book fans had been waiting for. Three of the world's most beautiful actresses slipping into second-skin spandex to take on a superpowered eunuch who wants to plunge a film noir world back to the dynasty system. His method: kidnap babies until he finds the reincarnation of the emperor.

The only thing between him and total domination is "Wonder Woman" (no, not *that* Wonder Woman), a deeply maternal acrobat who can hurl *shuriken* (throwing stars) faster than bullets, and runs across telephone wires; Thief Catcher, a money-grubbing mercenary in leather short-shorts who packs a mean sawed-off shotgun; and, eventually, Invisible Girl (no, *not* the one from the *Fantastic Four*), who starts the film working with the bad guys because they are holding her dying scientist boyfriend hostage.

The movie's very absurdity works in its favor as the rarely invisible Michelle, wondrous Anita Mui, and eye-catching Maggie Cheung leap all over the screen, supported by splendid visuals and an Oscar-worthy silent supporting performance by Anthony Wong as a monstrous henchman not averse to eating his own hacked-off fingers. The ending borrows heavily from the original *Terminator* (1984), but, as usual, who cares? The movie is so shamelessly thrilling, it more than makes up for its inspirations with original, uniquely Chinese action.

The pure exhilaration of *The Heroic Trio* raised expectations for the sequel, but no one expected the bleak, brutal, postapocalyptic world of *Executioners* (1993), wherein the trio returned, but now deeply changed and essentially suicidal. In their attempt to find unpolluted water and survive a clash between a religious deity and power-mad politicians, much blood is spilled. There is far more honest pain in the first five minutes of this than in the entire previous movie. On second, or third, viewing, once the shock of the mood swing between the original and the sequel wears off, there's some martial arts action to enjoy, but it is like visiting a loved relative who has fallen on hard times—the memory of previous joy keeps ruining the image.

Happily, Yeoh didn't trade in misery from then on. *Butterfly Sword* (a.k.a. *Butterfly and Sword*, as well as *Comet, Butterfly, and Sword*, 1993), is a far more enjoyable costume epic, with Michelle flying around with Donnie Yen, among others. By this time, however, honest kung-fu had given way to wire-enhanced fantasy. While Chinese "swordplay" fiction had always had flying blade-masters, the line between these films and martial-arts movies had become increasingly blurred as more non-Chinese discovered them.

Much more recognizable was *Project S* (a.k.a. *Once a Cop*, 1993), the semiofficial sequel to *Supercop*. In it, as you may remember, Michelle plays the same mainland police officer she had in the original, but Jackie Chan only appears in a jarringly strange cameo scene—having gone undercover as a woman to crack a jewelry store robbery ring, complete with snub-nosed revolver in panty hose between his legs! Once that wildly out-of-place comedy sequence is over, the story remains serious. Unbeknownst to Michelle, a fellow officer she once loved is now running a high-tech bank robbery gang. She chases him to Hong Kong, then all over it and even under it as they battle in an underground vault and the sewers.

With that out of her system, Michelle returned to mainland China for a pair of fairly pure martial arts epics by the venerable Yuen Woo Ping, the finest classical kung-fu filmmaker outside of Liu Chia Liang. The first was *The Tai Chi Master*, with Jet Li. The second was her very own: *Wing Chun* (1994) in which she plays the title character—the woman who invented the martial art of the same name.

"Although the film had many light

Sammo Hung (left) plays The Magnificent Butcher, *one of Huang Fei Hong's famous students.*

moments and was even silly sometimes," Yeoh related, "Yuen Woo Ping was very particular about the martial arts. Since I was playing Wing Chun and the movie was called *Wing Chun,* the movements had to be wing chun." All involved managed to make it so, despite obvious wire-enhanced leaping and spinning. Serious kung-fu fans wished for a less loopy story and were aghast that the great Donnie Yen was reduced to a comic

Sammo Hung shows the personal charisma and style that has made him one of Hong Kong's most notable filmmakers. A deeply felt moment from Close Encounters of the Spooky Kind.

supporting role, but even they enjoyed Michelle's repeated, climatic confrontations with a sexist bandit lord.

Her second movie of 1994 signaled another change in direction. *Wonder Seven* was done as a favor to director Ching Siu Tung, who was using the knock-off of *The Magnificent Seven* (which was, in turn, a knockoff of *Seven Samurai*) to showcase an Olympic-medal-winning Chinese gymnast.

Not surprisingly, the result was a mixed bag to say the least, with Yeoh as a lovelorn villain won over by the honest affection of the gymnast turned top secret operative.

After that, Yeoh knew she would have to find more serious roles if she wasn't to suffer the fate of Yukari Oshima, Moon Lee, and even Cynthia Rothrock, namely, to toil in increasingly cheap, unimaginative exploitation movies. Michelle knew it could happen;

Yukari Oshima had been in *Project S*, but only as one of many unnamed villains in the precredit sequence. So she put her extraordinary managers Terence Chang and Chris Godsick to work, and then waited for some serious scripts to come her way. In 1996 she only appeared in two films, only one of which was even nominally an action film. The nonaction movie, *The Soong Sisters*, was an important, heartfelt drama which proved that Yeoh was more than a pretty face, a great body, and fast limbs. But she was all that, and more, so her final Hong Kong film was especially disappointing.

Stuntwoman: The Story of Ah Kam seemed made for Michelle. It was directed by Ann Hui, who was known for such powerful dramas as *Boat People* (1983). It also featured Sammo Hung, playing an action choreographer. What could go wrong? Two things. First, the action was awful. Like so many movies about stuntpeople, the directors seemed loathe to show the audience the way stunts are actually done, creating absurd continuous action sequences instead. Any verisimilitude that could have been created is gone.

Second, and in a more personal vein, although Yeoh had suffered many bumps and bruises along the way, *Stuntwoman* was the only movie in which she got seriously hurt—all the more unfortunate since the movie's action is so ridiculous. After a completely unnecessary shot where she jumped from a bridge, she landed incorrectly, tearing ligaments, fracturing a rib, and nearly breaking her back. "I felt my spine bend," she said. "I was afraid I had broken it in two."

It would have been terribly ironic, since she was just months away from one of the greatest coups in movie history.

DOUBLE YEOH SEVEN

Never in the history of major action cinema had an established character allowed a veritable unknown to step in and share the spotlight the way star Pierce Brosnan and director Roger Spottiswoode did with Michelle Yeoh on *Tomorrow Never Dies* (1997). It was unprecedented, except for perhaps in *Supercop*.

Supposedly, the movie was set to be called *Tomorrow Never Lies*, and the wife of the meglomaniac media mogul villain was supposed to be sharing Bond's bed by the fadeout. But the "Die" was cast because it sounded better and, for whatever reason, the media mogul's wife was dead within fifteen minutes of her introduction on-screen. What was an aging action series to do? Call out Yeoh, apparently.

The day before Michelle was to report to the set, the rumor was that the producers were discussing cutting her action scenes so as to not upstage their Bond, but once she arrived that story, true or not, changed. The director and star were both charmed and impressed by their new costar, and the producers saw a prescription for a revitalized series. If many considered 007 out of fashion, then what about a woman who could match him kiss for kiss, bang for bang?

Thus the set was staged for one of the greatest introductions in the annals of action films. It was all the more incredible because, just years before, this sort of thing couldn't happen to a white Anglo-Saxon, let alone a "woman of color." And it wasn't just the film world which accepted Yeoh with open arms; it was Madison Avenue as well. It was Michelle's face alongside Brosnan's in the cosmetic ads. It was Michelle who was standing next to Pierce in the supermarket beer standees. It was her character who was made into an action figure along with Commander Bond.

If only the filmmakers had trusted Philip Kwok with Pierce Brosnan's action scenes as well. Kwok is better known to fans as Kuo Chui, the star of many a great Chang Cheh movie, and his cameo appearance in *Tomorrow Never Dies* gave fans of the *Black*

Belt Theater and *Drive-in Movie* series a thrill. He also choreographed Michelle's fight scenes, while stunt choreographer and arranger Vic Armstrong, of *Indiana Jones* fame, worked on Brosnan's battles. As a result, James looks old-fashioned, especially after the fine martial arts moves 007 showed in his first Bond outing, *GoldenEye* (1995), while the female Chinese agent looks better.

Even though director Spottiswoode chose to have the villain (ably played by exceptional actor Jonathan Pryce) make fun of Yeoh's kung-fu skill without giving her a chance for an audience-satisfying response in the climatic battle, all could be forgiven, since the crew was basically making up the film as they went along, and she was so lovingly showcased otherwise. Then, to add monetary success to critical success, the movie is the largest grossing film in the entire 007 series, grossing more than $300 million worldwide.

Now, what do *you* suppose the main difference between this one and all the others was? There was even talk of giving Michelle a parallel series to Bond, allowing a new 007-produced action movie to come out every year in a "boy, girl, boy, girl" sequence. Reportedly, Yeoh had also been offered leading roles in a feature film based on the *Charlie's Angels* television series and the movie adaptation of the *Danger Girl* comic book.

It seems that the really "bad" idea Dickson Poon and Corey Yuen had way back in 1985 was a pretty good one after all.

PAST, PRESENT, AND KUNG-FU FUTURE

The future is here, and I don't mean figuratively; I mean geographically. The future of Hong Kong kung-fu films is in America, because that's where the majority of its finest practitioners are. Since July 1997, when the British lease on Hong Kong ran out, many an upcoming martial arts movie has been announced, but few have appeared.

Sammo stands tough as My Lucky Stars *satirize kung-fu all around him (from left): Eric Tsang doing eagle claw, Richard Ng trying snake style, Charles Chin attempting crane, and Fiong Tsui Feng prepping dragon.*

For instance, a new mainland movie was announced, to be directed by Yuen Woo Ping and starring Jet Li. But then Yuen was seen in Australia, doing the action for *The Matrix* (1999), and Jet was in Los Angeles, co-starring in *Lethal Weapon 4.* So much for China. The money, and freedom, is better on other shores.

The logical thing would have been to reopen the Shaw Brothers movie units. They were closed down in 1985, reportedly because too many workers wanted to share the profits. Alledgedly, Run Run Shaw would rather disband his film crews than let his directors and actors join Jackie Chan in the superstar ranks. He could make just as much money, if not more, renting his studios to Chan as well as television producers.

Besides, what good would it do to reopen Shaw's? All the directing greats of its golden era were either retired, ailing, or dead. Chang Cheh was doubled over with arthritis. Liu Chia Liang was reportedly fighting cancer. His ex-partner in action choreography, Tang Chia, had only been able to make three movies before Run Run closed up shop, but

170

the last one—*Opium and the Kung-fu Master* (1984), starring Ti Lung as the drug-addicted head of the Kwantung Ten Tigers—was a doozy.

Tang Chia himself played Lung's blind sifu, who gives him the strength to beat his opium habit cold turkey and take revenge on the evil villain (Chen Kwan Tai) and his henchmen (Li Hai Sheng and Kao Fei). The final showdown, in which the teak grave marker of Lung's murdered student becomes the instrument of the villains' destruction, remains a fitting epitaph for the once mighty Shaw Brothers Studio.

After the delight of **The Magnificent Butcher,** *director Yuen Woo Ping starred Kwan Tak Hing in* Dreadnaught, *in which Huang Fei Hong captures a Peking Opera killer.*

It was, after all, the studio which also produced some of little-known director Sun Chung's best work. Sun was considered a poor man's King Hu, but unlike Hu, he didn't consider his kung-fu merely "dancing."

His trademark was a master shot in which two warriors are dwarfed by the glory of the landscape, reducing their conflict to a mere molehill in the mountain of Chinese history. In one great film after another, including the classic *The Avenging Eagle* (U.S.: *Avenging Eagles*, 1978), starring Fu Sheng, Ti Lung, and Ku Feng, he showed that, with a little luck, he could have been an international filmmaking favorite.

But he never got the chance. Even after leaving Shaw Brothers, his standards were too high to survive long in the dog-beat-dog world of the prolific Hong Kong movie factory. Even so, he still made the best Billy Chong movie. Billy (H.K.: Chuang Chuan Li) was probably the leading Jackie Chan "clone" to achieve stardom.

He was energetic, personable, and talented in his own right, and managed to elevate such inexpensive but very entertaining *Drunken Master* knockoffs as *Crystal Fist* (U.S.: *The Jade Claw*, 1979), and *Super Power* (1980). He even survived such unbelievable fare as *Kung Fu Zombie* and *Kung Fu From Beyond the Grave* (both 1981) with his credibility and reputation intact. In fact, these latter-day "Hellzapoppin' phantasmagoricals," complete with vampires, living dead, ghosts, and evil sorcerers laid low with soiled women's panties (you read that right) enhanced his star stature and even remain perennial favorites with the midnight-movie crowd.

They also led to his one shot at the (almost) big time. He starred in Sun Chung's independently produced feature *Wind, Forest, Fire, Mountain* (1983), a fine martial arts movie with fight choreography by Tang Chia. It wasn't their fault that, in America, it was pitifully renamed *A Fistful of Talons*. Okay, the talons come in when his hawk-keeping girlfriend helps out in an unconvincing finale with an obviously fake bird on a wire, but otherwise this was a beautifully filmed, strongly scripted effort.

There are times when Billy literally bounces off the wall in this tale of a young firebrand trying to prevent merciless Ching revolutionaries from plunging the country into civil war. At other times the powerful villain, played by the world-class kicker Wang Ing Sik, literally blasts people through those same walls. Their final battle in, on, and around a gigantic, candle-covered, reclining statue of Buddha is an unforgettable eyeful.

Even so, Sun Chung soon retreated into obscurity, and Billy Chong went to Malaysia to become a television star. The Shaw Brothers Studio, and Hong Kong, were left to the stronger and faster. One of those men is the oft-mentioned Yuen Kwai, also known as Corey Yuen, who first came to international attention with *Ninja in the Dragon's Den* (U.S.: *Ninja Warriors*, 1982), an amusing Hong Kong–Japanese coproduction starring the muscular Conan Lee and Hiroyuki "Henry" Sanada.

It was not only the first Hong Kong movie in years to feature a Japanese as a protagonist, but also one of the first major nonstudio efforts to concentrate on cinematography, lighting, and physical special effects. Although it sadly turns unconvincingly farcical in the final sequences, the initial fight is a classic (even though it is entirely incidental to the main plot). A fired member of a Peking Opera troupe tries to ruin their latest performance, only to be foiled by Conan, who dresses up as the mythical, mischievous Monkey King. To top it all off, the whole fight is accomplished on stilts!

Conan went on to cement his stardom with an appearance in Liu Chia Liang's best post–Shaw Brothers movie, *Tiger on Beat* (U.S.: *Tiger on the Beat*, 1988), a terrific, over-the-top, modern thriller which featured great kung-fu as well as a "shotgun yo-yo" which the hero used to shoot around corners. This star-making vehicle sadly became the instrument of both Conan and Liang's undoing, however. During the sequel (*Tiger on Beat II*, 1989), Conan suffered an on-screen accident (falling from a lamppost to the cement street below), after which neither he nor Liang was ever really the same.

Meanwhile, fellow director Yuen Kwai's skills never lessened. His speed and lack of pretention made him an enduring favorite amongst Chinese producers, so it was to him that Shaw Brothers turned when they wanted to test the cinematic waters after Hong Kong was returned to the mainland. Rather than risk presenting an entirely new film, however, Run Run and his longtime producer Mona Fong went the way of Disney—i.e., remaking a previous classic.

In this case it was *Killer From Shantung* (1968), a Chang Cheh action drama starring Chen Kuan Tai and David Chiang. It became *Hero* (1998) starring Japanese heartthrob Takashi Kaneshiro, with Yuen Baio in the Chiang role. As always, Corey Yuen created action sequences of verve and imagination, but somehow this depressing tale of corrupt bosses and downtrodden workers was not enough to herald a glorious rebirth of the Shaw Brothers Studio.

OH, NO, SAMMO!

Martial arts movie fans have to look elsewhere for classic, undiluted kung-fu. Their two greatest hopes are an arrogant upstart and a world-weary warrior. The latter (with a bit of the former thrown in) is the great Sammo Hung. Whenever anyone wondered why Sammo is not alongside his peers in Hollywood movies, some answer that it is because Hung is so overweight and facially scarred. The initial truth, however, was evident in the title of his last personal film: *Don't Give a Damn* (1994).

Although largely responsible for some of the greatest action movies, the most influential horror films, and simply the best individual kung-fu fights of all time, Sammo is consistently undermined by his own seething apathy—a bad attitude that sinks too many of his movies under the weight of unnecessary racism and sexism. A perfect and painful example is in the aforementioned *Don't Give a Damn*, when two Chinese cops vie for the opportunity to blacken their faces and put on "nappy" wigs (to unconvincingly impersonate the black villain's brother) by trying to outdo each other's descriptions of the woes that blacks have rained upon society. To make matters worse, the actor playing the black villain then had to pretend he didn't recognize that his brother was being absurdly impersonated by a Chinese in blackface. It was embarrassing and shameful, but, despite the protestations of the actors, Sammo went ahead with it anyway. The closest thing anyone could get to an explanation was that he was paying back Westerners for years of similar racism toward Asians. That explanation, while believable, didn't make up for his misjudgment—and misjudgments have kept him out of the pantheon of movie success.

It certainly hasn't crimped his output, however. Having been involved with at least eighty movies by the time of *Dragons Forever*, he went on to appear in, produce, or direct at least forty more, ranging from the beautiful *Eight Taels of Gold* (1989), a love story which garnered him acting awards, to the awful *Ghost Punting* (1992), in which the Lucky Stars seem inspired by the worst of the Bowery Boys. Before, after, and in between, he made some notable "pure" kung-fu films.

They include *Pedicab Driver* (1989), the best of his more recent personal films, which balanced comedy and tragedy on a razor's edge and featured an inspired bout between himself and the aged Liu Chia Liang. Sammo's company then went on to produce *Operation Scorpio* (1994), a throwback to Shaw Brothers traditions, featuring Liu Chia Liang in his best fighting role since, well, *Pedicab Driver*. Then came *Encounters of the Spooky Kind II* (1989), the fight-filled sequel to Hung's groundbreaking horror comedy of 1980.

He tried to recapture the pre-*Lucky Stars Go Places* magic of 1978's *Dirty Tiger, Crazy Frog* with *Skinny Tiger and Fatty Dragon* (1990), which featured the same costar,

Andy Lau (right) attempts to fight his way out of Lucky Stars Go Places, *the movie which nearly sank Sammo Hung.*

comic actor Karl Maka, and borrowed the plot of the 1986 Billy Crystal vehicle *Running Scared*, but it wasn't welcomed even half as much. He reacted to that rejec-

tion by really sticking it to the audience with *Pantyhose Hero* (1990), a variation on the Ryan O'Neal movie *Partners* (1982), in which a cop has to pretend he's gay to find a

175

Chow Yun-Fat (left) is the moral hit man. Danny Lee is the amoral cop. Together they have to blast their way through John Woo's unforgettable The Killer.

murderer of homosexuals. Daring the viewer to call him on his outrageous stereotypes, he also filled the movie with some of his most savage fighting and unbelievable stunts (such as actually being hit by a car in slow motion).

With that experience having not killed him or his career, he worked with Corey Yuen to fashion a vehicle for the new love of his life, Joyce "Mina" Godenzi, a statuesque, green-eyed Asian beauty pageant winner he had used to good effect in *Eastern Condors.* Her solo vehicle, *She Shoots Straight* (a.k.a. *Lethal Lady*, 1990), was way too overwrought to truly impress, although it did surprise Western eyes with a wedding-scene slaughter.

With half-hearted, overly familiar, subsequent efforts as *Slickers vs. Killers* (1992) which starts as a business-based comedy before degenerating into a mess about robbers holding executives and a psychiatrist hostage, the audience continued to stay away in droves. Still, Sammo knew he could wait them out, and, sure enough, within months producers were seeking him out as an actor and choreographer once again. He gained great credibility as an action choreographer on New-Wave director Wong Kar Wai's existential sword epic *Ashes of Time* (1994) before getting a hand up from old school chum Jackie Chan. First he directed the fights in Jackie's *Thunderbolt*, and then directed Jackie's 1996 movie *Mr. Nice Guy.*

Finally, with the direction of *Once Upon a Time in China VI,* he has come nearly full circle. Having directed the last Huang Fei Hong movie to star Kwan Tak Hing (*The Magnificent Butcher,* 1980), and having worked with everyone from Bruce Lee, King Hu, Angela Mao, and Jet Li to Jackie Chan and Yuen Baio, he is ready to see what the future holds.

Could he be the man to bring ferocious, authentic kung-fu back to mainland movies? If his many amazing martial arts classics, like *The Iron Fisted Monk* (1978), *Warriors Two* (1978), *Knockabout* (1979), and especially *The Prodigal Son* (1981) are any evidence, it's more than possible. Hung is not only a superlative martial artist and unsurpassed action filmmaker, he can focus laughs and gasps to a laser intensity, and sometimes within the same line of dialogue. In the latter title, especially, he shows his greatest strengths.

When the spoiled son of a rich man (Yuen Baio) meets an asthmatic Peking Opera wu dan specialist (Lam Ching Ying, in a star-making role), he learns not only humility but wing chun, often exercising with his new

Chow prepares to battle the Witch From Nepal, *a crazy Hong Kong knockoff of* Highlander, *which, in turn, borrowed some of its chops from samurai movies.*

Chow is stuck between Mira Sorvino and a hard place during The Replacement Killers.

master atop a small table. He also learns wing chun's tricks from the Peking Opera star's wily brother (Sammo himself). He'll need those tricks when confronting an even more arrogant prodigal son, played by Frankie Chan, who thinks little of including murder in his attempts to prove who is the best wing chun stylist of all. Once seen, never forgotten, *The Prodigal Son* ranks with the greatest martial arts films ever made.

When Hollywood came calling, Sammo's fans were still wondering if Hung would ever attain those creative heights again. It was with the knowledge of Sammo's incredible talents, not his occasional lapses in film-making taste, that Stanley Tong approached successful television producer Carleton Cuse. Cuse knew that CBS television desperately wanted to attract young male viewers to its Saturday night lineup, and Tong had a proposal for a series based on *Supercop*, the movie he directed, starring Jackie Chan.

When Jackie declined to play the role for American television, Tong turned to Sammo, while CBS executives gaped in disbelief. At first they gaped at his weight and face, but then Cuse and Tong showed them what he could do on camera. Desperate to fill a 9:00 P.M. time slot, CBS gave the team a green light, and within record time, production on *Martial Law* was started. Here Sammo Hung played Sammo Law, a top Chinese cop who comes to Los Angeles to track an Asian crime lord and then stays, thanks to an awfully convenient exchange program.

At first the series had some slight casting pains, but when Cuse killed off the Asian character Kelly Hu had played on his other hit series, *Nash Bridges* (starring Don Johnson), so she could join the *Martial Law* cast as Sammo's Hong Kong protégé, things started picking up speed.

Then *Rush Hour* made more than $100 million. Network executives, being network executives, saw that as a sure sign that adding a witty, fast-talking black costar would send *Martial Law* into ratings Valhalla. Happily, Arsenio Hall not only admired Sammo's skill, but was available. Soon the two shared top billing, and *Martial Law* not only became the network's most successful new drama of the year, but Sammo won the first *TV Guide* Award as Most Promising Newcomer.

It was an unexpected happy ending that Sammo himself would have been condemned for had he included it in any of his own films.

THE NEW WAVE

Naturally, where Jackie, Jet, Michelle, and Sammo led, others wished to follow. Donnie Yen leads the pack, and *Iron Monkey* (1993) is one of his best references. This "young Huang Fei Hong" film starred Donnie as the future master's father. Originally created as a way for producer Tsui Hark to get back at the departing Jet Li, director Yuen Woo Ping fashioned this tale of a young Huang Fei Hong and his father into a kung-fu showcase, having a cast of four heroes (two men, one child, and one woman) take on many powerful villains to save villagers from corrupt police and politicians. It displays Donnie Yen's best kung-fu since *Once Upon a Time in China II*, which had to be good indeed, since it was reported that Yen refuses to fight anyone on-screen who cannot defeat him off-screen.

"I don't know where that rumor came from," Donnie said. "I wanted to move on and try other things, specifically behind the camera, so I turned down a lot of films after that." It is possible that the rumor was the result of the mercenary and eminently practical Hong Kong film industry trying to explain to themselves why Yen didn't take immediate advantage of his success. It *had* to be ego; it *couldn't* be that he wanted to try new things!

Donnie was also vocal in his desire to save martial arts movies from special effects and wire trickery. He proved it again and again on two excellent miniseries on Hong Kong's ATV television channel. *The Kung-fu Master* (1995) was his version of the Hung Sze Kwan story, while *Fist of Fury* (1996) was a new version of the story Bruce Lee and Jet Li made popular in *The Chinese Connection* and *Fist of Legend*. "At first I was reluctant to do television because I was studying film-making," Yen admitted, "but I wanted to revolutionize TV action-fighting editing. After the success of the first series, I had total control on the action editing, and was very proud of it, because the *Fist of Fury* series had the highest ATV rating ever, and made the most money of any series ever telecast on ATV."

Even Donnie acknowledges the same problem as most everyone else in the industry: Where will the new Jackie Chans, Sammo Hungs, Liu Chia Liangs, and Jet Lis come from? The Shaw Brothers actors training course is no more. The Peking Opera schools have closed. Fewer and fewer students fill the mainland wushu academies every year. And, to hammer the final nail in kung-fu's coffin, the real Hong Kong cinema torchbearer is not named Jackie, Jet, or even Michelle. It is a soft-spoken, innocuous immigrant named John Woo.

With little doubt, John Woo is the most intelligent and technically gifted Asian action filmmaker. His step-by-step conquest of the American film market is more evidence of his intelligence. While he has made only a few actual kung-fu movies, he has used many of the genre's traditions to create a new genre: the "gun-fu" film.

Without a doubt, John Woo is the world's most serious action moviemaker. With the canny collaboration of Chow Yun-Fat, his most often-used star and the world's finest screen gunman, he consistently shows the passion, compassion, fear, and power that accompanies the pulling of a trigger. Only the emotion and effort Bruce Willis showed in *Die Hard* and Mel Gibson communicated in the original *Lethal Weapon* comes close.

In his revolutionary Hong Kong films, like *A Better Tomorrow* (1987), *A Better Tomorrow II*, (1988), *The Killer* (1989), *Bullet in the Head* (1990), and *Hard Boiled* (1992), Woo created fever-dreams of violence on the nature of brotherhood, betrayal, moral villains, and immoral heroes, all delivered with a filmmaking prowess that echoed the best of Francis Ford Coppola, Martin Scorcese, Jean-Pierre Melville, and Sergio Leone. Despite the strong box-office returns of his *Broken Arrow* (1996) and *Face/Off* (1998), these American films pale in comparison to what he did in the Far East.

And to think he started his career in Hong Kong with the likes of *Hand of Death* (a.k.a. *Countdown in Kung Fu*, 1975), costarring Jackie Chan. Chan suffered his first serious injury on that film, remaining unconscious for more than thirty minutes after a badly timed kick. He also almost never talks about Woo, especially since the director essentially walked by him, making $75- and $100-million American movies long before Jackie was toiling on films with even $25-million budgets.

Fellow directors Ringo Lam and Tsui Hark have followed Woo's lead (more on them in the upcoming Van Damme section, chapter 5), as has Chow Yun-Fat. Word has it that the director and his star cook Sunday breakfast together in Los Angeles, John instructing Chow on the "care and feeding of American movie executives." And, as always, Chow uses his own ample intelligence and ability to learn the lessons well, having starred in *The Replacement Killers* (1998) and *The Corruptor* (1999) as of this writing.

Meanwhile, director Stanley Tong, as well as actresses Michelle Yeoh and Maggie Cheung, have been launched in the United States through their affiliation with Jackie Chan. However, no matter who leads and who excels, the bottom line is that the sun which once shone brightly over the Hong Kong film industry now shines on American shores. Nearly all the greats of the martial art movie are either working in Hollywood or looking for work there.

In the original *Martial Arts Movies: From Bruce Lee to the Ninjas*, this chapter ended thusly: "it is just a matter of time [before] kung-fu movies receive their due. . . . in spite of many crummy kung-fu movies that make their ways to the States, mass audiences will

Meet the man who knows that great movie action equals effort and emotion: John Woo takes aim at his next cinematic conquest.

Chow Yun-Fat as film crews know him best: friendly, fun, and familiar, on the set of John Woo's weakest film, Once a Thief.

discover the great Hong Kong action films....There are kung-fu filmmakers who slave, putting their very limbs on the line, to create the world's most exhilarating cinema. And with the campy, unimaginative works of superheroics made in English-speaking countries, it's nice to know that Hong Kong movies have someplace to go."

They came. We saw. They conquered. It's good to be right.

Japan: Samurai Swordsmen and Karate Killers

There's a distinct difference between Chinese and Japanese martial arts movies. While the martial arts originated in China, great Oriental filmmaking originated in Japan. China had the history; Japan had the cinematic ability. The world discovered it in 1951 when Akira Kurosawa's *Rashomon* (1950) was shown at the Venice Film Festival (where it won first prize). Even the strangest of Japan's action films look wonderful. The big difference between the best and the worst of these genre movies lies in the approach. The subject matter is usually the same. It is how artistically and poetically the director portrays the violent images that does the trick in this country.

Let's establish something at the very outset. The martial arts movie is distinct from the samurai film—or, as it is known to aficionados, the *chambara* film. There are some samurai sagas that can be included on the basis of their violence. We'll create a simple distinction: if there's more argument than action, it's a mainstream chambara film; if there's more action than argument, it's a martial arts movie. Of course, some dialogue-laden movies will sneak in on the basis of their influence.

But first the foundation must be laid. To fully appreciate the films, it's best to appreciate the country they come from. The first hint of the Japanese came from the Chinese history of 108 B.C. The series of islands and its people were then called Wo. At that time it consisted of more than one hundred states. By 250 A.D. it was thirty states. Early in the 400s, it was unified into a single nation, with the *tenno* (emperor of heaven) as its leader. That's when the nation built on hypocrisy began to take shape.

Japan consists of four main islands: Hokkaido, Honshu, Shikoku, and Kyushu. To the south, there are the Ryukyu Islands between the East China and Philippine seas. By 550 B.C., Korea split off on its own, but not before introducing Buddhism to the islands. In the early 600s the country created a constitution, and imposing Buddhist temples were built. It had an emperor, a royal court, a Council of State (which took care of practical problems), and a Council of Deities (which was supposed to take care of heavenly ones).

The people were broken into two classes: freemen and slaves, while the land was broken into three classes: province, county, and village. Essentially, the government owned everything because it was charged with keeping the gods happy. In the late 700s, Buddhism was eliminated from affairs of

state, but it had served its purpose. The government was a powerful entity which controlled the populace, and the infighting within the ruling ranks was rampant.

Throughout the tenth and eleventh centuries, the emperors and aristocracy lived rich lives, while the common folk—farmers, mostly—survived the best they could. At this time came the first stirrings of the social class which would become the samurai. Dissatisfied youth began to seek power in the towns, acquiring land and pressing locals into service. Combined with this class's innate instinct were special teachings which could make a person a better fighter.

In the tenth century the Japanese developed an official language. No longer did they use complete Chinese lettering; instead, they used abbreviated Chinese lettering. The split between the leaders and the people became more and more pronounced, and even the religion was split. There were those monks who placed wealth over spiritual attainment, and therefore courted royalty's favors, and there were those "Pure Land" Buddhists who sought to purify themselves of negative desires.

Situations purely Japanese began to arise. Emperors would step down, supposedly to live a life of Buddhism, only to control the government from behind the scenes. Meanwhile, the temples were being infiltrated by people who had less interest in wisdom and virtue and more in personal success and wealth. By the time the warrior class emerged, the entire country was factionalized.

The samurai had become a sort of military police with connections in the royal court. Each different samurai family jockeyed for position, hoping to establish themselves by knocking another family off, or hoping to curry the emperor's favor by putting down someone else's uprising. By this time, to

Oceans of emotion could be read in Tatsuya Nakadai's expressive face, a visage that made him a memorable chambara actor.

become a samurai meant being born one. The lines were already established. Heaven help the common man.

By the 1100s, the samurai had become so powerful that the emperor instituted a military government, called a shogunate. There was still an emperor and an emperor's family, but real power now rested with the shogun and his samurai. There were military governors and military stewards and metropolitan guards, whose job it was to be policemen. Already the land was rife with thieves, gamblers, and other assorted scum. Again, pray for the common man.

In the 1200s, when Kublai Khan tried to invade Japan from his base in China, a typhoon destroyed most of his ships, and the samurai killed most of the survivors. Almost thirty thousand Mongols died, and the Japanese thanked the *kamikaze* (divine wind) for its protection. It filled the warrior class with the belief that they were blessed. At this point, the common man could forget about it.

The samurai were put in charge of entire districts and they ruled absolutely. Whenever they did a service for the shogun or fought bravely on the battlefield, they were often rewarded with more land. With time on their hands and the heavens on their side, the samurai developed the *Kyuba-no-michi* (The Way of Bow and Horse)—a creed which placed service to one's overlord more important than service to oneself, and then placed service to one's family even higher than that.

The government continued on its merry way, cheating, lying, and killing to get ahead, while the samurai learned more about their swords. The samurai swords were magnificent works of art, created by master designers and metallurgists. In a long, secret process, soft and hard metal was folded hundreds of times, creating an incredibly thin, incredibly strong edge.

At first straight and then slightly curved, the blades were tested, legend says, by cutting through a dead cow or a hanging corpse from shoulder to hip. If the blade slowed or

stopped, it was discarded or sold to a lesser-ranked warrior. If it moved cleanly through the corpse, it was deemed suitable for a true samurai. Little wonder that the sword came to be considered the soul of the samurai.

During the Ashikaga (or "Muromachi") shogunate, from roughly 1300 to 1500, cities grew to be strong commercial and manufacturing centers. But corruption came along with it. When the Spanish and Portuguese appeared and trade with China started, corruption grew even worse. Corruption is a natural extension of hypocrisy, and the Japanese system was based on that. Combining pride with paranoia led the country to a ridiculous, but poetic, situation.

By the mid-1600s the cycle was complete. Japan was locked into an amazing structure. The whole country belonged to the shogun, who was supposedly taking care of it for the emperor. The shogun divided the country up among his domain lords, in return for which the domain lords had to provide any service the shogun desired. *Any* service.

Beneath the domain lords were there retainers and feudal barons (called *daimyo*), who controlled the farmers. And everybody but the farmers had their samurai. And the samurai had their Bushido, their strict code of honor. There were certain things they could never do, the first of which was to go against their own clan (family) or the wishes of their overlord.

But all these people were human—too human for the scheme of things. No one seemed happy with his lot, so there was constant insurrection and intrigue, and outside influences didn't help. Along with the Portugese came Catholic Christianity, and with the Dutch and English came Protestant Christianity. The natural inclination of these religions is to make their influence felt, so to maintain their treacherous lifestyle, the Japanese enforced *sakoku* (national seclu-

Yojimbo *is no ordinary man. Toshiro Mifune cuts down his enemies.*

sion). In the 1630s they cut themselves off from the outside world.

With outside influences cut off, the system became rigid. There were the warriors, farmers, artisans, and merchants. The warriors (7 percent of the population of thirty million) levied taxes on the farmers (80 percent of the population). Although the economic foundation of the empire, the farmers and common folk were treated as less than dirt. The samurai could do what they wished with them.

In the samurai households, the head of the family was absolute ruler. Men were respected, women were chattel. Contrary to what male chauvinists might say, it was no way to live. Some managed to be content, essentially by ignoring these rules, but anyone who lived by Bushido was often forced to stare the hypocrisy of the system in its horrible face.

Therefore came the ninjas. The ninjas fell through the cracks of Bushido. They were families of spies and assassins who hired themselves out to do the dirty deeds that the samurai couldn't. Belief in the afterlife was powerful in feudal Japan, and to go against Bushido meant giving up one's soul; ergo, no afterlife. The ninjas had no place on earth and none in heaven. They only had their own pride and their own code, which was: Get the job done and never reveal family secrets. Die if captured.

Incredibly, this system—what was essentially a police state—lasted three hundred years. While the outside world developed guns and industry, Japan fought with swords and poisons. The central government was in Edo (what was to become Tokyo) on the largest island. And all life seemed to emanate from there. The collapse came in the late 1800s, heralded by, as usual, foreigners.

The Netherlands had exclusive trading rights with the Japanese at that time (they had what the Japanese needed), so they fought the British desire to open the country to other trade. The British empire's wealth was based on trade, so they always wanted other customers. The United States needed fueling outposts in the Pacific, so they had an interest as well. But when the shogun began to consider the offers, it factioned the country. Many saw trade as an invasion, a threat to the emperor. Others saw it as a way to gain power for themselves.

By the 1860s the country was plunged into civil war, the two sides being the shogun's and the emperor's. Samurai scrambled to be on what they hoped was the winning side, so Bushido crumbled around them. There was no "right" or "wrong" side. It soon became clear that the correct side was the one that wanted the warrior class to continue, and that was a toss-up.

The emperor won and established imperial rule, and the samurai were slowly phased out. The wearing of swords was soon banned. Japan crawled out of the eighteenth century and painfully into the twentieth.

JAPANESE MARTIAL ARTS CHART

Aikido: All movements are circular rather than linear. The fighter uses his opponent's force to either throw him or apply a joint-lock. The fighter will usually move along the line of attack and grasp the opponent's wrist, gaining control. Aikido relies on momentum. There are no attacks in aikido; only the opponent attacks.

Arnis: Originally known as *kali*. It is the most popular martial art of the Philippines. Although there are unarmed aspects to it, they are in the minority. It is usually practiced with a long wooden sword or short wooden dagger. Cinematically speaking, it is usually shown with one twenty-six-inch stick or two sticks of that same length.

Hapkido: A Korean martial art that resembles Japanese jujitsu. It is actually a forerunner of aikido. It is a synthesis of karate, judo, and *aiki-jitsu*.

Iai-do—The Way of the Sword:
1. Swordplay: Parry (*uke*)
   Exchange (*kawashi*)
   Attack (*kogeki*)
2. Sword position: Direct overhead (*dai-jodan*)
   Overhead left (*hidari-jodan*)
   Middle position (*chudan*)
   Pointed (*seigan*)
   Vertical right (*hasso*)
   Vertical left (*hidari-hasso*)
   Point lowered (*gedan*)
3. Sword cuts: Thrust
   Horizontal cut
   Vertical cut
   Diagonal up
   Diagonal down

Judo: Invented by Jigoro Kano and derived from jujitsu. It uses the fighter's opponent's weight against him. In sport judo, it uses throws, elbow locks, chokes, and hold-downs to score points. The striking aspects are practiced in the kata stage only.

Jujitsu: There are more than seven hundred styles of this self-defense art; most of them were practiced in the eighteenth and nineteenth centuries. Its basic concept is to do anything that is effective. Strikes, kicks, throws, chokes, joint-locks, and grappling techniques are all fair jujitsu game—anything that works.

Karate: Originated in Okinawa but brought to Japan in the 1920s. Brutal and direct, it is practiced as both a sport and a means of self-defense. Judo uses throws; karate uses punches, strikes, and kicks.

Ninjutsu: "The Art of Stealth." This is an ancient art that incorporates many ways of infiltrating an enemy's base and killing him. There are no opponents in ninjutsu. There are only enemies. Whatever is required to steal in, assassinate, and steal out again are part of ninjutsu. Related arts include how to escape after capture or to kill oneself if escape is impossible and interrogation is inevitable.

Savate: A French variation of karate that relies on lightning-quick kicks.

Tae kwon do: A Korean art that concentrates on kicks, and flying kicks at that. But it also employs punches, blocks, and jumps.

EARLY SWORD SLASHERS

The Japanese film industry was formed in the twenties and thirties, and then had to be reformed again after World War II. Japan's martial arts movies grew out of its ritualized theater—in this case the highly stylized Kabuki dramas. There were stacks of samurai movies in the 1930s, but most were staid glorifications of classical samurai heroes done in a very stiff, predictable style.

It wasn't until after the war that the particularly charged imaginations of the Japanese filmmakers conceived what was to become the most intense form of martial arts action. Keith Richards of the Rolling Stones rock group once said, "There's something about a naked blade that upsets people"—or words to that effect. In that he is correct. The chambara movie is the most personal of the martial arts films.

Kung-fu films portray an intricate ballet of move and countermove, its purpose to introduce the loser to the wonderful world of internal bleeding. But the chambara cinema portrays people who slash and chop with an incredibly sharp extention of their souls.

Here, the victims don't simply drop dead, the only clue to their destruction being blood-stained teeth (a mark of internal bleeding). Here, they lose arms, stomachs, heads.

Unlike the Chinese superhero cartoonists, the Japanese were artists, and were to do their killing on a grand canvas. In this country, after all, the martial arts movie genre was started, revolutionized, and then sustained by a certified cinematic genius—Akira Kurosawa.

Born in 1910, while the dissolution of the warrior class was still going on, Kurosawa was the youngest of seven children. As he grew he dreamed of being an artist, but when he graduated from school, he couldn't make a living in that field. In 1936 he answered an ad for assistant directors and was asked at the interview to write a paper on: "What is wrong with Japanese movies and what would you do about it?"

His answer was his films, but first he was assigned to assist Kajiro Yamamoto, an eclectic filmmaker who concentrated on crime dramas in his later years. In 1939 Yamamoto made his version of *The Loyal 47 Ronin*, a popular story of faithful retainers who first

Zatoichi, the Blind Swordsman, cuts down his enemies.

take vengeance for their lord's death and then kill themselves as per the code of Bushido. Kurosawa served as an assistant on this film, and two years later he worked himself up to writing and directing entire portions of Yamamoto's movies. Two years after that, he was assigned to direct his own first film.

It was *Sanshiro Sugata (Judo Saga)*, which he wrote himself and in which he tells the story of that art through the eyes of a disillusioned martial arts student. The screen was dense with multilayered images. Almost every visual Kurosawa created seemed to have easily graspable inner meanings. His characters also had depth and believability. Finally, the novice director seemed to have an inordinate grip on cinematic language—he knew how to say things with moving pic-

191

Zatoichi (Shintaro Katsu, left) prepares to launch into the final battle at the climax of The Blind Swordsman's Vengeance.

tures and he knew how to say them in the clearest way possible.

Filmmaking involves getting across information. The art of great filmmaking is getting across this information in such a way that the audience is both amazed and delighted with the clarity of the information. In other words, the scene has the look, feel, sense, and even stink of truth. Like all the finest martial arts moviemakers, Kurosawa also had the right morality, and his *Judo Saga* promoted the humanitarian philosophy of the art.

Kurosawa completed the second part of the *Judo Saga* in 1945, after having made another film called *The Most Beautiful*. His *The Men Who Tread on the Tiger's Tail* and the *Judo Saga* were banned during the American occupation after the war, and parts of the original prints were destroyed. Essentially, the entire film industry was put on

hold for a decade, until the early 1950s.

But then a curious phenomenon took place. The Japanese had experienced the modern nightmare of a nuclear attack. In a very short time they went from being a humiliated people to a growing world power. They had a past that was colorful (to say the least), and, perhaps more importantly, very recent. The country had remained frozen for three centuries, and was just thawing out during most of the populace's youths.

Whatever the reason, the Japanese film industry started producing warped visions—visions that were totally opposite to the Japanese manner on the streets. In real life, the Japanese were polite, considerate, moralistic, and humane, but in their fantasy life, it was a completely different story. Once they walked into a cinema for a chambara movie they were ready for some action.

And the Japanese film studios were ready

to give it to them. The major studios controlled all three aspects of motion pictures: production, distribution, and exhibition. Hollywood studios did the same until the antitrust laws of 1947, but the antitrust situation passed the Orient by. Studios made movies for their own theater chains, and the predominant chambara studio of the fifties was Toei.

The Japanese samurai have funny haircuts (called topknots) and wear funny clothes, but those are extensions of the Bushido malaise that both preserved and perverted the shogunate period. Like American cowboy movies, the chambara films rationalized what were essentially years of unfair slaughter—at first. Then came Saotome Mondonosuke, Tange Sazan, Kuro Genji, and Tengu Kurama.

Mondonosuke was "the Bored Samurai," a famous literary hero played by Utaemon Ichikawa. From the novel came the crescent-shaped scar across his forehead that interrupts his hair bangs. But his cinematic swordstyle came from Ichikawa the actor. It is the *moroha ryu seigan kuzushi*, a two-sword eye-slashing cut. In more than thirty movies made between 1931 and 1960, the Bored Samurai would leave his castle to go among the people and right wrongs.

Tange "Lefty" Sazan was one of the first samurai antiheroes—a subgenre most often credited to Akira Kurosawa. In a 1958 film, the character is shown losing his right arm and right eye to a jealous sword teacher. To most samurai, this would end their lives: The idea of using the left hand would mean putting the sword on the "wrong" side. Unthinkable! Because of the injustice done him, Sazan (who now has a scar across his closed right eyelid) rejects Bushido, becomes a *ronin* ("masterless samurai"), and slashes away at injustice with his one-armed style.

Kuro Genji was one of the first samurai superheroes. By day he was a gambler and general layabout, but by night he donned his white kimono and became a symbol of justice for all the downtrodden. He even had a

catchy motto he tells the bad guys: "Whoever needs help, call my name. Then the white wings of the Fighting Genji Butterfly will rise. This is my parting gift. To send you to hell! My family is Genji. My name is Kuro." The wings are the sleeves of his kimono as he raises his swords, one in each hand. The influential, emperor-related Genji family crest is a butterfly.

Finally, there was Tengu Kurama, the Japanese Lone Ranger. It is quite possible that George Trendle, the creator of the Lone Ranger, was aware of this Oriental character, whose first film was produced in the 1920s. He is the masked do-gooder on the beautiful white horse named White Dragon. He also is the man in black with the silver revolver fighting crime where e'er he roamed in the 1850s. He is Tengu Kurama!

It may already be apparent that the Japanese have as many varying sword styles as the Chinese have kung-fu styles. In truth, each major chambara star had his own unique form of swordplay, as did these four characters. And while this quartet established chambara concepts which would lead to their being resurrected time and again by different directors and played by different actors, it wasn't until Akira Kurosawa turned his eye back to the samurai genre that it took its next major leap.

It was with *Yojimbo* (*The Bodyguard*, 1961), starring Toshiro Mifune. In the intervening years, the eclectic director had done many dramas. He had also made *Seven Samurai* (1952), the influential epic which was to be remade into the inferior western *The Magnificent Seven* (1960), and the vastly inferior science-fiction film *Battle Beyond the Stars* (1980); *Throne of Blood* (1955), a Japanese period version of Shakespeare's *Macbeth*; and *The Hidden Fortress* (1957), a samurai movie whose characters helped inspire *Star Wars*.

All three prior films also starred Mifune, an actor who entered the industry in 1946 hoping for an assistant cameraman's job.

Instead, he accidentally stumbled into an audition and was hired by Toho Studios. In the years before *Yojimbo* was to turn the chambara cinema around, he starred in *Sword for Hire* (1952), a war movie set in 1573; *Miyamoto Musashi* (1954), the oft-told tale of Japan's greatest swordsman; and *Daredevil in the Castle* (1961), among many others. These films, however, were the work of chambara epic-maker Hiroshi Inagaki, who only directed samurai sagas, which ranged from small-scale mysteries (*Incident at Blood Pass*, 1970) to "cast of thousands" costumers (*Samurai Banners*, 1969).

But Inagaki's creations were traditional chambara. *Yojimbo* was something else again. The opening image of a stray wild dog sets the tone, as does the following image of Toshiro Mifune coming to a fork in the road and trying diffidently to decide which path to take. It is the end of the samurai era, and Mifune is playing a scruffy ronin out for a strange sort of fun. This was a Japanese western, and perfectly suited to the "stranger in town" cowboy films. In fact, *Yojimbo* was remade, plot twist for plot twist, into *A Fistful of Dollars* (1966)—the film that introduced Sergio Leone's "Man With No Name" and made Clint Eastwood a star.

Mifune, playing an ex-samurai with a number for a name, comes to a bad town filled with two warring gangs which are too cowardly to kill each other off. Mifune, enacting a man named Sanjuro (which means "Thirty"), plays both sides against each other, hiring himself out as a bodyguard to the highest bidder until he forces the issue. The arrival of a man with a gun (Tatsuya Nakadai) almost foils his plan, but in the climactic showdown—ten men and a gun against one—Yojimbo lances the man's gun hand and cuts through everyone else.

The earlier superhero samurai had established a fascinating form of screen swordplay, but *Yojimbo* and its sequel, *Sanjuro* (1962), added something more. Mifune had a vicious vitality to his blade in the first film. In the second, Kurosawa ends the more sedate story, of Sanjuro trying to save a clan, with a duel between the title character and a vaunted samurai (again, Tatsuya Nakadai). It consists of only one move each, the *iai* (fast sword draw), and ends with the two figures as still as statutes. Suddenly a spurt of blood erupts from the samurai's chest and he crumbles.

In all the years of chambara, in all the years of death by sword, no director had used blood so realistically. It would be almost ten years before directors would pour the scarlet stuff again. But when they did, they used buckets of it.

BLIND MAN'S BLOOD

The year 1962 was a great one. In that year two chambara series premiered which featured heroes probably born of *Yojimbo/ Sanjuro* influence. Yet these heroes went far beyond anything the Mifune character attempted. While director Kurosawa was subtle, these heroes were obvious. While other swordsmen fought against corrupt societies to create fine new ones, these heroes simply fought. Their aims were not to "save the society." The first of these new swordsmen fought to save individuals. The second fought to die.

The first was not blind the way most followers of Bushido were blind. The first was literally blind. He was Zatoichi, the justly famous blind swordsman. Rotund, scruffy, short-haired, he wandered the Japan of the 1800s, just barely surviving by gambling or hiring himself out as a masseur. Shintaro Katsu, the son of a musician, achieved stardom with this role, and little wonder. As the twenty-four films progressed between 1962 and 1972, his "playing blind" became more and more exact, filled with delightful nuances.

The audience never saw his eyes. Whenever his usually closed lids quivered, only the whites of his eyes could be seen. Still, the

Brother vs. brother in Zatoichi and a Chest of Gold *as Shintaro Katsu gets whipped up by his thespian brother Tomisaburo Wakayama (later to star in the* Baby Cart *series).*

character seemed to have a radar-exact sense of hearing. He could "see" with his ears and his incisive mind more than most people. And his ears seemed directly connected to his sword arm. He also used a cane sword that guided him in times of peace. But for Zatoichi, there were few times of peace. His hearing-radar also seemed to be a signal to which trouble and death would surely be attracted.

But he was prepared for it. The character was a master swordsman, a nearly unbeliev-ably fast and deadly fighter, and Katsu had the sword skill to pull this image off. The idea of a blind swordsman sounds ludicrous, but it has to be seen to be believed. And see-ing this *is* believing. Katsu would cut through three candles just by drawing his sword, and in the same motion, he would return the sword to its cane scabbard. There was no film edited; it was all done in one continuous take.

The character used the *gyakute-giri*, the reversed-grip sword cut, holding his blade in

a downward, defensive position at all times. All the other swordsman held their blades up, the point above their gripping forefingers. But the unassuming Zatoichi, who never wanted to fight but always had to, held the blade pointed toward the ground, below his gripping pinkie. When he fought, he would slice back and forth with his fist.

The Zatoichi movies were comedy-tragedies in which Ichi would play the buffoon until he came across evil, and almost always, his attempts to right wrongs are confused or complicated by people's emotions and desires. Zatoichi wants what is best for the common man and always puts his life on the line for the often misunderstanding, ungrateful commoners. This leads to both scenes of effective heartbreak and a final explosion of mass slaughter.

Throughout the series, Katsu would do a startling dance of death, the sword appearing and disappearing as he slashed it across the

bodies of his enemies—who almost always outnumbered him ten to one. Watching this innocuous, humble, shuffling lowlife turn into a whirling dervish of death was always exciting, and the filmmakers always put him in powerfully dramatic situations, which added volumes to the basic series structure.

In the first film, *The Life and Opinion of Zatoichi*, he is being hunted. Kan Shimosawa created the character and the story, while Minoru Inuzuka wrote the screenplay. Kenji Misumi, probably the greatest underrated Japanese action film director, helmed this first picture, as he would most of the series's first films. Through it and the subsequent movies, the character unerringly points out the injustice of the feudal system.

In the first film, the story of blind Ichi (*zato* means "masseur") is notably different than it is in the following films. (Ichi was not only famous to his fans, his character was also infamous on-screen. Almost everyone knew of him in these early stories.) He is being tracked by vengeance-seeking members of a gang whose boss he had killed when he stumbles across his brother—a man who reacted against Bushido as strongly as Ichi but is not taking the path of righteousness; instead, he is leading of life of crime, and he has gotten in over his head.

The two reminisce about their youth as the brother lies dying in Zatoichi's arms—

mortally wounded in a duel with his own brother. They remember the time when Ichi had his sight and they both loved the same girl. They remember how the brother stole her from Ichi and drove her to her death.

Ichi leaves his brother's body to confront the gang leader who hired his brother to kill him. In the very last second of the film, still surrounded by the gangster's henchman, Ichi swings his cane sword across the villain's neck in a freeze frame. It was an abrupt ending, but the following two sequels, produced in less than a year, added more to the character's history.

Both sequels seemed somewhat tenuous, as if the filmmakers weren't sure the series would last. At the end of 1962 came *The Return of Masseur Ichi*, and in early 1963 *Zatoichi Enters Again* premiered. The latter was directed by Tokuzo Tanaka, a regular on the series. This film establishes further Zatoichi traditions.

Most of the movies begin with the character minding his own business, but within seconds trouble finds him. Either a fight is going on nearby or enemies have finally tracked him down. For whatever reason, Zatoichi almost always finds himself fighting with someone for reasons he doesn't understand and then kills his opponent in self-defense. Or he rescues a relative of someone he's killed in a previous picture, as is the case in *Zatoichi Enters Again*.

It is the brother of a gangster he had killed earlier, who, although Ichi had saved him, follows the masseur for revenge. He follows him to the man who taught Zatoichi swordplay, Zatoichi's *sensei*. To the hero's horror, the man has been corrupted by lust for power. The sensei's sister loves the scruffy vagabond and wants to marry him. This is a seeming impossibility to Ichi, who thought an ugly low-ranked being such as himself would never find love. There's only one catch: she wants him never to fight again.

He agrees, leaving himself wide open to the vengeance of the gangster's brother.

Three ninja fall from the trees. They are dead before they hit the ground, killed by Tomisaburo Wakayama in Lightning Swords of Death.

Although his instincts scream at him to fight back, he lays his cane sword at the brother's feet and suggests that they gamble for his life. In a gut-wrenching scene, Ichi and his lady crouch at the man's feet in a side alley, throwing dice for the masseur's life. The vengeance-seeker wins, but he cannot bear to kill the honorable, humiliated man. He lies, saying the dice are in Ichi's favor.

But tragedy continues to stalk the hero. His own sensei forces him to duel, meaning to murder the man who constantly reminds him of how low he has sunk. Zatoichi's skill gets the better of him, and he kills his own teacher. This means that he must leave his true love, for he has killed a member of her family, and, in Japan, family takes precedence over all, even love.

Tokuzo Tanaka directed the next few films, with Kan Shimozawa supplying all the stories. They developed the character to a delightful degree, creating scenes that cleverly made use of both Ichi's blindness and his "seeing ears." Slowly but surely, Ichi was becoming a superman. Audiences flocked to the films, making them the greatest success of their time.

The fame grew to the point that *Zatoichi and the Scoundrels* (1964), the sixth in the series, the first to be filmed in color, and the first to be directed by Kimiyoshi Yasuda (who was soon to become the best director on the series) was dubbed into English and exported as *Zatoichi the Blind Swordsman.* But this translation didn't do as well as hoped, returning the character to Japanese cinemas and American revival theaters and art houses.

Even there, the movies often lost something in the subtitled translation. In one of the films, two kimonoed, top-knotted villains are discussing the masseur's arrival. "I hear Zatoichi is in town," the subtitles for

one say. "Yeah," says the other. "He's one tough hombre."

The "tough hombre" fought through five more movies until coming to *Zatoichi's Pilgrimage* (1966), directed by Kasuo Ikehiro—another series regular. This was a milestone, in that Ichi promises to visit and pray at eighty-eight temples along the road— one for each of the men he has killed. Before the movie's eighty-two minutes are up, he has about a dozen more temples to visit.

Just one film later, something else unusual happens. In *The Blind Swordsman's Cane Sword*, a master swordsmith warns Ichi that his blade is weak and will break if he kills just one more man. The masseur leaves it with the old smith for repair, not realizing that the master craftsman is making the Orient's strongest sword for a high-ranking official—a sword many people want.

Ichi does some razzle-dazzle with sticks and an umbrella to fight off the villains until the climactic confrontation with the corrupt official. With the now dead smith's words of warning booming in Ichi's brain, the men fight—and the evil man's sword breaks. The old smith had switched the blades. Now Zatoichi has the country's best sword. This was another excellent Kimiyoshi Yasuda film, one which many consider Zatoichi's best.

A personal favorite comes just two films later; after Zatoichi has continued to be both an amazing swordsman (in *Zatoichi Challenged* [1967] he cuts off the eyebrows of a corrupt official without breaking the skin) and an equally amazing humanitarian (in the same film he puts himself at the mercy of the shogun's agent to save the life of an innocent artist). It is *The Blind Swordsman and the Fugitives* (1968) wherein lie all of the series' traditions, along with a brand new one.

The astonishing ending of Lightning Swords of Death. *The Lone Wolf and son leave the battlefield after killing an entire army.*

It had been six years since the original film premiered, and already seventeen movies had been produced. By now Zatoichi is a masterful screen presence. After being hired as a masseur for the leader of a gang of cutthroats, the crooks purposely place things in his way, including a sword edge. Ichi nonchalantly avoids and replaces all of them, finally stepping over the sword nimbly. The men torture him by surrounding his face with their blades, then later try to kill him.

Their leader silently picks up a bow and arrow while talking loudly to Ichi. He silently pulls the drawstring back and lets the arrow fly. Zatoichi merely pulls his sword two inches out of his cane. The arrow hits the blade edge and goes off on either side of the sitting masseur.

Three men then try ambushing Ichi on the street. He swings his sword madly. The men freeze, certain that they have been killed. When they realize they haven't been touched, all three try to catch up with the shambling swordsmen. As they take their first steps, all their clothes fall off in tattered strips. Later, when a female assassin tries to cover Ichi with darts, he catches them on his sword hilt.

Directly Yasuda and story writer Shimozawa have thus far reestablished the character's excellence. Then they bring in a new ingredient: a villain with a gun. When the hammer clicks back, Zatoichi's ears do not recognize the sound. He holds up his blade to deflect the weapon, only to have the bullet ricochet into his shoulder. Escaping into the river, he digs out the lead and painfully cauterizes the wound by pouring sake into it.

Here was the rub: since Zatoichi had gotten so good, the filmmakers were introducing additional handicaps. This led to an especially involving climactic battle in which a bleeding Ichi, one arm in a makeshift sling, faces the mob. He always seems ready to collapse. The enemy attacks and he viciously slashes, and then immediately seems ready to collapse again.

No special-effects blood shoots out of his victims, but his speed and the excellence of the swordfight choreography give the impression that Ichi's blade is so fast that men die three seconds before they become aware of it, their wounds cauterized.

Ichi then slices right through a wall to reach the main villain. Thus ends another satisfying Zatoichi adventure. To keep the series going, Daiei Productions, and the series' producers, started using guest stars, as in *Zatoichi Meets Yojimbo* (1970, with Toshiro Mifune returning to the role) and *Zatoichi Meets His Equal* (1971, featuring Wang Yu as the One-Armed Swordsman). Yasuda directed the latter, but Kihachi Okamoto, director of some of the most wondrously violent chambaras (*Sword of Doom*, 1966; and *Kill!*, 1968, being two) both wrote and directed the former.

Daiei went out of business in 1971, and the series went over to Toho Films for two episodes. The final was *Zatoichi in Desperation* (1973), produced and directed by the star, Shintaro Katsu. Once again, the ever-faithful masseur tries to help someone, only to pay the piper. In this case, the villains drive spikes through his hands so that he will be unable to hold a sword.

In the climactic scene at a beach where Zatoichi is holed up in a shack, the smug villain sends in some men to kill the "helpless" blind man. To his amazement, the ruffians stumble back out, dying. Zatoichi follows like a hulking angel of doom: He had tied the

Katsu was to take his famous character onto a successful television series and a final Zatoichi remake, but the cinema had not seen the last of his particular skills. In 1972, Katsu Productions and Toho Films presented a series of *Sword of Justice* movies written by Yasuzo Masamura. These went way beyond Zatoichi. In them, Katsu played "Razor" Hanzo, the most extreme policeman of the late 1800s.

Softcore pornography had become the prevalent genre of the modern Japanese cinema. Almost 75 percent of the films made were high-quality sex-related stories. A major subgenre was that of "Roman porn," or as it is commonly known, SM/BD movies (Sado-Masochism, Bondage-Discipline). The *Sword of Justice* pictures were combinations of action and SM, but done in such a way that they seemed satirical.

The Snare, the second in the series, starts with Hanzo doing his morning exercises. He goes into his rock garden, puts on brass knuckles, and starts punching stone statues, sending up sparks. He then goes inside his combination gym, sauna, and torture chamber to exercise his "prodigious member." In these movies, he uses his private parts as an interrogation device. The treatment of female characters in the films is embarrassing.

Whenever he comes across a woman in his work, he almost immediately rapes her.

sword to his wrist and forearm! He chases the screaming villains, cutting them down as he goes. The final film image of Zatoichi shows him stumbling along the shore, the waves getting ever louder until they drown out all sound.

Whenever he comes across a reluctant female witness or suspect, he tortures, interrogates, and then has her lowered onto him. Then he spins her while she is (politely described) impaled upon him. In every case, the woman falls madly in love with him, desperately pines for him, and will do anything for him. All he wants, of course, are "Just the facts, ma'am."

In *The Snare*, Hanzo and his two bumbling assistants come upon a dead girl who recently had an abortion, and they trace the abortion to a church where the nuns practice nasty rituals. There they whip and molest captive women for the enjoyment of high-ranking officials. Because church land is sacred, Hanzo infiltrates the grounds by replacing the dead girl in her casket with himself and being buried alive in the church cemetery. The slight of him erupting from the ground is one of the great moments in martial arts cinema.

He attacks, breaks up the ritual, and takes the head nun back to his torture chamber. He discovers that the rite's organizer is a high-ranking treasury official he cannot legally touch. When reporting to his overlord, his jealous immediate superior demands he commit hara-kiri (or *sep-*

puku, as it is more accurately described in this case) for his failure to solve the girl's murder.

Hanzo immediately plunges his short sword into his stomach and pulls out some pulpy red stuff that he throws into his superior's face. Everyone, on-screen and in the audience, is shocked, but it turns out to be watermelon pulp that Hanzo had secreted there for this very purpose. To save his life he must bring to justice Japan's most horrible pirate, and he does so in an orgy of short-bladed violence.

Hanzo loves plunging his blade into enemies' joints (elbow or knee) and bending their limbs backward. He also has a pagoda-home filled with hidden traps and secret blades. When attacked in his bath, he pulls cords which send arrows and knives shooting into the ambushers. He finally manages to bring the treasury man up on irrefutable charges.

Now, this series has to be seen *not* to be believed. It is the kinkiest and strangest of a strange lot. But it did not appear full-blown, without any antecedents. Its way into the hearts of martial arts lovers was heralded by the second chambara series to premier in 1962—*Kyoshiro Nemuri: The Son of Black Mass.*

THE FULL MOON KILLER

Raizo Ichikawa could be called the Japanese James Dean. He was an intense young actor with glowing eyes, a weak chin, and a long nose. He was a commanding screen presence who also projected a great deal of vulnerability. His specialty was playing alienated characters, and audiences could clearly see great depths of sensitivity and suffering behind the tough exterior.

Arguably, Ichikawa's greatest role was that of Kyoshiro Nemuri, the halfbreed samurai. Again, Kenji Misumi directed the first of the series, introducing a red-haired master swordsman born of the rape of his mother by a Portuguese missionary during a black mass. Quite understandably, the man hates most everything, and especially Christianity. But again and again he voyages to towns where Christians are being persecuted by the Ienari Shogunate (1786–1838).

Nemuri is a seemingly amoral adventurer, intent on finding a situation or swordsman good enough to kill him. That is not easy, considering that "the Son of Black Mass," as he calls himself, is the master of the Engetsu Sappo—the dreaded, mystical (fictional) full moon cut.

In the later films of this eleven-film series, the full moon cut is pictured with a strobe effect so that Nemuri's sword seems to multiply. He moves it around in a circle in front of him, drawing the opponent toward him to deliver the killing slice. No opponent has been able to resist the hypnotizing effect of the full moon cut.

But it was used for one-on-one duels only. Usually Nemuri would cut down tens of men in the outlandish situations he sought out. In the first few movies he is pictured less nilhilistically than he would later become. These were fairly straightforward adventures of Nemuri protecting children and the like.

But it is in the third film, *Kyoshiro Nemuri at Bay* (1964), the first directed by Kazuo Ikehiro, that things get out of hand. There he kills dozens of Christians as well as those shogun men planning to kill the Christians themselves. The most memorable moment, however, comes after he has been imprisoned in a dungeon with a babbling white man who turns out to be his father. Upon their escape, he beheads the crazy man.

From then on, the Nemuri series got down to the serious business of mass slaughter. The filmmakers slaughtered dozens on-screen and the concept of Bushido in the

This man messed with Sonny Chiba, the Street-fighter, and got his teeth taken away.

207

The only man who can beat The Streetfighter is tiny, rotund Masafumi Suzuki.

scripts. The high point of the series might very well be *The Human Tarantula* (1968, directed by Kimiyoshi Yasauda). The first image is of a beautiful woman in plush surroundings having an epileptic fit. Her maids bring a young girl to her, and after she stabs the girl to death, splashing the walls with crimson streaks, the fit subsides. Toto, I don't think we're in Kansas anymore.

Here's the story: Two illegitimate children of the shogun have faked a suicide pact and then taken over a small town. The sister has

these blood fits. The brother is in love with his sister and is a master of poisons. They have taken all the young people from the town and placed them in dungeon cages, the men on one side and the women on the other. They spend their days thinking of interesting ways to kill them.

Enter Kyoshiro Nemuri. Hearing about the village, he decides it deserves a look. When the villains get word of his coming, they arrange all sorts of traps along the road. One is a veiled woman who begs Nemuri to make love to her. His reputation is one of a degenerate rogue—and he lives up to it. Even though the woman reveals herself to be a leper, he takes her into a hut and has sex with her under a mosquito net.

Only then does he pull off the "leprosy," which was actually makeup. At that moment three men chop down the net and slash at it with their swords. Nemuri rises behind them. They look down. The woman lies dead. All they've succeeded in doing is killing their bait. Then Nemuri quickly kills all three. A fourth runs in, looking at the woman in shock.

"I can see by the way you look that she was your woman," Nemuri says. Then he smiles. "But she gave herself to me before she died." The enraged man charges, and in one move, Nemuri slices him, spins, cleans his blade with a hanky, puts it away, and walks out of the hut. The fourth man stands, his sword raised, and then falls dead.

By the time Nemuri reaches the town, the insane sister will do anything to have him. She captures him, throwing open her kimono to reveal her naked form. In those days women were so well covered that the sight of naked skin could drive a man crazy with lust—a normal man, that is. Nemuri just glances at her chest. "I've seen that before," he says.

He escapes, only to come to a barn strewn with bloody corpses. Inside, tied to the ceiling beams, is a dead naked girl—the ropes making her body a cross. The sister again approaches him, and this time he takes her beneath the human cross. Then all the corpses jump up—they were live men playing dead bodies. Nemuri soon makes them real corpses.

He battles to the castle, where the villains have chained another halfbreed in the courtyard. He arrives to find that the young man's eyes have been gouged out. Behind him, a muscle man gloats that he did the deed and will do the same to Nemuri. Without turning, the full moon swordsman swirls his unsheathed sword and calmly returns it to his scabbard. He has cut through the muscle man's eyes.

He braves the castle, filled with traps such as spears coming through walls, to finish off the brother. Outside, the sister stands between him and the now-burning castle. Given a choice between facing Nemuri and the flames, she chooses the latter. She runs into the fire, and Kyoshiro Nemuri walks away.

Would you believe that these movies were done with high style and surprising taste? It's true. Although beyond the comprehension of many Western eyes, the Nemuri movies were done with demure sophistication. There was no complete nudity (even the girl in the barn was cleverly covered by the camera angles) and very little blood on-screen.

The Son of Black Mass movies stand on their own, without these defenses. At their heart, they promoted belief in oneself. They also soundly condemned the society that allowed such a tortured halfbreed as Kyoshiro Nemuri to exist. *The Human Tarantula* was Raizo Ichikawa's second-to-last Nemuri movie. After completing *Castle Menagerie* (1969), he died of colon cancer. Two more Nemuri movies were made with Hiroki Matsukata, but he paled in comparison to the beloved Ichikawa.

Ichikawa lived on in his movies, which included one of the most popular ninja series. Filmmakers on both ides of the world don't exactly know what to do with ninjas. They exist mostly in legend, and their legends dictate that they could disappear and sometimes fly. They were the most insidious creatures since the vampire.

Writers like Tomoyoshi Murayama and Hajime Takaiwa chose to portray the characters far more realistically. The concept of a person with no place on earth and none in the afterlife was fascinating. What kind of moral torture must their lives have been? Combining this intriguing character motivation with classic chambara ingredients led to the popular *Band of Assassins* series—seven films over three years tracing the lives of three ninja, all played by Raizo Ichikawa.

The story is a true one: In the mid-1500s, a powerful warlord named Nobunaga tried to eradicate certain sects of Buddhism that stood in his way to the shogunate. The Iga family of ninjas were descended from these sects and fought back for their lives, seeking to assassinate the warlord while working for Nobunaga's enemy.

All seven films were downbeat, in keeping with the ninja legend. Even when the black-garbed killers won they seemed to lose. Part one chronicled their unsuccessful assassination attempts. Part two ended with the ninja hero (Ichikawa) being led to a boiling pot of oil. In reality, the ninja died in the pot, but on-screen he escaped to fail again.

In the third episode, in which Ichikawa plays another ninja, he is assigned to kill his own sensei, whose daughter is in love with him. In the last four episodes, the third ninja Ichikawa plays decides to reject his heritage and try to take sides, rather than go with anyone who pays him. But first he must fight all manner of enemies.

After Ichikawa died, several more ninja adventures were filmed, the one immediately following his death starring Hiroki Matsukata (who seemed to be making a living playing Ichikawa's parts for awhile). It was called *Mission: Iron Castle* (1970) and told of the ninja's attempt to escape the title location after having been captured. One of the most memorable ninja gimmicks here was to eat ten days' worth of unboiled rice in order to stay alive while digging a tunnel out in nine days.

BABY CART TO HELL

With the success of Zatoichi and the Son of Black Mass, martial arts sword movies became livelier and livelier. Also, with the dawn of the 1970s came an increased Jap-
anese public consumption of comic books. These weren't the kind that English-speaking countries were accustomed to; these were as thick as telephone books and came out weekly in mass quantities. Even today, comics make up 40 percent of the entire Japanese publishing industry.

The Japanese comics range from love stories through sports stories to samurai adventures. One of the most popular of the latter was the *Kozure Ogami* (Lone Wolf and Cub) series, written by Kazuo Koike and drawn by Goseki Kojimba. The most popular Japanese comics are later bound into volumes, and the Ogami series was to fill twenty-eight of them. It is generally regarded as the standard for samurai comic stories.

It told of a disgraced shogun executioner of the early 1600s who takes his revenge on an evil clan by becoming a hired assassin. That, in itself, was not enough to distinguish the series. In addition, this killer brings along his three-year-old son for the ride in a wooden, weapon-laden baby carriage. In 1972, Katsu Productions bought the rights for the film version. Shintaro Katsu hired Koike to write the screenplay, Kenji Misumi to direct, and his own brother, Tomisaburo Wakayama, to star. The *Sword of Vengeance* series was off and rolling.

The first film told of the "Lone Wolf's" creation. Itto Ogami, a rising samurai in the ranks of the Iemitsu shogunate, was dueling with Gunbei Yagyu—one of the six Yagyu family sons—to see who would become the official decapitator. When someone committed seppuku (the more respectable form of hara-kiri), the decapitator was to cut the head from the suicide's body as per ancient traditions.

Gunbei wins the match, but Ogami is declared winner because he has maneuvered the Yagyu son into pointing his blade toward the shogun—an inexcusable offense. To satisfy the shogun, the Yagyu father must bring him the head of Gunbei. The cunning, corrupt father merely sends for his son's double

The Streetfighter stares down his arch-enemy Jungo (Milton Ishibashi).

(all his sons have doubles for this very purpose) and beheads him. Then he starts seriously planning to frame Ogami.

But first he must kill a lord who has become aware of the Yagyu family's treachery. He arranges another bout between Ogami and himself. Ogami uses his Suioryu Zambatto style (Sea Gull-Horse Slashing cut) while Yagyu uses a wooden staff. This time the villain manipulates Ogami so that the cut tip of his pole lances the suspicious lord, killing him.

Only then does the plan go into effect. Ninjas attack Ogami's home in order to plant a memorial tablet with the shogun's name on it in the Ogami family shrine. Any hint of disloyalty—even this extremely questionable sort—is seen as betrayal and punishable by death, and since the Yagyus are essentially the shogun's secret police, it'll be easy.

Ogami's wife discovers the ninjas and is killed. When the trap is sprung the next day, the shogun is fooled and Ogami is told to commit seppuku. He cannot decide whether to loyally die or take vengeance—go "on the road to Hades," as he calls it. He leaves it up to his baby son by putting a ball to one side and his sword on the other. If the boy touch-

Sonny Chiba dresses up for his final appearance as Terry Surugy in The Streetfighter's Last Revenge.

es the ball, he and his father will die. If he touches the sword . . .

The child reaches for the ball but touches the sword. The next day, in the official seppuku ritual, Ogami goes wild, killing everyone around him and taking his son away. The Yagyu father is waiting for him outside. He suggests a duel with Gunbei and places the adversaries so that his son's back is to the sun. The plan is to blind Ogami, but the tables are turned. The samurai places his son on his back, the child outfitted with a metal headband which reflects the light back at the superior swordsman.

Itto Ogami kills the real Gunbei Yagyu, and then the adventure truly begins. He builds the baby cart and places a sign on it reading, "My arm is your arm." For five hundred gold pieces he'll take on any assassination job, secure in the knowledge that any problem that requires that much expense would be created by the Yagyus. The succeeding films in the series tell of the Lone Wolf and Son's assignments, as well as duels with the remaining Yagyu family members.

The films so impressed Americans David Weisman and Robert Houston that they bought the rights for the first two, reedited them together, rescored them, dubbed them, and released them as one feature, *Shogun Assassin* (1980). Here the head of the Yagyu family has become the shogun who kills his official decapitator's wife as a test of loyalty. Itto Ogami fails but accepts a duel with the Shogun's son to attain freedom—with the results previously described.

Enraged, the shogun sends all manner of ninja after Ogami, who has taken an assignment to kill the shogun's brother. Ogami defeats all the ninja and faces the brother's bodyguards, "the Three Masters of Death." One master uses a studded club, another a studded glove, and the third a razor-sharp claw. Ogami throws his sword into the first (an unthinkable act for a samurai) and uses another sword to chop the second's head down the middle, and then opens the third's neck.

Weisman and Houston do an exceptional job scripting and dubbing the American voices—one of the best jobs ever—and the new musical soundtrack by Mark Lindsay and W. Michael Lewis is terrific. Unfortunately, without the interconnecting pure Japanese sequences, *Shogun Assassin* becomes one gory scene after another. The original language versions have a sense of epic poetry about them missing from this otherwise effective work.

The Japanese version of the second *Sword of Vengeance* film, *Baby Cart at the River Styx*, is considerably different in plot from *Shogun Assassin*, but not in picture. Ogami still faces the Three Masters, but they are bodyguards of a man who has enough evidence to abolish a clan the Yagyus want out of the way. The female supreme ninja of *Shogun Assassin* is actually a Yagyu daughter in the original version. In both versions, Ogami seduces her by his honorable nature, and she cannot bring herself to kill him.

And the violence is the same in both versions—excessive. The screen blood pours, spurts, and drools in the Baby Cart movies, so much so, in fact, that the films become . . . cartoonish. In his review of *Shogun Assassin*, Chicago critic Roger Ebert said, "No one bleeds like this unless they have garden hoses for veins." And he's right.

An unadultered version of the third in the series, *Baby Cart to Hades* (1973), was dubbed and exported years before *Shogun Assassin*. It played in America under the suitable title *Lightning Swords of Death* (1974). This episode had some notable highlights, including the opening.

Ogami walks in a bamboo forest and then suddenly, inexplicably, swings his sword madly. He then replaces the sword and waits. Three bamboo trees suddenly collapse and three ninjas fall from them. Whipping out his sword a second time, he kills all three before they hit the ground. In an ensuing duel with another Yagyu son, he defeats that superior swordsman by leaping upside down over the man and hurling his blade into the top of the Yagyu's skull.

Finally, he turns the corner with the cart to face a literal army of opponents. In an exhausting but beautifully sustained fight scene, he kills every single one of them.

Number four, *Baby Cart in Peril* (1972), had an interesting premise. Ogami has been hired by a father to kill his own daughter. The woman, once a promising martial artist, was tricked by her sensei and raped. To take revenge, she had an ornate tattoo placed on her chest. When she is losing a duel, she throws open her shirt and kills her opponent while he's distracted. Unfortunately, her burning desire for vengeance is threatening the safety of her clan. It is either her death or everyone's death.

Ogami waits until she has exacted revenge before killing her, then he again confronts the head of the Yagyus. In this battle the villain wounds Ogami, so he is too weak to kill the old man when he pushes his sword into

admits it was a test of Ogami's skill, and each tells him a different part of his assignment.

One dies beneath a waterfall. One dies in a river, a circle of blood growing wide around him as he sinks lower and lower. One dies at a campsite, his leg in the campfire. As he speaks, the flames eat away at him. Finally, Ogami gets the full story. A warlord has gone insane and has fallen in love with a prostitute. He has locked his own son and heir up, and then disguised the prostitute's daughter as a boy so she can be the heir. To save the clan, Ogami must kill the man, the woman, and the female child.

The finale is nothing short of magnificent. Ogami has entered the insane lord's lair to try and talk the old man out of his insanity before all is lost. As he speaks, surrounded by enemy samurai, his son and the prostitute's daughter are making faces at each other, happily playing as children. When Ogami finishes, all eyes turn to the little girl for a decision. "Kill them," she says brightly.

The following fight scene is impressionistic, experimental, inventive, and one of Misumi's best. After the last man has been mortally wounded, the dying samurai basically suggests that now that the guards had fulfilled their duty to defend their lord, Ogami should go and kill the senile maniac. The guards themselves had hired Ogami, and all had died doing their best—knowing the truth all along. That is why they were so intent on testing Ogami at the opening—they wanted to be sure he was good enough to kill them all!

The following movies couldn't live up to that classic. They were excessively violent

the Yagyu father's eye. Following that bloody picture, Kenji Misumi took the writer's fifth script, *Baby Cart in the Land of Demons*, and made it the best in the series, if not one of the greatest martial arts movies.

The fifth Lone Wolf film is special, not only because of the ample action, but because it is such a trenchant statement on the feudal era. The opening is riveting. Five men attack Ogami in five atmospheric locations. As each is mortally wounded, each and clever, but number five said it all. They started resorting to the supernatural, with Ogami versus Yagyu zombies and Ogami versus Ninjas on skis. The series finally followed Zatoichi to television, where Kinnosuke Nakamura—one of the great veterans of chambara cinema—played the leading role.

However, now it can be told. Recently the final volume of the comic series was published in America, and the fate of Lone Wolf and son became known. As the final book opens, the shogun has become aware of the Yagyus' duplicity. He sends an army out to find and kill them. Knowing the end is near, the Yagyu father throws all he has left at Ogami. Ogami slaughters the rest of the Yagyu family but suffers mightily in the process. In a weakened condition, he then faces the Yagyu father, one of the most hated villains in Japanese comic and cinematic history.

As they square off, the shogun's army surrounds them. They watch in tears as the antagonists battle. The sword fight is brutal, but no one can get the upper hand. The Lone Wolf feigns death, but even that doesn't work. Finally, Itto Ogami expires from his wounds. Daigoro, his tiny son, picks up a blade that has fallen from the cart and charges. The Yagyu father, seeing the army around him, opens his arms to accept his fate. The child plunges the knife into the man's chest. The Yagyu father dies, embracing the child.

ENTER THE STREETFIGHTER

"I want karate fighters, not karate dancers!"

—Shinichi "Sonny" Chiba,
Champion of Death

The 1980s were not good years for the big-screen chambara stars. Zatoichi, Kyoshiro Nemuri, and Itto Ogami went on television,

and the sword-slashing genre all but died out in movies. They were just too expensive to make, there were no new stories, and the Japanese public seemed far more interested in such softcore pornography as *Red Rope Rape* (1981).

The era might very well have died with Kenji Misumi, in 1975. However, before Misumi died he made a fitting final movie. It was *The Last Samurai*, a two-hour-and-twenty-minute story of the end of the warrior class. Hideki Takahashi, a tall, muscular actor, starred as the title character who must fight battles, lose loves, and take revenge (by chopping the villain completely in two down the middle) before becoming a barber in the brave new world.

No one could make movies move like Misumi. His final work was an involving, exciting action picture with strong characters and affecting performances. No one can make them quite like Hideo Gosha, either. In 1978 and 1979, he made two samurai thrillers, *Bandits vs. Samurai Squad* and *Hunters in the Dark*, both starring Tatsuya Nakadai—an actor many feel is even superior to Toshiro Mifune.

Gosha's work is highly emotional, with violence to match. While he doesn't always keep the action coming, when it does come it is often teeth-grindingly intense. In *Hunters*, an amnesiatic hero charges through a half-dozen rice-paper walls before coming upon a group he means to kill. When he attacks, the first move chops an opponent's arm off at the elbow. The opponent's sword had stuck into the ceiling, so for the rest of the scene the arm hangs down like some sort of perverse chandelier.

Later in the same film, the amnesiac is attacked in his bath by a female ninja whom he kills by slowly, agonizingly pushing a bamboo tube into her side. Finally, the Nakadai character must challenge the man who had caused all the suffering—a corrupt member of the shogun's staff—and the two kill each other in a farmyard. The villain of the movie was played by a brooding, strong figure with thick eyebrows and dark eyes. This was Shinichi Chiba, the man who had been known as the Streetfighter for years.

For many, the mention of that name is like pulling fingernails across the blackboard. Many remember the movie in disgust for its excessive violence. Many remember it with distaste for the editing job that came after its initial American release. Many remember it with disdain for Chiba's lack of martial arts grace. Many remember it with pain for the jumping, confusing camerawork that filmed it.

No matter how it is recalled, the original *Streetfighter* (1975) was an unforgettable theatrical experience. It was the first film ever to receive an X rating for violence instead of sexual content. Although some reports made this first release appear to be an amazing success, history bears it out as a dismal failure. Most theaters wouldn't show it—relegating it to cinemas that usually showed sexual pornography. Those audiences certainly didn't have the stomach for it.

The original, unedited *Streetfighter* is now out on video. Shinichi Chiba is not. He was born in 1939 and entered the film business in 1961 after having won a Toei Studios "New Faces" contest. He gained his higher education at the Japanese University of Physical Education under the training of Mas Oyama Koncho—the World Karate Grandmaster. Chiba studied gymnastics and kyokushinkai karate, respectively.

Kyokushinkai karate is a formal competition version that requires knock-downs for points. It is one of the harsher forms of an already harsh art. *Harsh* is a word that doesn't quite do Chiba's film work justice. He came to the attention of the Japanese masses with *Karate Kiba* (1970, also known as *Bodyguard Kiba* and *The Bodyguard*), which set the tone for his future films. In it he plays a master of an unusual form of "ken-karate" who foils a skyjacking singlehandedly. When interviewed by the television press, he takes the opportunity to offer himself out as a paid bodyguard.

From there he runs afoul of complex plots and the Oriental underworld, and succeeds by being the toughest guy around and not being afraid to get physical. From there it was on to the *Gambler Cop* movie series (1971)—an extension of the Japanese crime genre generally known as the *yakuza* film. That led naturally into the *Lone Wolf Gambler* series, in which he plays a cigar-chomping assassin of yakuza gangsters.

Then came a long stream of lookalike movies and television shows. By the time he became known in this country, he had reportedly done over seventy-five features. The feature he became known for was originally called *Sudden Attack: The Killing Fist*. Here it was named *The Streetfighter*. Chiba, now deemed Sonny, played Terry Surugy (also spelled Tsurugi), a man who survives in modern Japan by his wits and fists. He is a professional "jobber"—for a price, he'll do anything.

That is not to say he is always successful. While rescuing a murderer named Jungo (Milton Ishibashi), he accidentally kills the man's brother. Surugy goes on to other work, but Jungo promises revenge. Surugy's other work is protecting an oil sheik's daughter from the Five Dragon Society, headed by an Englishman named King Stone. He's not too good at that, either. She gets kidnapped, he gets captured, and his good friend Ratnose gets killed trying to save him.

Escaping from torture, Terry tracks the villains down, only to find Jungo waiting for him. He leaves him in a pool of blood and rips the Five Dragon Society apart. Summarized this way, the movie seems like just another thriller, but during the proceedings, a man pushes a knife through his own sister in an attempt to kill Surugy. Surugy himself tears a man's genitals off, tears out another

Sue Shiomi is a stranger in a strange land. Lucky she knows karate, in Sister Streetfighter.

Hiroyuki "Henry" Sanada in action, leaping over the roaring fire.

man's adam's apple, and, in the nauseating climax, smashes a man's head open—a scene which is both shown in slow motion and in X ray! At the climactic moment, the screen becomes an X-ray machine showing internal effects.

Anyone who saw this picture either loved it or hated it, but New Line Cinema, its

American distributor, hated the box-office returns. In a hurried negotiation with the rating board, they promised to do anything to get an R rating. The result, which is available on videotape, was just short of incomprehensible. The rating board demands required the elimination of all screen blood, not just some of it.

The result was confusion. Fight scenes started and then almost immediately ended without the audience seeing what had happened. The same was initially true of *Return of the Streetfighter* (1976). This never had a chance of being seen in its complete form until recently. What remains intact is the Streetfighter's youth. A flashback scene shows his father being killed by a firing squad. Surugy is a halfbreed and becomes a renegade. About the only man he respects is karate master Masaoka (Masafumi Suzuki), a tiny, fat expert who fights Surugy to a standstill.

A new employer hires Surugy to kill the karate master and then attempts to kill the Streetfighter when he refuses. It is all because the villain is embezzling money from a fund to build an All-Asian Military Art Center. Surugy kills all the attackers except one. Jungo has returned, seemingly from the grave, to battle his enemy on a rain-soaked roof. The antihero falls off the building but is nursed to health by the love interest (Yoko Ichiji).

Although not fully recovered, he goes after the villain, cornering both him and Jungo on a ship. The final fight also occurs in the rain. Surugy is shot in the back. He does something which is edited out, and the film ends with him standing and the villains dead, the ship's deck awash in blood. What director Shigehiro Ozawa and writers Koji Takada and Steve Autry originally intended is clear enough, but the result was frustrating.

What remained was a potent performance by Chiba. Martial arts lovers were captivated by his screen persona, which was several notches more severe than Bruce Lee's. As Chiba played him, Terry Surugy was an animal, and not a tame one. Surugy's face would contort, incomprehensible cries, grunts, and groans would burble out of his mouth, and then he would try to tear something off. Surugy wasn't a graceful fighter, either—he went for the jugular every time, and if he couldn't get that, he'd shoot for a less polite target.

Someone that practical and unforgiving was attractive to jaded filmgoers. A certain *Streetfighter* fever occurred, leading to some ludicrous publicity. Sonny Chiba's official American biography had him sired by an unknown father. According to this public relations release, his mother was a dancer, and he was the leader of a street gang called the Kamikaze Lords. He learned kung-fu on the streets, but after a motorcycle accident he became a serious student of karate. The one-page bio went on to say that because of the public adoration following *The Streetfighter*'s release, Chiba became a Shinto monk living in the foothills of Mount Fuji.

Chiba left the mountain retreat long enough to make *The Streetfighter's Last Revenge* (Japan: *The Streetfighter Counterattacks*, 1977), by far the worst of the lot. This time the violence wasn't that bad, it was the story. The basic idea of a company creating synthetic heroin is workable, but the remainder of the picture was incomprehensible junk. His subsequent films weren't much better.

Champion of Death should have been a great film. It purported to tell the life story of Mas Oyama, and started well: Shambling into a 1940s karate tournament is an unkempt bum who surprises everyone with his karate expertise. But when it comes time for the final "no injuries" bout (against "Jungo" actor Milton Ishibashi), his opponent cheats by hitting him in the stomach and he retaliates by smashing the cheater in the eye.

From there the film goes right down the drain. After World War II, Oyama sees a

His uncle shoots him in the arm, and Henry Sanada bumps the guy off the cliff at the end of Roaring Fire.

beautiful girl with an American general. He rapes her and is arrested. In jail he's forced to fight another prisoner while handcuffed. When he is released, he apologizes to the woman he raped and she becomes his girlfriend. Then, one day a bull goes wild in the street (!) and Oyama saves a small child from a trampling by beating the rampaging bull to death.

When a student is killed defending Oyama's reputation, Oyama gets drunk and kills someone else. After his second imprisonment, he goes to the murdered man's farm and helps his wife and child until she says it's all right. Finally, the jealous karate man Oyama defeated at that first bout sends hired killers to get revenge. Oyama defeats them all, kills the villain, and stumbles away. The end.

Oyama should sue and Chiba should be ashamed. Of far more importance to the genre, Chiba created the Japanese Action Club, a combination martial arts school and stunt association. The members are stuntmen and instructors on Japanese films, and several of the students have contributed more to the genre than Chiba himself.

The first of these is Etsuko "Sue" Shiomi, who initially played the girl stabbed through by her brother in *The Streetfighter*. She went on to star in *Sister Streetfighter* (1978), playing a karate student searching for the murderer of her brother. Since her sibling was a narcotics agent, she stumbles across a drug ring. In tried-and-true Streetfighter tradition, she is at first beaten and thrown off a cliff. Coming back, she attacks the villains' headquarters with the help of Ninja Sonny Hibaki (Chiba), who knows the secret of invisibility.

Coming soon after that was *Sonny Chiba's Dragon Princess* (1980), which starts like a Streetfighter film but ends like *Champion of Death*. Chiba plays Shiomi's father, a bitter karate teacher who was crippled and handicapped years before in a rigged fight. The prologue shows the Tokyo fight, which took place in an atmospheric barn.

After the father defeats his opponent fair and square, villainous henchmen stab him in

the eye, hand, and chest. He survives and escapes with his infant daughter to New York, where he raises her on karate. On his deathbed he tells her to seek revenge. Shiomi goes back to Tokyo and teams up with a handsome young fighter played by Shoji

Kurata, and they eliminate the bad guys who harmed her father.

Although a person may be an accomplished fighter and a good actor or actress, parts like these can impede a career. The modern Japanese action film industry tried to do that with Chiba's second major protégé, but it just wouldn't stick. Hiroyuki "Henry" Sanada first starred in *Roaring Fire* (1981), a movie so dreadful it is fun to watch. Norry Suzuki wrote and directed the film, which billed Hiroyuki as "Duke" Sanada.

Duke is called to his father's deathbed to hear that he was kidnapped from his rightful family by the dying man. The false father tells him that his real parents and brother have been murdered by the Tokyo syndicate and that he should take revenge. Duke returns to the Orient to discover that his uncle is the head of a drug ring. Now the bad guy wants the family jewels to pay off his supplier, but only blind Chihiro (Sue Shiomi), Duke's sister, knows where they are.

Both brother and sister are taken hostage and tortured by Orientals dressed as Nazis. Duke escapes, but Chihiro is given an overdose. Teaming up with "Mister Magic" (Sonny Chiba), a ventriloquist, magician, and cop, Duke corners the villains on a cliff and knocks his evil uncle off. *Roaring Fire* could kill a normal man's career, but Sanada's talents were too great.

In 1982, Chiba was finally convinced to do a period piece of his own. This was *Shogun's Ninja*, and while it has some of the laughable ingredients that sank the earlier productions, it mostly showcased Sanada's martial arts skill. Chiba played the villain this time, and Shiomi played Sanada's heroic partner. Everyone but the hero and his love interest dies by the fade-out.

Following quickly was Sanada's call to China to make *Ninja in the Dragon's Den.*

Although a protégé of Sonny Chiba, Henry Sanada's best film was Ninja in the Dragon's Den, *where he got to spar with Conan Lee (right).*

Upon his return to Japan, he found a growing audience for his films. Plans were quickly made for Chiba himself to direct Sanada in subsequent movies. It was hoped that these films would be about something other than a cheated fighter taking revenge for a relative's death.

Meanwhile, the Japanese movie industry became less and less interested in quality of any kind. Akira Kurosawa had to look to Francis Ford Coppola and George Lucas to get enough money to make his monumental *Kagemusha: The Shadow Warrior* (1980). Other notable directors had to slave to find their budgets. Actors had to work on television or in pornography to survive.

The Chinese and Japanese cinema started at opposite poles and moved in opposite directions. The Chinese started with junk and worked toward excellence. The Japanese started with excellence and are moved toward junk.

America: From Texas Rangers to Power Rangers

The history of American martial arts movies is very simple. There was nearly nothing before Bruce Lee. The history of America and how it relates to martial arts films is also very simple. U.S. history is not about "excellence of self," it's about "excellence of *aim*." To put it bluntly, Americans have never been without the gun, and the huge majority of filmgoers really can't understand why two people would engage in a dance of death with limbs or swords when they could pull out a handgun and resolve matters much more easily.

To be fair, America's history is shorter than China or Japan's, and whenever the U.S. movie audience sees authentic martial arts in exciting, emotionally-involving films, they always respond. The man who proved that long before the name Bruce Lee was ever heard on American shores was Tom Laughlin.

Born in 1938, Laughlin became an actor in the 1950s, and was featured in several major Hollywood productions, including *Tea and Sympathy* (1956), *South Pacific* (1958), and the original *Gidget* (1959). His destiny, however, was in the exploitation genre. Giving up the rat race in "Tinseltown," he decided to make a movie on his own terms. He wrote, directed, produced, edited, and starred in *The Young Sinner* (1965), establishing his

ongoing theme of misunderstood youth.

Two years after that he hit the mother lode. *The Born Losers* (1967) was ostensibly about a motorcycle gang, but in it he played a heroic halfbreed named Billy Jack. The laconic, karate-trained wanderer keeps a gang from beating up a kid, only to get arrested for assault himself. This scenario was perfect for 1960s viewers, already all too frustrated by the establishment and the government.

The Born Losers made more than $10 million—an extraordinary amount of money for a mere exploitation film. It financed Laughlin's dream project, a movie he spent the next four years making and then distributing himself outside of the major studios' stranglehold. This would be the movie he is most remembered for: *Billy Jack* (1971).

He timed it perfectly. This story of an ex–Green Beret who fights rednecks and a corrupt sheriff's office to protect a Freedom School for hippie runaways (located on an Indian reservation, yet!) pleased alienated audiences. Obvious and superficial, yet heartfelt and well-meaning, *Billy Jack* pulled off an audacious accomplishment. It not only had the audiences cheering when Billy kicked in the faces of guffawing bigots who were pouring ice cream and flour over the heads of innocent Native Americans, it also introduced them to America's first martial arts hero.

Although Laughlin's movie making skills were only slightly better than his karate, he also featured real-life martial arts expert Bong Soo Han in a featured role. That allowed Bong to do the really fancy stuff while Billy got down to the serious business of kicking racists through walls. The movie cost $800,000 to make, and made more than $18 million.

The stage was set for *The Trial of Billy Jack* (1974), another labor of love from Laughlin and company. By this time, however, the director, writer, and star was replacing most of the action with strident sermons on equality. Though slicker than his previous fare and universally panned by confused critics, it made more than $28 million.

Laughlin should have quit while he was ahead. Instead, he announced extreme expansion plans into every media arena, heralded by *The Master Gunfighter* (1975), his pretentious remake of Hideo Gosha's great Japanese epic *Goyokin* (1969), transposed to the American West. Wandering all over the screen for a seemingly endless two hours, Laughlin's brooding, ruminating title character, armed with both a six-shooter and an incongruous samurai sword, did not excite his fans.

Naturally, another Billy Jack sequel was called for to recoup the losses. But *Billy Jack Goes to Washington* (1977), all two hours and thirty-five minutes of it, was too much talk and too little action, way too late. By this time, Bruce Lee and Lo Lieh had reached American shores, as had dozens of their poor relations. Inner-city movie theaters were filled with films that featured the words *Black Belt*, *Chinese*, or *Kung-fu* in their titles.

With the success of *Enter the Dragon* but the death of Bruce Lee, producer Fred Weintraub and director Robert Clouse tried nearly everything to keep riding the kung-fu

Bong Soo Han was brought to the public's attention by Tom Laughlin, and then made audiences laugh in the "Fistful of Yen" segment of the Kentucky Fried Movie.

wave they helped start. First, they featured Bruce's *Enter* costar Jim Kelly as *Black Belt Jones* (1974). The movie is still fondly remembered but was really pretty unimaginative. And why would the mob want to take over a martial arts school in the middle of Watts anyway?

Next they tried *Golden Needles* (1974). The burly Joe Don Baker starred as a brutish mercenary out to find a fabled Asian statue that held the promise of eternal youth. When that didn't work, they were all set to bring over Liu Chia Hui, also known as Gordon Lui, the charismatic star of *Master Killer* (H.K.: *Thirty-Sixth Chamber of Shaolin*) to star in *The Ultimate Warrior* (1975), only to have Warner Bros. pull another *Kung-fu* on them, that is, chicken out on casting a Chinese and replace him with a Caucasian instead.

In this case, it was that Gordon Lui look-alike Yul Brynner, who wound up wasted in the postapocalyptic sci-fi adventure. This fight-filled flop would have been great with Gordon strutting his martial art stuff. Unfortunately, Brynner made a much better king than kung-fu master. Following that fiasco, Weintraub reteamed with Jim Kelly for *Hot Potato* (1976), a dreadfully titled, painfully mediocre film with the actor demoted to playing one of three mercenaries hired to rescue a senator's daughter held captive in Thailand.

When that flick died at the box office, Weintraub and Clouse decided to shoot the works. Taking the plots from *Enter the Dragon* and *Hot Potato*, they hired three of the country's best real-life martial artists, threw in a burly black, a beautiful blonde, and a heinous Asian villain. They called it *Force Five* (1981), and it was not good. Their hearts were in the right place, but their filmmaking skills were not.

This painful waste squanders the abilities of World Heavyweight Karate Champion Joe Lewis, World Kickboxing Champion Benny "the Jet" Urquidez, and Richard Norton, not to mention Bong Soo Han, who played Reverend Rhee, an evil minister who lived on an island and had his own "Maze of Death." Sound familiar? Despite its obvious origins, had the script been half as clever and the fights half as good as they were in *Enter the Dragon*, the movie might have had a chance. It wasn't, they weren't, and it didn't.

Weintraub and Clouse never gave up, bless them. They tried Jackie Chan in *The Big Brawl* and, more recently, Cynthia Rothrock in *China O'Brian* and its sequel, but with similar results. It seemed that without Bruce Lee, Weintraub, Clouse, and the American martial arts movie was in a maze of death without a map.

NASTY, NEARLY NONEXISTENT NINJAS

American action film fans were in the head-lock of exploitation filmmakers. Relegated to the disdained genre called "chop-socky," even great classics from the Shaw Brothers Studio were constantly deemed "turkies" and "stinkers of the week" by *Siskel and Ebert*. Things seemed about to change with the publication of *The Ninja* (1980), Eric von Lustbader's evocative espionage novel which introduced mainstream fiction readers to the ancient sects of Japanese magician-spies.

Even though 007 fans had discovered ninja in *You Only Live Twice* (1967), it took Lustbader's novel to inspire Richard Zanuck and David Brown, producers of *Jaws*, to mount a multi-million-dollar, top-grade adaptation of the book thirteen years later. But it was not to be. Instead of the exotic, long-suffering, tragic, antiheroic spies they historically were, ninja were portrayed in cheap American exploitation films and lousy television shows as ludicrous superheroes and supervillains in hooded black pajamas who threw metal star-shaped darts like Frisbees. It was all because Cannon Films'

Israeli producers Monachem Golan and Yoram Globus rushed out *Enter the Ninja* (1981), dooming the American martial arts movie to more years of abuse.

"It was originally a script I wrote called *Dance of Death*," said undefeated karate champion Mike Stone. Golan made Stone the star, collected a crew, and sent everyone to the Philippines to start shooting. Three weeks later he fired them all. "Golan brought in a completely new crew from Israel, save for the sound man. He brought in Franco Nero to star and then rehired me for more money to stay on as action choreographer and stunt double."

Golan's rationale may have been that he didn't like the way the film was coming out. Stone had another point of view. "Apparently it's just the way they are," he explains, referring to Golan, who served as *Enter the Ninja*'s new director, and Yoram Globus, the producer. "From what I hear that's just their standard operating procedure."

The procedure continued to the patently absurd sequel, *Revenge of the Ninja* (1983). "*Enter the Ninja* turned out far better than I thought it would during filming," said Stone. "But when I got back to the States, I was told that Golan and Globus thought they had made a mistake: the ninja was the star, not the actor. They could have starred me and made just as much money. So they promised to do another film with me as the lead. They wanted Sho Kosugi, who I had hired to play the black ninja in the first film, to costar. Sho promised that he would not sign before I signed. But then Cannon promised to feature his son in the second film."

Suddenly, Stone was out of another picture and soured on the exploitation film business as a whole. Kosugi went on to a series of increasingly ineffectual ninja films, as did Cannon, releasing *Ninja III: The Domination* to a stunned audience in 1984. This tale of a ninja spirit who possesses a bodacious white woman was hilariously bad, but not so funny that it scared up much profit. It

Tom Laughlin kicks the stuffing out of rednecks in The Trial of Billy Jack.

served as the final coffin nail for any reputable ninja movie. In fact, the concept of the ninja was such a joke by the end of the century, that the only major movie featuring them was the lame comedy *Beverly Hills Ninja* (1997), one of the last films starring *Saturday Night Live* alum Chris Farley. Fittingly, the ninja movie disappeared almost as effectively and completely as the ancient ninja magician-spies themselves, though the insidious effect of Cannon Films on the development of American martial arts films was far from over.

NICE GUYS KICK FAST

After Bruce Lee died, everybody wanted a piece of him. To extend his legacy, some pro-

ducers used "clones." Others used his costars. Chuck Norris had worked with Lee in *The Wrecking Crew*, and, of course, in *Return of the Dragon*. As a result, Lo Wei, the prolific Chinese filmmaker who proclaimed to all who would listen that he launched Bruce as well as Jackie Chan, cast Norris as the beating, raping, robbing, and laughing villain of *Yellow Faced Tiger* (U.S.: *Slaughter in San Francisco*, 1973).

It contains some of Norris's best acting, despite the crudity of the movie as a whole. Chuck had started learning karate seventeen years prior and had become a respected world champion in 1968—holding the title for an impressive six years. After that, he decided to become a movie star in his own country, a decision he pursued with the same dedication with which he had pursued fame in the

martial arts arena.

In 1977 he got his big break in the aptly named *Breaker, Breaker*. It was a mediocre movie slapped together to take advantage of the minor trucking–CB radio–convoy craze that was sweeping the nation, but Chuck was likeable and his spinning back kick was top-notch. In this movie, as in almost all of its successors, many stuntmen would wait around just to get his cowboy boot in their faces.

Although his first movie came and went like a passing truck, *Good Guys Wear Black* (1978) got more attention. Director Ted Post, who had helmed Clint Eastwood's *Hang 'Em High* (1968) and *Magnum Force* (1973), decided to make Chuck his new "poor man's

Clint." He put Norris through his paces as John T. Booker, leader of the Black Tiger unit in Vietnam. Years later, after Booker had become a political science professor—a role that fit Norris like a sleeping bag—he discovers that a corrupt politico agreed to have his unit killed as part of the peace treaty negotiations.

Filled with plenty of movement, action, and violence, capped by the great stunt of Norris leap-kicking through a car's windshield, *Good Guys Wear Black* established Norris's credibility. He did the fight choreography himself in his next film, *A Force of One* (1979). It was a grateful flashback to his karate days, as he battles in a martial arts competition that serves as a front for drug pushers. In it, he fights Bill "Superfoot" Wallace, to much the same tepid response as when Jackie Chan fought Superfoot in *The Protector*.

Although not as exciting as his previous film, *A Force of One* was superior to anything else that could have been termed an American martial arts movie. Although limited as an actor, Norris cared about the movies he made, and he was intent on creating a breakthrough film—something that would bring him to the attention of the major studios.

The Octagon (1981) did it. With his wooden delivery and stolid screen presence, Norris seemed born to play a ninja, whose job is not to be noticed. Here, he plays a nearly somnambulistic fighter who resists taking on a present-day ninja camp despite the fact

Ken Takakura finishes off the Yakuza, as Robert Mitchum slumps exhausted behind him.

that all his loved ones are dropping like flies around him. It turns out that he was trained by a great ninjitsu sensei, whose own envious son decided to turn evil when Chuck beat him in their final teenage challenge.

The climatic assault on the Octagon-shaped ninja camp is a good one, reminiscent of the opening Vietnam War sequence in *Good Guys Wear Black*. And, despite the fact that several protagonists die because Norris's character refuses to take action through most of the film's first half, *The Octagon*

became his best-looking and one of his best-loved movies.

Following that, he reportedly wanted to do *The Destroyer*, the satiric, male-action, paperback book series about Remo Williams and Chiun, two masters of Sinanju—the sun source of all the martial arts. But the authors, Warren Murphy and Richard Sapir, weren't selling to Norris.

No, *Remo Williams: The Adventure Begins* began and ended in 1985, when Fred Ward and Joel Grey played the roles in the

Ed Parker tries to tear a guy's head off during Kill the Golden Goose. *And he's just the guy to do it, too.*

uninspired first film in an aborted series. "You could have made Rambo, instead you made Dumbo," author Murphy was quoted as saying to the film's producer after he left a screening.

Instead, Chuck Norris made *An Eye for an Eye* (1981), with Mako as Chan, an Asian mentor to the martial artist taking revenge for the killing of his policewoman girlfriend. Even with fights choreographed by Chuck and his brother Aaron, the result was tired. But, as uninspired as it was, the "Eyes" finally brought Norris to the attention of a major studio.

Columbia Pictures wanted him to star in

seemingly the worst script they could find: *Silent Rage* (1982). Here Chuck plays a stiff, honorable small-town sheriff whose justifiable killing of an insane ax murderer is complicated when some scientists in the town, for reasons that still defy explanation, bring the nutcase back to life as an unkillable monster.

While Chuck is breaking up a barroom brawl with his patented spin kick, the monster is running around town killing people in gruesome and gratuitous ways. Finally Norris kicks the guy down a well and the film ends with a freeze frame of the monster struggling in the water, where he apparently

is to this very day.

Words cannot describe the pandering nature of this production: stultifying to even fans of slasher movies. The only irony was that Chuck Norris was playing a live man like a zombie while Brian Libby, who portrayed the killer, was playing a zombie like a live man.

So much for Columbia, but Chuck wasn't out of the majors yet. MGM/UA released *Forced Vengeance* in 1983, which was originally called *The Jade Jungle*. Under any title, it was Norris's return to form under the direction of James Fargo, whose main claim to fame was helming the third Dirty Harry movie, *The Enforcer* (1976). Once again, Norris had been relegated to the role of a poor man's Clint Eastwood, but as each successive film was asking more and more from him in the way of acting talent, it was a part he seemed content to play.

Here he plays it as a Vietnam vet who goes berserk in a Hong Kong casino, only to be nursed back to mental health by the gambling den's kindly owners. Only after the casino operator and his son are killed by a mob eager to take over does Chuck exact the title action, protecting his mentor's surviving daughter and his own gorgeous girlfriend. This was a cautious, self-conscious attempt to distill everything that had been considered successful thus far in Norris's career, from the title on down to the lackluster fights, again choreographed by the Norrises.

Like Columbia, MGM/UA passed on Chuck's next picture. It was Orion who released *Lone Wolf McQuade* (1984), the movie which proclaimed to all the world that Norris *wanted* to be "Clint Lite." The plot, obstensibly based on the real-life exploits of Texas Ranger "Lone Wolf" Gonzales, was really a patchwork of Eastwood's Dirty Harry and "Man With No Name" spaghetti westerns. Even the soundtrack was reminiscent of Ennio Morricone's brilliant music for Sergio Leone's trilogy, *A Fistful of Dollars*, *A Few Dollars More*, and *The Good, the Bad, and the Ugly*.

The final affront to martial arts movie fans was that David Carradine played the villain. However, Carradine, who had been given Bruce Lee's role in both the *Kung Fu* television series and the awful film version of *The Silent Flute* (1974), would only sign on if he was not seen beaten on-screen. So he was blown up off-screen instead.

Norris was quoted as saying that Carradine was about as good a martial artist as he, Norris, was an actor. While that is a very brave thing to admit, it really doesn't say much for either man. Still, Chuck Norris had come far as a screen idol. He always tried his best and was a conscientious worker and an honorable professional. Of all the action stars of the time, he was one of the nicest to be around.

It was his inherent promise that attracted producer Raymond Wagner. Wagner was working with a remarkable young man named Andy Davis, whose only directing credit up until that time was a minor movie called *Stony Island* (1977). But they had a workable script called *Code of Silence* (1985), which Davis knew he could make great if it was filmed in his favorite city, Chicago. Surrounding Norris with veteran "Windy City" actors, and playing to his strengths, Davis made Norris's best movie—a crackling good, emotionally involving cop thriller.

Although low on martial arts, it was high on stunts and solid dialogue, probably the most memorable of which had Chuck growling, "If I need any advice from you, I'll beat it out of ya." Finally, after more than a decade, Chuck Norris had made a fine film—one that he could have used as a foundation for a career that could place him alongside the greats.

In the annals of action-film history, there have been some notable turning points. One of the most painful was George Lazenby choosing not to continue in the role of James Bond after *On Her Majesty's Secret Service*. One of the saddest was Burt Reynolds deciding to concentrate on increasingly stupid car chase movies despite great reviews in serious

acting skills, Norris may have doubted his ability to stand alongside the greats. Besides, would major studios allow his brother to continue choreographing and directing his pictures?

Whatever the reason, it was a terrible shame. While Andy Davis and Norris's action peers went on to bigger and better things, Chuck toiled in the slums of filmdom for years more. *Missing in Action* (1984), released prior to *Code of Silence*, but made afterward, was the first of his Cannon Films. Exploiting the real pain of missing-in-action Vietnam veterans, but cheering armchair soldiers of fortune, Chuck played a hero who went in to get them out.

Now forty-five years old, Norris went the way of so many martial arts stars by downplaying karate for gunplay. He cowrote his next Cannon loss leader, *Invasion U.S.A.* (1985), which had him taking on foreign terrorists in Florida. Not stopping for breath, 1985 also saw the release of *Missing in Action 2: The Beginning*, a middling prequel.

Norris was rapidly oversaturating himself in cinemas and video stores, so he decided on a different tact for the following year. *The Delta Force* (1986) was his best Cannon Film, as

dramas and romantic comedies. And then there was Chuck Norris deciding to turn his back on *Code of Silence* to make down-and-dirty movies for Cannon Films.

The rationales I've heard for this decision were manifold. Supposedly coming from a poor background, Norris chose to take money in the hand rather than pie in the sky. Golan/Globus apparently paid him $1 million for signing and promised $1 million a film. Then there was the question of insecurity. Always self-effacing when it came to his

well as one of Cannon's best. Monachem Golan returned to the director's chair for this combination of *The Dirty Dozen* and *Airport*, filling the cast with familiar but talented actors, ranging from *The Dirty Dozen*'s Lee Marvin to *Airport*'s George Kennedy to *The Poseidon Adventure*'s Shelley Winters. In the mix was also the great Martin Balsam, Robert Forster, and even Joey Bishop.

At two hours and ten minutes long, Golan was able to make two movies: one a fairly credible docudrama about the real skyjack-

Franco Nero doesn't look at all happy replacing Mike Stone as the star of Enter the Ninja.

ing that the film was based on, and the other a patriotic revenge fantasy that had Lee and Chuck saving the day. Wanting to follow up this milestone with something unexpected, Norris tried his hand at action comedy. *Firewalker* (1986) had the right idea, teaming him with Oscar-winning actor Louis Gossett Jr. to play wisecracking treasure hunters, but

234

it had a script that did no one justice.

Having shot their Cannon's load, it was back to the cinematic cellar for Chuck, whose filmography degenerated rapidly from there. He wrapped up his initial contract in 1988 with *Braddock: Missing in Action III* and *Hero and the Terror*, both which showed a creeping indifference on the part of cast and crew alike. It only got worse. *Delta Force 2* arrived in 1990, after a dreadful on-location helicopter accident which killed a stuntman. Norris's screen work would never be the same.

The Hitman (1991) was an embarrassment, combining a greater violence and profanity quotient with the "heartfelt" tale of a boy looking for a father figure. But even it wasn't as bad as *Sidekicks* (1993), with Chuck training a kid to be a responsible martial artist. But neither of those efforts could compare to the nearly unknown U.S.-Canada-Israel coproduction *Hellbound*, which went directly to video in 1993 and had Chuck fighting a demonic spirit. Finally, there was *Top Dog* (1995), a sad attempt to team cop Norris with a police pooch.

Thankfully, the saga of Chuck Norris has a happy ending. *Walker, Texas Ranger* went on the air in 1993, and was immediately decried as the most violent show on television. Its millions of watchers didn't care. Recycling *Lone Wolf McQuade* into a teen-friendly action hour, the nearly sixty-year-old karate champion found the success he had longed for in a medium that didn't intimidate him. Few expected greatness of Norris on television—his fans wanted good times and his bosses wanted good ratings—and that's what he gave them, in spades. With a spinning back kick, of course.

BRUSSELS MUSCLE

Back in 1986, when *The Delta Force* hit theaters, a little movie called *No Retreat, No Surrender* also came out. It was a laughable effort, ripped off from *Rocky IV* (1985), with an American martial arts team fighting a seemingly unstoppable Russian bruiser. The filmmaking skill on display was barely above home-movie level, but there was something about the intensity of the actor playing the Russian that stood out.

That was no accident. Twenty-five-year-old Brussels, Belgium, native Jean-Claude Van Varenberg had been preparing for that moment almost all his life. "I'd been dreaming of working in show business since I was ten years old," he said. "I started to work in France, but I thought America was the best place in the world to succeed as an action-film actor." The reason he felt that way could be summed up in one name: Arnold Schwarzenegger.

If Chuck Norris was the poor man's Clint Eastwood, Van Damme was certainly Arnold Lite. Like Schwarzenegger, he was a heavily muscled man with a heavily muscled accent. The comparison was not lost on Van Damme, who came to Hollywood with little money, no English, and the laughable Westernized name "Frank Cujo."

"I tried to look as charming as I could and started knocking on every door. It took me three years to even begin making a name for myself. I was obliged to take a lot of odd jobs, including as a taxi driver and a bouncer." He also got work in *Missing in Action 2*, where he asked Chuck Norris to serve as his agent ("I was very naive at the time," he admits) and in Schwarzenegger's *Predator* (1987), where he worked inside the alien suit.

"I was wearing the suit for three weeks before Kevin Peter Hall took my place," he explained, "because he's a lot taller than I am. This experience was a big step in my career. I remember that they asked me to do a very dangerous stunt and I was obliged to say no, because I had just been hired for *Bloodsport* and I was afraid I'd break my leg!"

Van Damme saved his leg for this Mark DiSalle production, which appeared in 1987. The earnest, decent-looking variation on

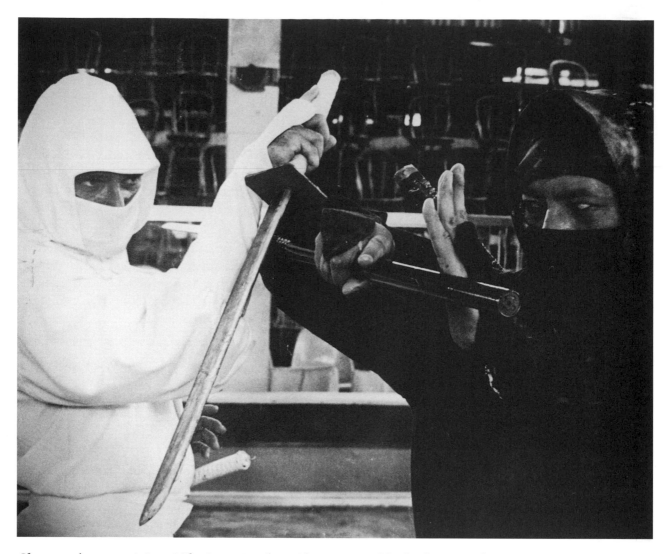

Close-up of enemy ninjas—Mike Stone in white, Sho Kosugi in black—for Enter the Ninja.

Enter the Dragon, which told of international martial artists competing in an illegal battle to the death, was silly and predictable, but enjoyable for all of that. And, of course, it had Van Damme giving it his all. Van Damme saw Chuck Norris's spinning back kick and raised him one: Jean-Claude could not only do a 180-degree flying front kick, ballerina-style, but he could do splits like nobody's business.

Van Damme hoped *Bloodsport* would be his ticket to the major leagues, but he toiled in independent exploitation features for years more. Up next came *Black Eagle* (1988), in which he played villain to one of Sho Kosugi's last gasps as a ninja hero.

Cyborg (1989) treated Van Damme a little better, in that it was Albert Pyun's bargain basement variation on *Terminator* (1984). On the one hand, Van Damme found his new director even more inspiring than the man who made *Die Hard* and *Predator*.

"John McTiernan is a wonderful, hardworking director," he said. "But I'm more impressed by Albert Pyun's work because he gets wonderful results without a big budget. He's a very resourceful person."

On the other hand, Pyun was not resourceful enough to avoid being second-guessed by his star. "I was very disappointed in *Cyborg* because I didn't like the editing," Van Damme admitted. "I had to go back and reedit it myself to make something coherent out of the film."

It would not be the last time Van Damme felt the need to do that to his director, nor would it be the last production Van Damme worked on where a stuntman was reported hurt. For the moment, however, he returned to work with Mark DiSalle, who directed his next picture, *Kickboxer* (1989). It worked along the same lines as *Bloodsport*, but to lessening returns. Even so, Van Damme's first five movies established him as an ambitious actor willing to do almost anything to get ahead.

Death Warrant (1990), coming from Canadian director Deran Serafian, was Van Damme's first movie with any real credibility. This was the old chestnut about a French-Canadian mountie being sent undercover into a prison to see who's killing convicts, but even aside from the clichéd plot, Van Damme's films were already of a recognizable type. He would glare, lose the first fight, do a split, do a slow-motion leaping front kick—and then win the second fight for no real reason other than the script said so.

Glare, splits, slow-motion kicks, and inexplicable victory was in abundance in his next film, the seminal *Double Impact* (1991), his first major-studio film. Although a man named Sheldon Lettich directed it, Van Damme contributed the screenplay and was credited as fight choreographer in this two-headed Universal Pictures release. Two-

What the ninja craze wrought: such minor movies as Beverly Hills Ninja *and the* Three Ninjas *series of kid flicks, such as* Three Ninjas: High Noon at Mega Mountain, *featuring J. P. Roeske II, Michael O'Laskey II, Matthew Botuchis, and Victor Wong.*

headed because in it Van Damme played twins separated soon after birth who are then reunited years later in Hong Kong to avenge the death of their father.

Given his script credit, Van Damme was more than likely responsible for the totally gratuitous dream sequence in which he cavorts in the nude with beautiful costar Alonna Shaw, as well as the scene where a bevy of leotarded beauties coo over his spandex-covered buttocks (while he does a split, naturally). Otherwise it was business as usual, with Van Damme inexplicably losing his first fight with Bolo Yeung, but winning the second despite discovering no new technique or any of his enemy's weaknesses.

As unfocused as *Double Impact* was, it had nothing on Van Damme's next movie, a story concocted by Van Damme himself, which has been called *A.W.O.L.*, *Wrong Bet*, and, finally, *Lionheart* (1991). Sheldon Lettich was still in the director's chair for this tale of a foreign legion deserter who descends into the world of illegal street fighting. And it, like its predecessors, is full of loving close-ups as well as repetitive fights that have no discernible dramatic structure. When the evil manageress bets against him in the final fight, Van Damme barks, "Wrong bet!" and trounces his opponent with, you guessed it, a slow-motion leaping front kick.

"*Lionheart* was my first film with a good publicity campaign," Van Damme maintained. "After it, people started taking me seriously in the industry."

It was hard to tell from his next movie. Its title, *Universal Soldier* (1992), was apt, because he had, by then, become Universal

It's Bill "Superfoot" Wallace as the villain versus Chuck Norris (left) in A Force of One.

The originally hairy Chuck Norris has met his match in Way of the Dragon.

Studio's good soldier, willing to appear in all manner of predictable, ultimately unsatisfying action fare. Here he shares the screen with Dolph Lundgren, whose *Rocky IV* role of the seemingly unbeatable Russian fighter Van Damme had borrowed for *No Retreat, No Surrender*. Their teaming did nothing to improve the uninventive tale of two super-soldiers, one who goes berserk and one who becomes heroic. Guess who played who.

Following that tepid tale, Van Damme wanted singular credibility, and he felt he knew the best way to get it. Having worked in Hong Kong, he was aware of that city's most kinetic and important action director. He also knew that the great filmmaker wanted to get out of Asia in the worst way. "I know the new government won't allow me freedom of speech nor freedom of creation," said John Woo before Hong Kong was

Chuck Norris (right) starts his solo star career in Breaker Breaker.

returned to mainland China in 1997. "I can't approve of totalitarianism, and I know people like myself will be crushed by the new regime."

Jean-Claude Van Damme and Universal Pictures gave him a way out. But it came with a price. That price was *Hard Target* (1993), and the version which eventually made it to American screens could not honestly be called "a John Woo Film." Reportedly, Woo delivered an over-two-hour first edit of this modern variation on *The Most Dangerous Game* (1932), i.e., people hunting people for sport. He was supposedly told that "We don't release Van Damme films which last over two hours." Weeks later he delivered an edit that was only about ten minutes shorter.

Despite enthusiastic responses from test audiences, Van Damme was said not to like it—not enough close-ups, apparently. Allegedly, Woo was locked out of the editing room, and Van Damme recut it himself. The final version came in at ninety-four minutes,

and could more honestly be called a Jean-Claude Van Damme film. The kind of emotion, effort, passion, and compassion which drive the complex heroes in Woo's other films was missing here. John Woo went on to make *Broken Arrow* (1996) and *Face/Off* (1997) for 20th Century–Fox, both of which made over $100 million each. *Hard Target* leveled out at about $30 million at the box office.

The aptly named *Nowhere to Run* (1993) came next, after Van Damme made an ironic cameo appearance in Arnold Schwarzenegger's first major bomb, *The Last Action Hero* (1993). Van Damme was reported to be very proud of the former, boring, film because it was based on a story by famous, wealthy screenwriter Joe Eszterhas (who gave us *The Jagged Edge* and *Basic Instinct*). It started a string of setbacks for Eszterhas, which included the reviled, campy failure *Showgirls* (1995). By this time, Van Damme was hardly doing any martial arts at all in his films, doggedly repeating the split and leaping front kick only when pressed.

240

The box-office returns for *Nowhere to Run* gave ample evidence of the dwindling audience's displeasure. Lucky for Van Damme, although unlucky for the audience, studios were embarking on a string of adaptations. Adaptations of great novels? Landmark television shows? Maybe even classic movies of the past? No, adaptations of video games.

Yes, the martial art movie maven's fondest wishes were coming true: great kung-fu video games were being made into big-budget motion pictures. Now, we would finally get to see some fast, exciting, authentic kung-fu action on the American screen, right?

Of course not. Viewers were better off playing the video games in the theater lobbies rather than sitting through the dreadful *Double Dragon* (1994), *Super Mario Brothers* (1993), and Van Damme's own *Street Fighter* (1994). Not even the respected screenwriter Stephen E. de Souza could help *Street Fighter*, especially since he was also directing. It was even more tragic that this was Raul Julia's last film before his untimely death. The movie also wasted the talents of Benny "the Jet" Urquidez, who is merely glimpsed in one mob scene. One stuntman reported that he was told not to kick so well, lest he show up the foreground stars.

Still, Van Damme didn't have to worry about the flat box-office take, since he was already working on *Timecop* (1994), the first of two collaborations with director Peter Hyams. This effort seemed initially promising, since the director was known for both jaunty action comedies (*Running Scared*), as well as exciting, if implausible, sci-fi thrillers (*Capricorn One*, 1978, and *Outland*, 1981, among others). And, for awhile, it appeared that *Timecop*, a tale of time-traveling police, might be the breakout movie Van Damme had been waiting for.

Then the finale arrived with all the logic of a Bugs Bunny cartoon. Jean-Claude had gone back in time to save his murdered wife, seemingly setting the stage for a clever climax in which he could counter every villainous ploy, since he knew what was going to happen. But that wasn't the way it turned out. Instead, Van Damme's character stumbled through an absurd climax where, just as in every other disappointing Jean-Claude effort, things occur simply because they do.

Although a woeful disappointment, the movie did spawn a television series, minus Van Damme's participation, which didn't last its first season.

Before all the critical and box-office drubbing occurred, however, Van Damme and Hyams were already hard at work on their next film, a *Die Hard* knockoff titled *Sudden Death* (1995). Jean-Claude plays a fire inspector whose daughter is taken hostage by a quipping extortionist who threatens to blow up the Stanley Cup Playoffs, as well as the attending U.S. vice president. Incredibly, the film doesn't even wait for the climax to squander its credibility. Things start getting stupid within the first half-hour, and never recover.

Drastic measures needed to be taken. Prior to Hyams, Van Damme had worked with some of the greatest action directors, and the results were still impotent. There was only one thing left to do: he would have to be directed by the person who knew him best—himself.

"Directing is my dearest wish," Van Damme proclaimed. "When I am the director, I'd love to hire unknown actors and make them stars. I think it's a wonderful thing to do and I'm sure it's possible with a good script."

The Quest (1996) made no new stars, and the script was a warmed-over 1930s version of *Bloodsport*. Although the production proudly proclaimed the participation of fifteen of the world's greatest martial arts champions, you couldn't tell by the finished work. As usual, Van Damme merely swings his arms and legs the same way from the first fight to the last—the only difference being when his opponent falls down. It wasn't so

The great images of Good Guys Wear Black. *First there was this picture of Chuck Norris leading his Black Tigers into battle.*

much that *The Quest* was awful, it was merely unremittingly dull and uninvolving.

Jean-Claude knew what to do, however: he turned back to Hong Kong. If he was the poor man's Schwarzenegger, then he would get the director known as the poor man's John Woo to helm his next production. Ringo Lam directed *Maximum Risk* (1996) and managed to invest what action scenes there were with some verve. Unfortunately, all too much of this middling thriller was taken up with intrigue as Van Damme falls back into his *Double Impact* ploy of an identical twin brother.

Although everyone who saw it agreed that this was probably his best film in a long time, not *enough* people saw it. More drastic measures needed to be taken to get people to the theaters. Okay, what if a script called *The Colony* was written, borrowing heavily from Patrick McGoohan's cult TV show *The Prisoner*? And what if Van Damme got Tsui Hark, the man known as the Steven Spielberg of Hong Kong, to direct it? And, just to be on the safe side, what if National Basketball Association "bad boy" Dennis Rodman was somehow crammed into the plot?

The result would be *Double Team* (1997), and the result would be bad. Tsui Hark, like John Woo, was anxious to get out of Hong Kong, but, unlike Woo, he didn't just have Jean-Claude to contend with. He had Van Damme, Dennis Rodman, *and* Mickey Rourke to control. Rourke played the slimy villain of the piece, a man so addle-brained that he lures Van Damme to a crumbling coliseum where Jean-Claude's newborn son is being held hostage amid littered land mines as well as a roving killer tiger(!).

Then, what should appear to an astonished audience's eyes but an inexplicable row of soda machines, which the heroes use to protect themselves from the exploding land mines. It is one of the most incredibly arrogant product placements in film history, but

finally released, the muddled, boring story of spies trying to smuggle miniature bombs in counterfeit designer jeans strained the credulity of even Van Damme's (not to mention Tsui Hark's) biggest fans.

Following that fiasco, Jean-Claude's next film, *Legionnaire* (1999) was released directly to video. It showed that Van Damme is still kicking, albeit barely. Although, at the time of this writing, he had just finished filming the long-delayed sequel to *Universal Soldier*, he really cannot be considered a great martial arts movie star. His true interests, and talents, seem to lie elsewhere.

THE AIKIDO ACE

The rumor is intriguing. Arguably, the most powerful man in the Hollywood of 1987 was Michael Ovitz, agent extraordinaire. Some have said that he was learning aikido from a man named Steven Seagal. Some have written that a man named Steven Seagal was serving as Ovitz's bodyguard. In either case, shortly after Ovitz reportedly arranged to secure the director (Richard Donner) and star (Mel Gibson) of *Lethal Weapon* for Warner Bros., the story goes that the agent strongly suggested that they consider making his aikido teacher and/or bodyguard their next great action star. Whether or not this story is true, a very entertaining movie called *Above the Law* premiered in 1988. It starred a thirty-six-year-old aikido expert named Steven Seagal who was absolutely fascinating to watch. Aikido seemed designed for American action movies, since it took the roundhouse punch-

it was obvious by that time that no one behind the camera really cared. They just wanted this circus to get out of town. Audiences, apparently, felt the same way.

Even so, Tsui Hark was so anxious to stay out of Hong Kong that he even signed on to direct Van Damme's following film, accurately titled *Knock Off* (1998). Those this insane film didn't repel, it perplexed. Originally rumored to be an action musical comedy (!?), when the finished work was

Chuck Norris has the sword and Tadashi Yamashita has the sais, *in* The Octagon.

es that had been U.S. fight choreographers' stock-in-trade for more than fifty years and turned them back on themselves.

It was the hand-to-hand equivalent of a wild-mouse roller coaster, spinning the antagonists in tight, fast, vicious circles. Unlike some other so-called American martial arts movie stars, it was instantly apparent to audiences that this guy, whoever he was, knew what he was doing.

Who he was, was a man who had been learning karate and aikido since he was seven years old. By the time he was thirty-one he had opened an aikido dojo in Sherman Oaks, California, and whether he was teaching or guarding Michael Ovitz, by 1987 he was working with Andrew Davis on a story which would become the script for his first starring role.

That wasn't all. Not only would he help write the story, he would also be the producer and martial arts choreographer, while Davis would direct. It was more than possible that the studio didn't expect much from this collaboration. After all, what had the two done before? Seagal had been the martial arts coordinator on the samurai sword picture *The Challenge*, while Davis had merely managed to make Chuck Norris look great in *Code of Silence*. But other than that, what?

Mako (left) looks tired and Chuck Norris looks pained in An Eye for an Eye.

Davis had been the director of photography on some minor independent exploitation movies like *Cool Breeze* (1972), *Hitman* (1972), and the gangster thriller *Lepke* (1975). Since the Norris picture in 1985, he had no major credits to speak of in three long years. The odds were that *Above the Law* would drop into the ocean of cinema without causing a ripple.

The odds were wrong. From a final screenplay penned by himself, Steven Pressfield, and Ronald Shusett, the fledgling director spun gold. Set in his beloved Chicago, Davis weaved an entire life around Seagal, whose career-long concerns were already evident. More than just a well-trained, no-bull cop, his character was also a caring and religious husband and father.

Long before Quentin Tarantino worshiped actress Pam Grier in *Jackie Brown* (1997), Davis cast her as Seagal's partner in this tale of an obsessed cop trying to take down an FBI-protected drug lord. And long before she hit gold in such films as *Total Recall* (1990) and *Basic Instinct* (1992), Davis cast Sharon Stone as Seagal's understanding wife. The rest was up to Seagal, and he delivered.

Whether blasting away with an automatic or clothes-lining some thugs, the aikido ace made all the other Hollywood action stars look like pretenders. Outside of a rushed, perfunctory climax, and a strange finale

where Seagal lectured the press on corruption, *Above the Law* was a complete success. Critics and fans alike sat up and took notice, while Seagal moved quickly to show that he needed neither Ovitz nor Davis to shine. Warner Bros., however, seemed less than enthusiastic about acknowledging their new star's charisma.

For the aptly named *Hard to Kill* (1990), the basically unknown Bruce Malmuth was in the director's chair, while the star took the additional credits of screenwriter and martial arts choreographer. Both the script and action were in good hands. Its martial arts

Chuck Norris flashes his famous foot in the face of a villain in An Eye for an Eye.

highlight was an engaging scene set in a liquor store where Seagal taunts a punk into attacking him, because the best aikido requires an attack to react against.

Playing another take-no-prisoners cop,

Seagal is blasted into a coma by a corrupt politician who he had been investigating. When he awakens seven years later, his muscles haven't atrophied, but his family has been slaughtered. The remainder of the

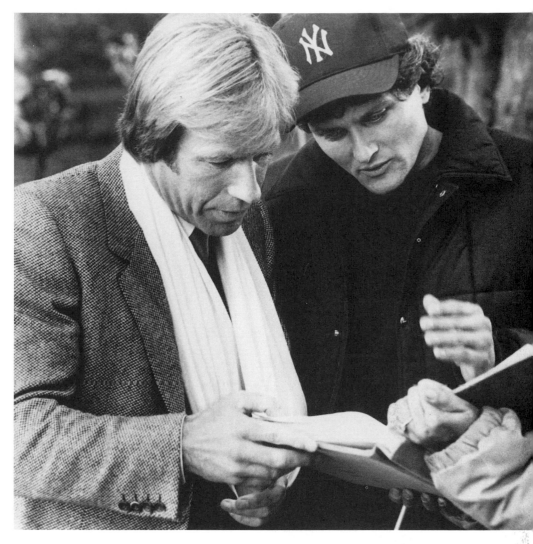

film's ninety-five minutes was a very satisfying hunt for revenge.

Less satisfying was some *The Making of Hard to Kill* footage, which showed a frustrated Seagal complaining about the studio's apparent lack of cooperation with the actor and writer's vision. It was not surprising, then, that for his third movie, *Marked for Death* (1990), he was back in the producer's chair and Warner Bros. was not involved. Unfortunately, it was the actor's weakest film thus far, with an uncomfortable plot pitting Seagal against Jamaican voodoo drug runners. Nevertheless, the aikido on display was just as enjoyable and kinetic.

To rectify the plot problem, Seagal returned to the screenwriter role for a new movie he called *The Price of Our Blood*. The studio, however, didn't want to lose the catchy three-word titles of his filmography, so when the movie reached cinemas in 1991 it was titled *Out for Justice*. Basically a very busy twenty-four hours in the life of a Brooklyn cop, the film was aptly named. In fact, Seagal interrupts his credit sequence stakeout to hurl an abusive pimp through the windshield of the creep's own Cadillac.

From there the plot unfurls into a *mano-a-mano* confrontation between Seagal and a drugged-out mob maniac who was once the cop's childhood friend. Perhaps knowing that this would be his last word in the aikido department, Seagal does some beautiful hand-to-hand work, tearing up a pool hall not once, but twice. He also saves the best for last. Finally cornering the villain (William Forsythe) in a tenement kitchen, Seagal very carefully, very methodically, takes him apart in a series of master shots—camera angles that take in the entire room—so you can see his every move and every result of those moves.

Forsythe is beaten and humiliated through the power of aikido, creating one of the most pounding, brutal, and memorable scenes in Seagal's filmography. After that, it appeared as if he knew that he would be forever relegated to the subcellar of chop-socky movies if he didn't make a major change. Director Andrew Davis seemed to realize the same thing. Following *Above the Law*, he had had

247

CHUCK NORRIS

DAVID CARRADINE

LONE WOLF McQUADE

AN 1818 PRODUCTION of a STEVE CARVER FILM · CHUCK NORRIS · DAVID CARRADINE · BARBARA CARRERA · LEON ISAAC KENNEDY
LONE WOLF McQUADE · Also Starring L.Q. JONES · Music by FRANCESO DE MASI · Screenplay by B.J. NELSON · Story by H. KAYE DYAL and B.J. NELSON
Produced by YORAM BEN-AMI and STEVE CARVER · Directed by STEVE CARVER · Prints by DE LUXE

Chuck Norris has a problem. He seems to want to be Clint Eastwood. First there already is a Clint Eastwood—the public doesn't need another. Second, Chuck Norris's personality is not Eastwood's. Norris has to fake it—something he is not good at. Nowhere is this problem more apparent than in Lone Wolf McQuade.

In this case, the so-called little man was a disgraced ex-Navy SEAL who had become a battleship cook.

According to an article by the scripter, it was Jones's idea to disguise himself as a rock singer, while it was Busey who chose to kill the captain of the ship while dressed in drag. Seagal's contribution was the demand that a bare-breasted *Playboy* bunny be brought onboard in a hollow cake, instead of sticking to Lawton's subplot concerning a female Coast Guard officer's heroics.

That bunny was played by real playmate-of-the-month-turned-actress Erika Eleniak, who gave a winning performance despite her less than demure entrance. She is then left to marvel at Seagal's mayhem along with the rest of the audience. There is less aikido than ever before, but the stars and director more than make up for it with big booms and many, many bullets. It turned out to be the most successful movie of Steven Seagal's career, as well as its apex.

With its popularity came the freedom for Seagal to call the shots on his next picture. That movie didn't appear until two years later, and left audiences gaping in wonder. *On Deadly Ground* (1994) was Seagal's first directing job, and he promoted it as a serious ecological statement. Being the story of an oil rig specialist who tangles with an insane corporate polluter, it had all the ingredients of a solid, socially-redeeming spectacle. It became, however, a spectacle of another sort.

From the very moment Seagal appears on-screen, background characters literally can't

another few frustrating years. He managed to get *The Package* (1989) made, but it was a forgettable suspense thriller starring Gene Hackman as a military man trying to prevent the assassination of Boris Yeltsin. After that, nothing.

Taking a script by J. F. Lawton, Davis hired Tommy Lee Jones and Gary Busey to play villains. Together with Seagal, they added level upon level of characters until *Under Siege* (1992) became the best "big" action movie of its type since *Die Hard*. Its "type" was the terrorists-take-over-something-big-so-a-lone-"little"-man-can-save-the-day plotline.

248

"David Carradine is about as good a martial artist as I am an actor," Chuck Norris was quoted as saying. Sadly, they were evenly matched in Lone Wolf McQuade.

stop talking about how great he is. What at first appears to be an odd directing and editing choice becomes an annoying distraction by the middle of the movie. Finally, when an evil mercenary team's leader interrupts the climax to deliver a monologue on how incredibly talented Seagal's character is, it becomes a laughable sign of insecurity. Adding fuel to that theory is a perplexing dream sequence in which Seagal's character

is "reborn" in a river of life wearing neck-to-ankle leather while all the sexy "Indian" girls in the background are totally nude.

Seagal destroys an entire oil foundry, kills all the corporate executives affiliated with it, and what happens? Is he arrested and jailed like some sort of latter-day Billy Jack? Oh, no: He is celebrated and caps the film with a speech about alternate energy sources—a diatribe that comes off less than credibly because

Jean-Claude Van Damme prepares to break a stuntman's elbow under the watchful eyes of the Hard Target *crew and director John Woo (center, in white shirt).*

of all the absurdities which preceded it.

Suffice to say that the film did not reach the box-office heights of *Under Siege*. Therefore, a sequel of that hit was hastily called for. Thankfully, Andrew Davis did not need to direct it. He had gone on to direct the wildly successful movie adaptation of the television show *The Fugitive* (1993), starring Harrison Ford and Tommy Lee Jones, so *Under Siege 2: Dark Territory* (1995) was directed by Geoff Murphy. It placed Seagal's cook character on a train, which was soon to be taken over by many incongruous terrorists.

Although far better than *On Deadly Ground*, the effective and entertaining new thriller also didn't approach the financial success of the original. Drastic steps were required and, to his credit, Seagal took one. He put in a guest-starring stint in the suspenseful *Executive Decision* (1996), starring Kurt Russell and directed by longtime editor Stuart Baird. Playing a self-sacrificing government

The stare that launched a dozen movies: Jean-Claude Van Damme.

commando, Seagal appeared in only about fifteen minutes of the thriller, but to great effect.

That successful gambit completed, the next step was supposed to be a comic "buddy cop" picture along the lines of *48 Hours* (1982), but when *The Glimmer Man* appeared in 1996, it was light on the comedy, very light on the "buddy," and extremely heavy on the kind of action which had become associated with Seagal in the films prior to *Under Siege*. There was only one major difference: rather than film Seagal's aikido in one long shot, each of his fights were now torn by dozens of fast editing cuts, so the beauty and smoothness of the moves were all but obscured. It was hard to tell what was actually happening anymore, and even harder to care.

The good feelings Seagal had engendered in *Executive Decision* were all but dashed by his 1997 effort, *Fire Down Below*, which was, for all intents and purposes, a sequel to *On Deadly Ground*. Here Seagal was a full-fledged Environmental Protection Agency agent (seemingly with a license to kill) going up against another apparently psychotic corporate polluter. Only this time, producer Seagal throws in as much country music as he does aikido, seemingly trying to create a latter-day B western in the tradition of Roy Rogers or Gene Autry pictures. He even dons a buckskin jacket, pulls out an ol' guitar, and sings a couple of tunes he penned himself.

The film's lack of success at the box office

251

made an orphan of Seagal's next movie, *The Patriot* (1999), which could find no distributor to schedule it in movie theaters. It finally had its American premiere on the Home Box Office cable channel. There, fans could enjoy Seagal as one of the world's top immunologists (?!) who becomes a small-town doctor to get away from the machinations of big-government disease-control types. But when a militant crackpot spreads a deadly disease, he needs all his killing and healing skills to save the day.

The twenty-first century finds Steven Seagal in a quandary. As he becomes more intent on making socially relevant action films, his unconvincing plots, characters, and contrived action only serve to trivialize his important messages.

TWENTY-FIRST CENTURY U.S. ACTION

So if not Norris, Van Damme, or Seagal, who will drag the American martial arts movie kicking and chopping into the new millenium? There is certainly no shortage of candidates. Thanks to the insatiable need for product on cable movie channels and in video stores, earnest amateur actors like Tae-bo master Billy Blanks, Gary Daniels, and Don "the Dragon" Wilson are filling the airwaves and the racks with titles ranging from *Bloodmoon* to *Ring of Fire*—not to mention their inevitable sequels. New talents, like Robert Samuels, Ron Hall, and Vincent Lyn are waiting for their chance to show what they can really do.

On other channels, syndicated television series like *Hercules: The Legendary Journeys* and *Xena: Warrior Princess* gleefully "borrow" from Jet Li and Jackie Chan movies,

Steven Seagal in the days just prior to Above the Law, *showing what he can do in his West Hollywoo dojo.*

even going so far as procuring Huang Fei Hong's patented "no shadow kick" for their screeching heroine. Gleaning dramatic concepts from Pro Wrestling, the syndicated TV series *WMAC Masters* imagined a world where martial artist battles martial artist when they aren't trying to help teens discover their self-esteem.

In the meantime, kung-fu managed to make its way into American cinemas in "disguise." It started in 1989, when Jackie Chan was rebuffed by U.S. theater owners. His producer was told that they would never show a film with an all-Asian cast. Golden Harvest Studios considered its options and decided, "Well, what if they don't know that the heroes are Asian? What if the kung-fu fighters were turtles?"

Kevin Eastman and Peter Laird had originally created the *Teenage Mutant Ninja Turtles* by accident, but when this hodgepodge of seemingly incongruous themes took on a life of its own, they independently produced a black-and-white comic book which showcased their love of great martial arts movies. The public responded to these "heroes on a half shell," and especially to Eastman and Laird's honest conviction.

Once a savvy marketing genius ran with the idea, these pizza-loving creatures, Donatello, Leonardo, Michelangelo, and Raphael, named for famous artists, were everywhere—which was where producer Kim Dawson and writer Bobby Herbeck found them. Making a deal with all concerned, they hit real paydirt by signing director Steven Barron. Barron became famous with a series of innovative music videos, including Dire Straits' *Money for Nothing*, A-ha's *Take on Me*, and Michael Jackson's *Billie Jean*. His first movie, however, was a different story. *Electric Dreams* (1984) was hobbled by a silly script, but there was no question that it was the work of an original thinker.

His thought for the Turtles was simple: the more outlandish the characters, the more

Jr., and Kenn Troum. "You could hardly see in there and you could hardly breathe," said Troum, an enthusiastic newcomer. "And, oh yeah, you sweat buckets as well."

While Pat Johnson, veteran of all four *Karate Kid* pictures (1984, 1986, 1989, and 1994) handled the stunts and martial arts, the kung-fu consultants were Chun Wai "Brandy" Yuen and Tak Wai "Billy" Liu. "They all conferred together," said Troum, "but it was usually Brandy and Billy who worked with us on the more intricate kicks and hits." This combination of American and Hong Kong experience lent an authenticity which audiences around the world appreciated. The rest depended on Herbeck and Todd W. Langen's script, which balanced just the right amount of heartfelt plot with humorous absurdity. After all, these were five-foot-tall turtles. Helping along was Barron's casting of likeable unknowns like Judith Hoag and Elias Koteas in the human roles of reporter April O'Neil and merce-

realistic the atmosphere and photography had to be. It would be a concept that he had to continually fight for, but one that helped make the first *Teenage Mutant Ninja Turtles* (1990) the only one worth watching. The animatronic suits for the leading characters were made by teaming up with Jim Henson's Creature Shop. But to fill those tiny suits required very small, very capable martial artists.

They were three Asians and three Americans: Yuen Mo Chow, Choi Nam Ip, Chi Wai Chiang, Reggie Barnes, Ernie Reyes nary Casey Jones. It came together in an international hit, which the producers then squandered with two inferior sequels that upped the level of absurdity while diminishing the realistic look of the original.

Meanwhile, Tokyo producers were desperately trying to convince American television stations—with little success—that the many teams of costumed superheroes that were beloved in Japan would be as big a hit in America. The biggest costumed superhero in Japan, in both size and success, was Ultraman, but despite many attempts to

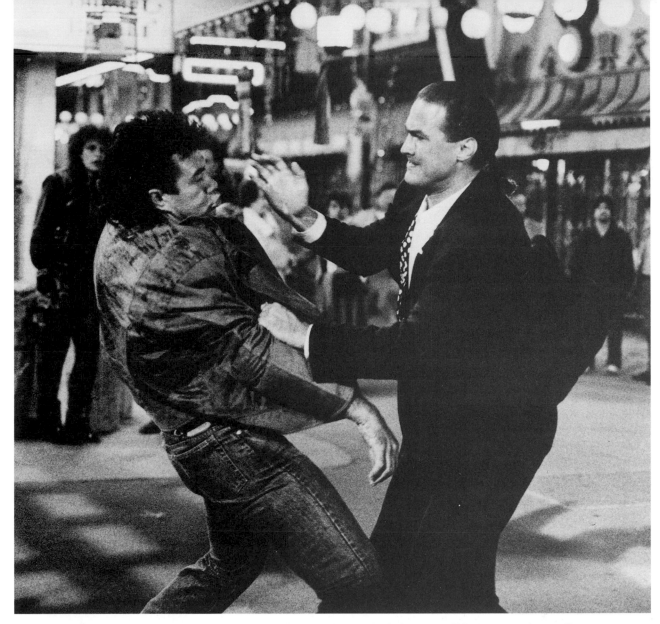

Steven Seagal wants a pesky thug to hear a little something aikido has to tell him in Hard to Kill.

Westernize him, his truncated, dubbed appearances on English-speaking television and in American comic books were quickly forgotten.

The problem seemed to be the pesky differences between Eastern and Western cultures. To see one of these Japanese superhero shows was essentially to see them all. They all started with an interchangeable alien villain deciding to take over the earth. The only thing standing in their way is a group of supernaturally powered teenagers. So every week a new monster is dispatched to defeat the heroes and destroy the population.

The first half of these efforts was all setup and the second half was all action. Mobs of biodegradable thugs are thrown against the heroes to "soften them up," only to be defeated easily. The main monster would then appear and trash the town as well as the costumed teens, until the kids banded together into a gigantic robot. The monster would then grow magically to giant size and slug it out until the team blew him up. Then there would be just enough time for a joke or important life lesson.

Television executives took one look at these redundant, silly shows—albeit colorful and action-packed—before laughing them out of their offices. They even tried getting

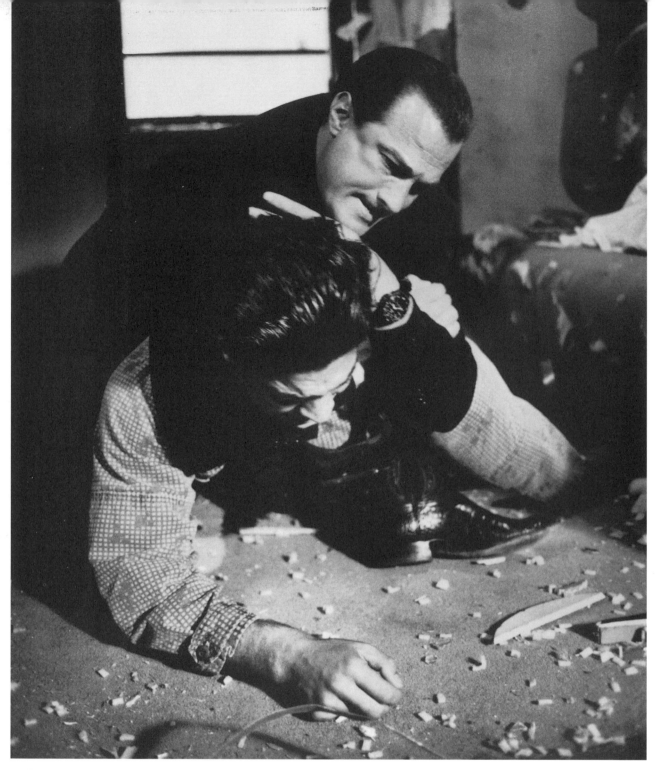

A henchman gets all choked up when he meets Steven Seagal during Under Siege 2.

American producers to laugh with them rather than at them. One team of costumed heroes was redubbed as a joke. Following the lead of Woody Allen's *What's Up Tiger Lily* (1966), in which Allen hilariously redubbed a bad Japanese espionage movie, members of the SCTV comedy troupe did the same for thirteen half-hour episodes of a high-flying Japanese television series. The result was shown very late on weekend nights on the USA cable network, and then disappeared entirely.

Finally the Saban company convinced Fox television to air what they were calling

Seagal shows off his disarming personality in Fire Down Below.

Mighty Morphin Power Rangers. They had cleverly kept the Japanese action sequences while refilming the noncostumed moments with an interracial, English-speaking cast. In fact, to make it even more attractive to its young audience, they made one of the boy heroes—the yellow ranger—into a girl. In the first few seasons, it was obvious to anyone who knew the show's origins that the fully-suited yellow ranger was not much of a woman.

It didn't matter. As the long-suffering producers figured, the series was a big success in the States, spawning two movies as well as several different series. By the time the first film, *Mighty Morphin Power Rangers* (1995), appeared, the series had run out of original Japanese footage. Instead, California film-makers were producing one hundred percent of the material, allowing an actual woman in the yellow ranger's suit and more home-grown acrobatic martial arts to carry the day.

Director Bryan Spicer kept things colorful and in motion, while filling the supporting cast with personable, attractive actors. He also added some nice feature-film touches, such as having the fodder villains splatter when they were defeated, as opposed to just disappearing, which they always did on the TV series. The final nod to an adult audience came with the in-joke ending in which victory was won by pushing the "big red button" inside the struggling robotic power ranger, causing the big machine to knee the monstrous villain in the groin.

Turbo: A Power Rangers Movie (1997) was

A conscientious sculptor at Jim Henson's Creature Shop prepares the mold for a teenage mutant ninja turtle.

Mortal Kombat (1995), the only halfway decent movie adaptation of a video game. It helped that the video game itself had more of a back story than most, but it didn't help that it featured more blood than a date with a starving vampire.

The filmmakers, led by director Paul Anderson, wanted to attract the under-seventeen crowd, so meaningless movement replaced the bone-snapping thrills of the game. Aiding greatly in the film's acceptance was costar Robin Shou, the only one of the leads who actually knew a little kung-fu, and the pounding musical soundtrack, which raised goose bumps if nothing else did.

Although Shou contributed some decent wushu to the special-effects-laden mix, nothing made much sense in the finished film, and the seemingly slapped-together script constantly undercut whatever involvement the audience might feel. It was even worse in *Mortal Kombat: Annihilation* (1997), which made almost no sense and wasn't even remotely exciting. By then the kung-fu had been reduced to mere movement, with no intellectual or emotional reason for being. For all its meaning, the fists and feet might as well have been guns.

released to celebrate the ongoing success of the series, but it, like *Teenage Mutant Ninja Turtles II: The Secret of the Ooze* (1991) and *Teenage Mutant Ninja Turtles III: Turtles in Time* (1993), suffered from too little involving action, too many campy characters, and too much cheesy comedy.

Finally, as the world has rolled relentlessly toward the new century, a final hope of martial arts movie mastery appeared with

Then *Rush Hour* premiered in movie theaters, one month after the success of the martial arts–vampire movie *Blade* (1998), while, a month after that, *Martial Law* premiered on CBS television. With their success, the martial arts genre was suddenly fair game for producers all over the world. Within the season, *Mortal Kombat* was a syndicated television show with its mysti-

The Teenage Mutant Ninja Turtles—*Raphael, Leonardo, Michelangelo, and Donatello—celebrate success with Splinter, their Aged Mutant Ninja Master Rat.*

cal, mythical setting intact, and Wesley Snipes was already planning a return to his role as the half-vampiric, sword-slashing vampire killer, Blade.

Meanwhile, on other TV channels, handsome Adrian Paul had set female fans' hearts aflutter with his samurai-sword stylings in a long-running *Highlander* series, while Elizabeth Gracen did the same for male viewers in the *Highlander II* follow-up series, filled with sword slashing of all sorts. Finally, despite the tragic death of Brandon Lee, *The Crow* was given new life on television with Mark Dacascos—a veteran of many martial arts exploitation films—as the avenger from beyond the grave.

The very existence of all these movies and television shows have proven just how pervasive martial arts movies have become around the world. The influence of Bruce Lee, Jackie Chan, and all their contemporaries have permeated world cinema from Australia to Zanzibar. Kung-fu moves from Jet Li and Michelle Yeoh are being attempted in French cinema, as well as the crazy three-hour action-musical-romances which premiere in India every day.

The kind of filming and editing Sammo Hung can create is being taken apart and put back together by everyone from Oliver Stone to Sylvester Stallone. Every actor who picks up a prop gun remembers the cool, charming style of Chow Yun-Fat, while their action directors try to copy the sizzling emotion of John Woo. And, although no one has managed to create the *Star Wars* of martial arts movies in America, it hasn't been from a lack of trying.

Johnny Yong Bosch, David Yost, Karan Ashley, Jason David Frank, Amy Jo Johnson, and Steve Cardenas star as one group of Mighty Morphin Power Rangers.

As long as mild-mannered actors strive to be supra-heroes with powers and abilities far beyond the normal man, there will be great martial arts in movies. As long as Batman and Spiderman strive to become cinema icons, there will be great martial arts in movies. As long as heroes strive to vanquish evil, there will be great martial arts in movies.

Why the martial arts movie? Because it can excite, engage, inspire, and free an audience like no other genre. Because martial arts, quite simply, is the optimum in human defense. There is no better or more effective way for a protagonist to use their body to set things right or to see that justice triumphs. Then, as now, that is what it is all about—exhilaration.

Afterword

A lot has happened since I finished writing the new version of this book. The Hong Kong-ing of Hollywood moved at an ever-increasing pace at the same time that there were unavoidable publication delays.

Jackie Chan followed *Rush Hour* with *Shanghai Noon* (2000) and *Rush Hour 2* (2001), not to mention his Hong Kong–based productions of *Gorgeous* (1999) and *The Accidental Spy* (2001). He even got a Saturday morning animated series, Jackie Chan Adventures, on television.

Jet Li followed *Lethal Weapon 4* with *Romeo Must Die* (2000), *Kiss of the Dragon* (2001), and *The One* (2002) as well as coproducing his own syndicated action series alongside Mel Gibson. *The Matrix* begat two martial-arts-filled sequels while influencing such other kung-fu-flavored successes as *X-Men* (2000) and *Charlie's Angels* (2000).

But all that paled in comparison to the most unlikely yet most important American martial arts movie of the century. Many people would say that the most important and influential U.S.-produced kung-fu film was *Enter the Dragon*, but even that didn't slap the derogatory term of "chop-socky" out of cinema mainstreamers' mouths. Nor did it discourage even inveterate fans from referring to kung-fu movies as "karate flicks" (which is like calling football baseball—yes, it's still a sport, but totally different).

No one is calling *Crouching Tiger, Hidden Dragon* a chop-socky karate flick. It won the People's Choice Award at the prestigious Toronto International Film Festival, from among more than three hundred movies screened. It probably would have won the same award at the even more prestigious Cannes Film Festival if it had been an official entry (as it was, the jaded international audience burst into spontaneous applause within minutes of its start). It was honored as the official closing-day feature at the influential New York Film Festival. It was on virtually every top ten list and was nominated on every award program.

Who would have thought that a subtitled Mandarin romantic epic made by a man who had found international success with family dramas set in nineteenth-century England and twentieth-century American suburbs would be the one to make all film lovers take the martial arts genre seriously? And who would have thought that the renowned filmmaker would be the lone Taiwanese

261

native who refused to be pressured into making action movies by the sledgehammer Hong Kong powers-that-be.

He was the one who followed his heart and head to make such insightful and charming films as *Pushing Hands* (1992), *The Wedding Banquet* (1993), and *Eat Drink Man Woman* (1994). And he was the man who, when recruited by American studios, decided to make films in the Merchant/ Ivory and Robert Redford tradition, rather than be categorized as an "Asian filmmaker." The results were the surprising and stunningly effective *Sense and Sensibility* (1995) and *The Ice Storm* (1997).

Finally, after all that, Ang Lee tested the action waters with his underrated Civil War adventure *Ride With the Devil* (1999). With the weak box-office response to that film, one might imagine that Lee would return to the genre where he initially made his fame. Instead, he surprised everyone again by returning to China and making a mainland, Mandarin-language, Qing dynasty "flying swordsplay" *wu xia pian* (literally "martial chivalry film") with the unwieldy title of *Crouching Tiger, Hidden Dragon*.

He paid for that choice with a long, arduous production that was fraught with setbacks, including the exit of its original male star, Jet Li, due to a scheduling conflict. Li's loss was our gain and Chow Yun-fat's, too, as the great actor went through the same thing Keanu did on *The Matrix*, with the same teacher, Yuen Woo Ping. Further complicating matters was that both Chow and his costar, ex-Bond girl Michelle Yeoh, didn't know the source material's original language, Mandarin, which Ang insisted be spoken.

Sets burned down and blew away. Cast and crew froze, sweated, and got lost in the desert. Each shot was an agonizing trial of multiple languages and cross purposes. Not a frame was created with computerized digital effects. Instead, the actors were outfitted with thick cables and hoisted from construction cranes. Like human yo-yos they were lifted and thrown across ceilings, lakes, and trees— often to heights greater than sixty feet.

And when it was all over, after more than two years of intense work, only the most obtuse asked "How come they're flying?" Within a half hour of this magical entertainment, the audiences knew that the kung-fu warriors' bodies were doing what their hearts could not. Soar . . . leap . . . fly . . . fall.

One might again assume that this laborious oddity would only be embraced by Asian audiences and rejected by the rest of the world. Wrong: In the wake of the deservedly huge sword-and-sorcery hit *The Storm Riders* (1999) not to mention fifty-five years of literally thousands of *wu xia* novels and *wu xia pian*, Lee's labor of love was greeted with Asian appreciation, but not passion.

But European and then Canadian audiences were galvanized by the soaring images which embodied the powerful passions of the fabulous swordswomen, desert bandits, perverse villains, and heartsick martial arts masters who filled the film. Of course it didn't hurt that the beautiful Zhang Zi Yi was introduced to the world in an unforgettable starring role either.

The result is the first real kung-fu "art film," which allows even the most cynical and snobbish of cinephiles to enjoy the exhilaration we've been championing for years. While critics can celebrate the exceptional cinematography, musical score (running the gamut from pop singer Coco Lee to classical idol Yo Yo Ma), and acting, they can secretly thrill to the amazing bouts between Yeoh and Yi—and the sequence where the latter takes apart a tea house in true *Deadly Venoms* tradition.

It is a great kung-fu movie, a wonderful tragic romance, and simply a remarkable film made by an exceptionally courageous and dedicated filmmaker. It is the only movie that could fittingly finish this volume, and so it does.

My job is done.

January 2001

The Ultimate Martial Arts Movie Collection

ONE HUNDRED FILMS TO MAKE YOU A TRUE MARTIAL ARTS MOVIE MASTER

And remember: uncut, subtitled, and letterboxed-widescreen is best!

Liu Chia Liang

1. *Master Killer*—(H.K.: *The Thirty-Sixth Chamber of Shaolin*)—the first movie to show how these amazing Shaolin monks became supra-natural fighters.

2. *Legendary Weapons of Kung-fu*—(H.K.: *18 Legendary Weapons of China*)—still the quintessential martial arts movie, which introduced the top secret concept of the Mo Sha, the Chinese origins of the Japanese ninja.

3. *Challenge of the Ninja*—(H.K.: *Heroes of the East*)—a kung-fu *Kramer vs. Kramer* as a Chinese groom and Japanese bride test their skills against one another. Gives new meaning to the term *family feud*.

4. *Mad Monkey Kung-fu*—Involving tale of a wounded Liu Chia Liang teaching Hsaio Ho how to get revenge, monkey-style.

5. *Dirty Ho*—Some of the most imaginative fight scenes ever put to film highlight this tale of a street thief and undercover prince battling imperial court corruption.

6. *Executioners of Death*—(H.K.: *Executioners From Shaolin*)—Liu Chia Liang tells the tale of the Shaolin Temple's destruction and the betrayer's defeat, as only he can.

7. *My Young Auntie*—A kung-fu *My Fair Lady*, as a traditional small-town girl meets her Westernized nephew, and both battle to pre-vent an evil relative from claiming the family fortune.

8. *The Invincible Pole Fighter*—(H.K.: *Eight Diagram Pole Fighter*)—Liu Chia Liang's bleak, brutal, final Fu Sheng film.

Liu Chia Hui/Gordon Lui

9. *Fists and Guts*—Inexpensive, but fast and fun action helmed by brother Liu Chia Yung.

10. *He Has Nothing but Kung-fu*—Another cheap but fast-moving action comedy with that Liu Chia touch.

Chang Cheh

11. *Five Deadly Venoms*—Half kung-fu fantasy, half crime thriller, with a totally unforgettable premise: What if there were five masked, mythical animal fighters?

12. *Super Ninjas*—(H.K.: *Five Element Ninja*)—The ultimate comic-book movie, as the master of matter-of-fact mayhem pulls out all the stops in this battle between honorable Chinese and dirty rotten Japanese tricksters.

13. *House of Traps*—Gory goings-on in the title abode make for fascinating and fun viewing. Even the wildly overdone bloodshed isn't off-putting, since all the characters deal with it in such an "Okay, now what do I do?" manner.

14. *Kid With the Golden Arm*—So how do you defeat a man whose skin can't be pierced? Practice, my friends, practice.

15. *Mortal Combat*—Blind, deaf, and dumb (stupid, not speechless) fighters team with a man with metal feet to kill their tormentor. Wall-to-wall training and fight sequences.

Bruce flies above it all in The Big Boss/Fists of Fury.

16. *Masked Avengers*—A stunning display of weapons prowess as a team of heroes defeat a gang of killers at their own game—every one of them hurling eight-foot-long tridents back and forth like so many frisbees.

Bruce Lee

17. *The Chinese Connection*—(H.K.: *Fist of Fury*)—Arguably Bruce's best, most rounded, and effective film.

18. *Enter the Dragon*—King of the hill. Still works, probably always will.

19. *Return of the Dragon*—The most "Bruce" of them all. His baby all the way.

20. *Fists of Fury*—(H.K.: *The Big Boss*)—Crude and lewd, but unforgettable once Lee starts strutting his acting chops and fighting skills.

Jackie Chan

21. *Project A*—Brought the kung-fu film kicking and screaming into the twentieth century.

22. *Police Story*—Revolutionized the modern martial arts movie and still has the best shopping-mall battle ever conceived.

23. *Drunken Master 2*—Speed, complexity, and emotion don't get better than this in the final fight sequence—and the rest of the movie is pretty darn good, too.

24. *Project A 2*—Jackie's most obvious homage to the films of Buster Keaton and his last real stab at complex screenwriting.

25. *Drunken Master*—The movie that cemented Jackie's superstardom and perfected his brand of kung-fu comedy. Chan's energy and desire to please has never been greater.

26. *Young Master*—Jackie's final word on the kind of kung-fu comedy that made him famous. Plot? Who needs plot? Just watch as Chan juggles fans, swords, pipes, and skirts instead.

27. *Police Story 2*—Solid, involving work from all concerned—but things were getting just a trifle taken for granted right about now.

28. *Rush Hour*—A deceptively ingratiating crowd pleaser. Jackie's sweet-and-sour chemistry with motor mouth Chris Tucker delighted and satisfied all races, ages, and sexes.

264

Sammo Hung

29. *Eastern Condors*—Every war movie cliché imaginable, but once *The Dirty Dozen* meets *You Only Live Twice* ending hits, you won't care.

30. *The Magnificent Butcher*—Classic Sammo in a tale of Huang Fei Hong's famous fat student. Comedy, tragedy, romance, unrequited love, and incredible kung-fu—all on a razor's edge.

31. *Pedicab Driver*—Hung's last "Real Sammo" movie, with some show-stopping sequences. It came too late for his alienated Hong Kong audiences, but not for appreciative Western eyes.

32. *Encounters of the Spooky Kind*—Dueling sorcerers, laughs, and frights combined to create bigger goose bumps, and, of course, amazing kung-fu as only Sammo can do it.

33. *Encounters of the Spooky Kind II*—Not interested in the patent Chinese brand of gorgeous lovelorn ghosts, funky monsters, and warring Taoist shamans? Let Sammo make it easy on you in this fight-filled spook saga.

Tomisaburo Wakayama cuts through armies in the Baby Cart *movies.*

Legendary villain Shih Kien claws his way out of Enter the Dragon.

Yuen Baio

34. *Prodigal Son*—A classic directed by Sammo Hung, with a spoiled rich kid learning humility and wing chun excellence. Watch for the standout performance of Lam Ching Ying as an asthmatic wu dan specialist.

35. *Righting Wrongs*—*Death Wish* meets *Dirty Harry* as barrister Yuen Baio takes on homicidal police corruption, with a bloody vengeance.

36. *Kickboxer*—Yuen returns to the role of Huang Fei Hong's student in this, one of his last solo kung-fu action comedies. Lots of funs and fights.

37. *Knockabouts*—More brilliantly likable early Sammo, featuring Yuen Baio in one of his most delightful performances.

Jackie, Sammo, and Yuen

38. *Dragons Forever*—The trio's final word in martial arts action. The Japanese weren't crazy about it. You will be.

39. *Wheels on Meals*—The best of the trio's bunch. The final fight with Keith Vitale and, especially, Benny "the Jet" Urquidez, is a classic.

40. *Winners and Sinners*—The movie which started it all, with a standout roller-skating sequence.

Toshiro Mifune, the "Japanese John Wayne."

Jet Li

41. *Fist of Legend*—Jet's politically correct, more balanced version of *The Chinese Connection*, and his last word in "hard" kung-fu.

42. *Once Upon a Time in China 2*—Although a sequel, it even outranks the original in plot, character, romance, and action.

43. *Once Upon a Time in China*—Huang Fei Hong is reborn for a new generation as a powerful, politically savvy healer.

44. *Shaolin Temple*—The classic classic of mainland martial arts mastery.

45. *Shaolin Temple 2*—More charm and humor than the original, though less plot, but just as much authentic action.

46. *Shaolin Temple 3*—Liu Chia Liang nearly dances with joy at being able to choreograph hundreds of kung-fu masters, and it shows. The greatest martial arts you'll ever see in the Forbidden City or on the Great Wall.

Donnie Yen

47. *Iron Monkey*—Starting as a Huang Fei Hong rip-off but ending as one of the great screen kung-fu adventures.

John Woo

48. *The Killer*—An immoral cop versus a moral hit man in a riveting cinematic dance of death, complete with one of the greatest climatic black-comedy moments in movie history.

49. *A Better Tomorrow*—A bullet-splattered fever-dream on the nature of brotherhood, as a honest triad gangster tries to gain the forgiveness of his bitter policeman brother. The film that deservedly made Chow Yun-Fat a superstar.

50. *Bullet in the Head*—The director's masterpiece of brotherhood and betrayal set in 1970s Saigon, as three friends are (literally) torn apart by power, greed, and desperation. The creation and execution of the "title character" separates the men from the boys.

51. *A Better Tomorrow 2*—An insane sequel (sometimes literally), featuring a fiery climactic attack on the villains' lair, where white-suited gunsels are mowed down like so many clowns falling out of circus Volkswagens.

Chow Yun-Fat

52. *God of Gamblers*—*Rain Man* meets *The Cincinnati Kid* meets *Lethal Weapon*, as a supreme cards-man regresses into amnesia before wreaking vengeance on his enemies. A masterpiece of action acting.

53. *Tiger on Beat*—Kung-fu meets "gun-fu" as cowardly cop Chow teams with Conan Lee to battle bad guys. Watch out for the "shotgun yo-yo" and dueling chainsaws finale.

Michelle Yeoh

54. *Yes, Madam*—Probably the best all-around woman warrior pic. Now if only someone would release a "director's cut" with all the excised action returned to its rightful place.

55. *Heroic Trio*—The best superheroines movie Marvel Comics never made.

56. *Wing Chun*—Though the plot is just a little too silly, there's no faulting Yuen Woo Ping's action and Michelle's charisma.

Yukari Oshima

57. *Outlaw Brothers*—Delightful plotting and exceptional martial arts make up for a sour ending. Otherwise, a most entertaining time.

58. *Angel*—Cheap, tacky, down and dirty, but it has Moon Lee versus Yukari, and that's all anyone really needs.

Fantasy

59. *A Chinese Ghost Story*—A gorgeous ghost promised to "the big evil" by a three thousand-year-old unisex tree demon with a thousand-foot-long tongue, and a break-dancing warrior-priest with a magic sword who can blast bombs out of his arms like a battleship's ack-ack guns. You'll never forget this one!

60. *Mr. Vampire*—The vampire legend started, like so many things, in China, and this wonderful action comedy plumbs the depth of the myth. It also introduces two great antagonists: the Taoist feng shui expert known as the Priest With One Eyebrow, and the unforgettable hopping blood-suppers known as *gyonshi*.

The Chinese could have an astonishing team of high-kicking Rockettes, if Hsia Kuang Li (right) is any evidence. She's the other pair of The Incredible Kung Fu Legs.

"Master Killer" Liu Chia Hui.

61. *Bride With White Hair*—One of the greatest fantasy films ever made, with star-crossed lovers, an intersexual Siamese-twin villain(s), and one of the funniest death scenes ever dared.

Swordplay

62. *Zu Warriors of the Magic Mountain*—Edited like a comic book, with demons and demigods bouncing around like pinballs, as the forces of good and evil slug it out for the fate of the human race. A real eyeful, wherein the color red is the main bad guy.

63. *Duel to the Death*—Hordes of exploding ninja highlight this stunning tale of the centennial battle between Japan and China's greatest martial artists, all capped with a climax that is literally earth shaking.

ETC

64. *Naked Killer*—The supremely sexy Chingmy Yau gets caught between two warring lesbian hit women in this incomparable Category-3 thriller.

Kwan Tik Hing returns to the role of Huang Fei Hong in The Magnificent Butcher *during a dazzling "calligraphy" fight sequence.*

65. *Seventh Curse*—Ridiculous, silly, gory, and sexy, this "anything goes" action horror film features loads of action as well as a bazooka-touting Chow Yun-Fat featured as the sci-fi author and adventurer known as Wisely.

66. *The Invincible Kung-fu Legs/The Leg Fighters*—One of the talented Korean kicker Tan Tao Liang's best films, where the title says it all. Wall to wall high steppin'.

67. *Ninja in the Deadly Trap*—Shaw Brothers Lite: the remnants of Chang Cheh's second team reunite for their own handmade film, featuring the mighty Shoji Kurata as a ninja master.

68. *Hitman in the Hand of Buddha*—World-class kicker Hwang Jang Lee's one major starring role. Worth the dross of a plot just to watch him in action.

Billy Chong

69. *A Fistful of Talons*—Billy's classiest film, directed on a grand scale by the underrated Sun Chung and featuring top kicker Whang Ing Sik.

70. *Kung-fu From Beyond the Grave*—Insane, stupid, but wonderful. Must be seen *not* to be believed.

71. *Crystal Fist*—Billy makes the best Jackie Chan "clone," showing that even rip-offs of *Drunken Master* can be vastly entertaining in their own right.

72. *Super Power*—Another Jackie Chan rip-off, but if they were all this good, it wouldn't matter.

Yung Wang Yu

73. *Dirty Kung-fu*—Yung Wang Yu was being groomed as the "new Fu Sheng" and showed a lot of charm. Even though he never quite scaled the heights, he left a lot of fine entertainment behind.

74. *The Young Avenger*—Another try at establishing Yu as Fu Sheng's successor. Hong Kong never bought it, but their loss is our gain.

Casanova Wong

75. *The Master Strikes*—Another kung-fu take on *Rain Man*, as a bodyguard is driven insane by betrayal. Wong is an incredible talent, but disappeared after only a handful

Wu Ma essays the Taoist superpriest in A Chinese Ghost Story.

Two of the Five Masters of Death: the great Wang Lung Wai (left) battles one of his favorite fellow actors, Fu Sheng.

of promising films, making each of them even more notable.

76. *Story of the Drunken Master*—A *Drunken Master* rip-off, but with the real Drunken Master, Simon Yuen. Add the great Wong and lovely Yang Pan Pan and you've got a good time for all.

David Chiang, Lily Li

77. *The Bloody Tattoo*—Chiang and Li try to recapture some of the fun and fights of the Shaw Brothers' golden era in this independently produced gem. The plot is secondary to the imaginative choreography, which was designed to show off everyone's best attributes.

78. *The Deadly Challenger*—Ranging from the truly amusing to the downright silly, this standard story of a fighter trying to show everyone who's best is elevated by great fighting, and plenty of it.

The Streetfighter

79. *The Streetfighter Collector's Edition*—An Adam's apple being torn out, teeth flying everywhere, an X-ray image of a hand going through a skull into the brain—it's all here in glorious, unedited color as Shinichi "Sonny" Chiba growls and spits through his greatest role.

80. *Return of the Streetfighter*—More mayhem and gore in the great Sonny Chiba tradition.

Akira Kurosawa

81. *Seven Samurai*—The magnificent epic which inspired *The Magnificent Seven*.

82. *Yojimbo*—The brilliant minimalist classic which inspired everything from *A Fistful of Dollars* to *Last Man Standing*.

83. *Kagemusha*—One of the most gloriously colorful movies ever made, as well as probably the best Japanese war movie.

84. *Ran*—The genius director's feudal, war-torn, Nippon version of *King Lear*, gloriously realized.

Zatoichi

85. *Zatoichi's Cane Sword*—Who has the strong-

The ultimate confrontation between Chinese and Japanese martial arts came in Golden Harvest's visually splendid Duel to the Death.

est sword in all of Japan? Not the wandering gambler-masseuse, who must battle without a blade when a deadly crack appears in his weapon.

86. *Zatoichi and the Chess Master*—Has the deceptively humble swordsman met his match in an evil genius of strategy? Don't count on it.

87. *Zatoichi and the Fugitives*—Some razzle-dazzle swordplay as masseuse Ichi discovers the power of the gun for the first time—but it doesn't slow him down for long.

88. *Zatoichi Meets His Equal*—An extremely rare coproduction in which the Japanese blind swordsman meets Jimmy Wang Yu's Chinese one-armed swordsman. Jarring in the clash of styles but endlessly entertaining.

Lone Wolf and Cub

89. *Baby Cart in the Land of Demons*—The Japanese feudal society gets lambasted in this terrific action classic, as an entire clan hurls itself at Itto Ogami so he will kill their illegitimate four-year-old leader.

90. *Baby Cart to Hades*—Itto Ogami marches around a corner—and an entire army is waiting for him. Guess what? He kills them all. Incredible.

Son of Black Mass

91. *Trail of Traps*—Pretty much just what the title says. Kyoshiro Nemuri wants to see what's what, and everybody wants to stop him—but they didn't count on his deadly full moon cut.

92. *The Human Tarantula*—Kyoshiro Nemuri happily faces off against two illegitimate children of the shogun—the blood-frenzied daughter and her brother, the master poisoner.

Razor Hanzo

93. *Sword of Justice 2: The Snare*—Someone high up in the feudal government is using novice nuns as sex slaves. This looks like a job for Tokyo's most savage cop.

94. *Sword of Justice 3*—More sexual torture, more razor-sharp blades plunged into knees and elbows, more "fun" with feudal Tokyo's most unforgiving investigator.

Chuck Norris

95. *Code of Silence*—Chuck's one "classy" action film, helmed by Andrew *The Fugitive* Davis. If only Norris had decided to stay on the "high road."

96. *The Octagon*—Probably Chuck's best martial arts movie (outside of *Return of the Dragon*, of course).

Steven Seagal

97. *Above the Law*—Discounting the rushed, perfunctory climax, a really cool aikido action picture, ably delivered by action expert Andrew Davis.

98. *Under Siege*—Andrew Davis does it again, directing the aikido ace through his best "big" action pic.

Jean-Claude Van Damme

99. *Bloodsport*—Predictable, unbelievable, derivative, and not even particularly well choreographed, but somehow it hits the right buttons.

100. *Maximum Risk*—A little too chatty and slow moving, but director Ringo Lam handles what action there is with verve, and costar Natasha Henstridge is a welcome eyeful.

270

HONORABLE MENTIONS: FIFTY MORE TO GROW ON

Liu Chia Liang

1. *Instructors of Death* (H.K.: *Martial Club*)—A Huang Fei Hong film capped with an amazing Wang Lung Wai vs. Liu Chia Hui fight.

2. *The Lady Is the Boss*—A reversal of *My Young Auntie*, with Kara Hui Ying Hung as a modern girl and Liu Chia Liang clinging to the past.

3. *Operation Scorpio*—Sammo Hung produced this throwback to the Shaw Brothers' style with fine satire and exceptional kung-fu.

4. *Deadly Mantis*—Liang's most insidious story, where the hero turns out be the villain. A brilliant action rumination on Chinese history.

5. *Challenge of the Masters*—Liang's first Huang Fei Hong tale.

Chang Cheh

6. *Chinatown Kid*—A tacky modern thriller set in San Francisco, featuring the amazing Fu Sheng.

7. *Five Masters of Death*—The aftermath of the Shaolin Temple's destruction, with Ti Lung, David Chiang, and Fu Sheng.

8. *Spearmen of Death*—The incredibly versatile "second team" struts their stuff, only this time with long, heavy spears and killer flags!

9. *The Destroyers*—Patriots vs. Manchus, second team–style. Plot? No. Fights? Yes!

10. *Shanghai 13*—Chang's fortieth anniversary film. Cheap, tacky, and hardly more than a TV movie, but where else can you see Cheh's three teams fighting each other?

Jackie Chan

11. *Fearless Hyena*—Jackie's version of *Drunken Master* and *Eagle's Shadow*. His first exuberant fully-credited directing job.

12. *Eagle's Shadow* (H.K.: *Snake in the Eagle's Shadow*)—The first formative stab at superstardom.

13. *Supercop* (H.K.: *Police Story 3: Supercop*)—Michelle Yeoh matches Chan move for move, stunt for stunt.

14. *Dragon Lord*—The best "street-style" kung-fu ever filmed.

15. *Rumble in the Bronx*—Jackie's successful

Even water isn't safe from the savage choppers in Tsui Hark's The Blade.

assault on American sensibilities.

16. *"Operation Condor Two"*; *Armour of God*—Retitled for an American video release, this prequel to *Operation Condor* becomes its sequel in name only. In any case, it shows how Jackie Chan can come back from an opening-sequence on-set broken skull to create a fight-filled finale par excellence.

Sammo Hung

17. *Pantyhose Hero*—Bigoted, stereotypical "comedy," but whoa, those fights!

18. *Skinny Tiger, Fatty Dragon*—Sexist, cheap, derivative, but whoa, those fights!

19. *Millionaires Express* (a.k.a. *Noble Express*)—Lurching plot, but whoa, those stunts and fights!

Yuen Baio

20. *Dreadnaught*—One of the last Huang Fei Hong films starring Kwan Tak Hing, featuring Yuen as the plot's linchpin.

A blind dance of death ensues as the wandering masseuse and gambler uses his cane sword to mow down enemies in Zatoichi and a Chest of Gold.

Jackie, Sammo, Yuen

21. *My Lucky Stars* (U.S.: *Winners and Sinners*)—No Yuen, but a great Jackie roller-skating sequence.

22. *Twinkle, Twinkle Lucky Stars*—Andy Lau shows up for a second, and Jackie gets wounded, but Sammo shines.

Jet Li

23. *Fong Sai Yuk*—Too much comedy and wire-assisted stunts, but when the man moves, watch out!

24. *Fong Sai Yuk 2*—More action, so more better.

25. *The Tai Chi Master*—Too much plot and wires, but the last half-hour cooks.

26. *Once Upon a Time in China 3*—Silly and overblown, but still epic and watchable.

John Woo

27. *Hard-Boiled*—Woo's final Hong Kong film, fittingly filled with the kind of overblown action he's loved for.

Chow Yun-Fat

28. *The Postman Strikes Back*—Extremely rare, extremely effective period kung-fu effort from the admitted non–martial artist.

29. *Full Contact*—Director Ringo Lam's best "John Woo Lite" thriller, with a climax where the camera follows the bullets into people's heads.

30. *God of Gamblers Returns*—Sometimes stunningly sadistic, sometimes annoyingly silly, but almost always effective.

31. *Treasure Hunt*—Chow's Hong Kong "farewell" film, combining all of his other movie's genres. A great action–sci-fi–comedy-romance film!

Tsui Hark

32. *The Blade*—Hark's remake of the classic Shaw Brothers' *One-Armed Swordsman* in

272

the style of mainland China. Incredible hacking, slashing—and flying bear-traps!

33. *Peking Opera Blues*—A wonderfully colorful action comedy adventure with three of Hong Kong's most beautiful actresses: Brigette Lin, Cherie Chung, and Sally Yeh.

Michelle Yeoh

34. *Royal Warriors*—Great beginning, sizzling middle, over-the-top ending.

35. *Magnificent Warriors*—Sometimes eye-filling, sometimes silly, but Michelle is in there kicking.

36. *Project S: Once a Cop*—Michelle continues her mainland cop character from Jackie's *Supercop*.

Swordplay

37. *Swordsman 2*—Jet Li explodes in this crazy, gender-bending eyeful.

38. *Bastard Swordsman*—A terrific Shaw Brothers fantasy with a hero who can spin cocoons.

Zatoichi

39. *Zatoichi's Fire Festival*—Lots of flames and flashing blades.

40. *Zatoichi in Desperation*—Particularly sadistic installment, with the blind swordsman's palms pierced. But does that stop him? Hardly.

41. *Zatoichi Meets Yojimbo*—Toshiro Mifune both battles against and with our hero. Longer, more sedate, but much more classy, too.

Lone Wolf and Cub

42. *Baby Cart on the River Styx*—A half-naked, tattooed swordswoman starts slicing.

43. *Baby Cart 6: White Heaven in Hell*—Itto Ogami hacks ninja on skis as well as zombies. Go figure.

Son of Black Mass

44. *Castle Menagerie*—Will Kyoshiro Nemuri survive a palace of traps? Could Bruce Lee cha-cha?

Chuck Norris

45. *Delta Force*—Chuck and Lee Marvin kick skyjacking terrorist butt.

46. *Missing in Action*—Chuck breaks out of 'Nam.

Steven Seagal

47. *Hard to Kill*—Like it says: even after seven years in a coma, he's at his aikido best.

48. *Out for Justice*—Don't get cornered in a tenement kitchen by the aikido ace. It gets messy.

Jean-Claude Van Damme

49. *Hard Target*—The John Woo touches that manage to survive the final edit make it worth watching.

50. *Sudden Death*—Well, we had to finish this list with something, didn't we?

Steven Seagal proves it in movie after movie: he's Hard to Kill.

Appendix: Sources

Tell them I sent you!
www.thebestonly.com
1/888/RICSTUF

Tai Seng Video Marketing
170 S. Spruce Ave., Suite 200
S. San Francisco, CA 94080
(800) 888-3836

The Forty-Third Chamber
681 8th Ave.
New York, NY 10036
(212) 582-8685

JARS Video Collectibles
(718) 456-0663
Fax: (718) 631-6549

Video Action/Chambara Video
708 1st Ave.
Los Angeles, CA 90012
(800) 422-2241

Samurai Video
P.O. Box 372
Suffern, NY 10901

We know that being a true martial arts movie fan can be a lonely, misunderstood vocation. Feel free to write (clearly and kindly) with any questions or comments—but be sure to include a self-addressed, stamped envelope if you want an answer!

Ric Meyers
The Story Co.
P.O. Box 885
Southport, CT 06490

ABOUT THE AUTHOR

Ric Meyers has been called "America's foremost expert on Asian action movies" by the *Boston Globe* and "one of the men most responsible for the importation of Hong Kong films to America" by international film authority Peter Chow. Generally considered the dean of martial arts film experts because of his pioneering work in the field, Meyers first brought the genre to the American public's attention with his groundbreaking book *Martial Arts Movies: From Bruce Lee to the Ninja*, published by Citadel Press in 1985.

Millions more were made aware of the genre's thrills when Meyers inspired and contributed to several Asian movie episodes of *The Incredibly Strange Film Show*, shown on the Discovery cable channel. He went on to appear on the Bruce Lee and Jackie Chan episodes of *Biography* on the Arts and Entertainment cable channel. Presently he writes film columns for both *Inside Kung-fu* and *Asian Cult Cinema* magazines. He is also the coauthor of *The Encyclopedia of Martial Arts Movies* and cocreator of *Jackie Chan's Spartan X* comic book. In 1998, he was inducted into the World Martial Arts Hall of Fame for "Outstanding Contributions to the Martial Art Movie Industry."

Outside the genre, Meyers was twice nominated for the Mystery Writers of America Edgar Award for his nonfiction books *TV Detectives* and *Murder on the Air*. His book *For One Week Only: The World of Exploitation Films* inspired a British television miniseries of the same name, and *The Great Science-Fiction Films* was cited by *The Encyclopedia of Science Fiction*. His novels include *Doomstar*, *Dragon Rising*, *The Kohga Ritual*, *Fear Itself*, and *Murder in Halruaa*.

Meyers continues to celebrate the joys of martial arts movies by hosting kung-fu film festivals around the country every year. He has no social life, and lives in Connecticut.

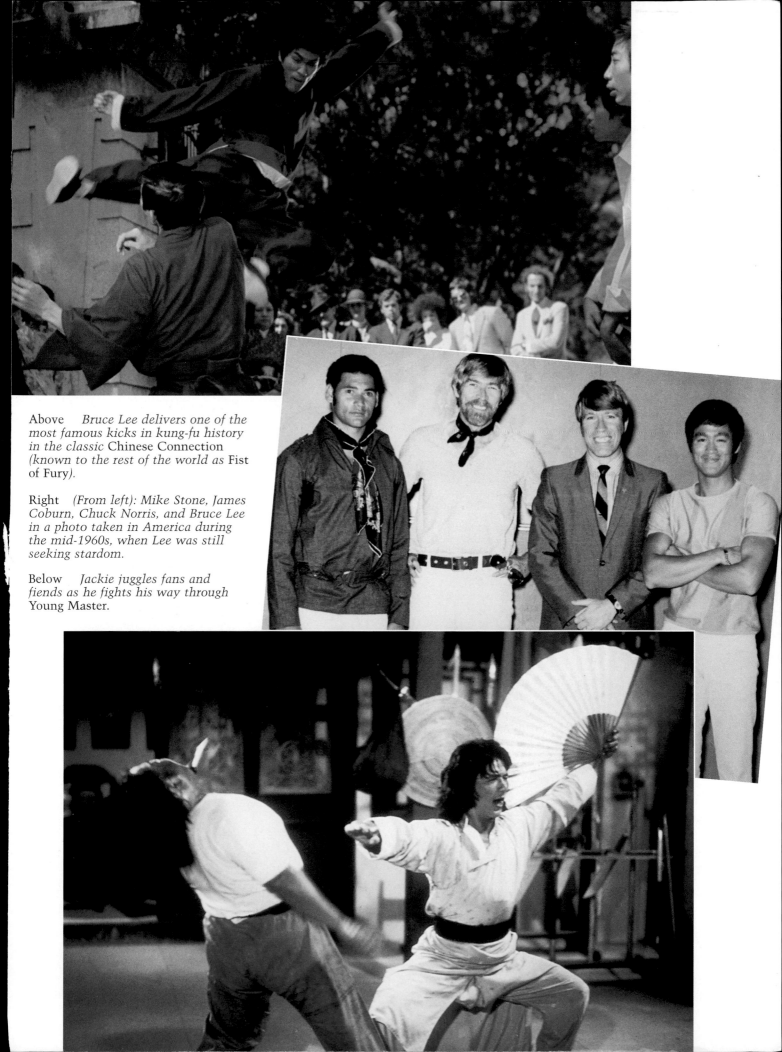

Above *Bruce Lee delivers one of the most famous kicks in kung-fu history in the classic* Chinese Connection *(known to the rest of the world as* Fist of Fury*).*

Right *(From left): Mike Stone, James Coburn, Chuck Norris, and Bruce Lee in a photo taken in America during the mid-1960s, when Lee was still seeking stardom.*

Below *Jackie juggles fans and fiends as he fights his way through* Young Master.

Above   *Scene not seen: the closing sequence in the Japanese version of* Police Story *shows the mall-battle's aftermath, with a bruised Jackie (center, with girlfriend Maggie Cheung) handcuffed along with witness Brigette Lin (far left).*

Below   *Scene not seen 2: Andy Lau (far left) appears with Jackie and Yuen (far right) in this sequence edited out of* Twinkle, Twinkle Lucky Stars.

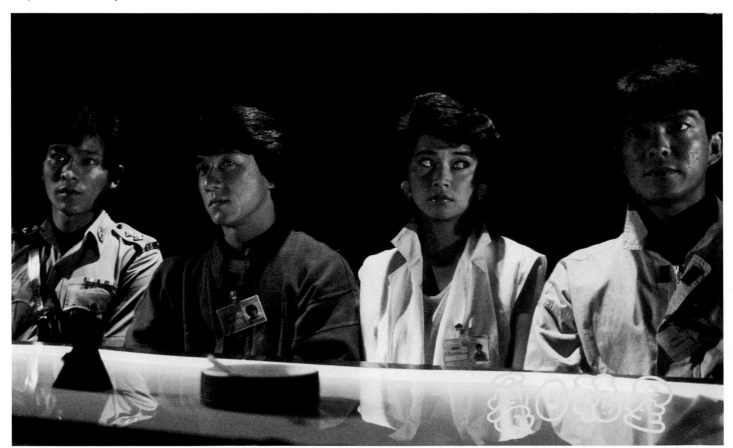

Above *The fateful
opening sequence from*
Armour of God—*note
the ear-exposing hair-
style, which the super-
stitious crew blamed for
Jackie's accident. The
hair miraculously grew
in time for every subse-
quent scene.*

Right *Fast action from
the* Project A II *battle
royal.*

Left *Vincent Lyn (left) and Jackie take a breather during the agonizing wind-tunnel sequence in* Operation Condor.

Below *Jackie and the* Operation Condor *cast and crew try to stay cool in the one-hundred-degree-plus temperatures on location in the Sahara.*

Above   *Vincent Lyn would kick Yukari Oshima a mile for a camel in this shot from* Outlaw Brothers.

Above Left   *A true sign of American stardom—a page from Jackie Chan's own comic book,* Spartan X: The Armor of Heaven, *published by Image Comics in 1998.*

Below right   *Despite wearing an explosive-filled vest, Michelle kicks her way out of* Supercop.

Above   *Brigitte Lin is the delightfully dangerous* Bride With White Hair.

Top *Sammo and Kenny Bee (right) blast away with a urine-cooled Gatling gun (see the movie!) in* Millionaire's Express.

Above *Chow Yun-Fat as audiences know him best: bloodied but unbowed, fists full of "gun-fu."*

Left *The great Donnie Yen does what he does best in* The Kung-fu Master.

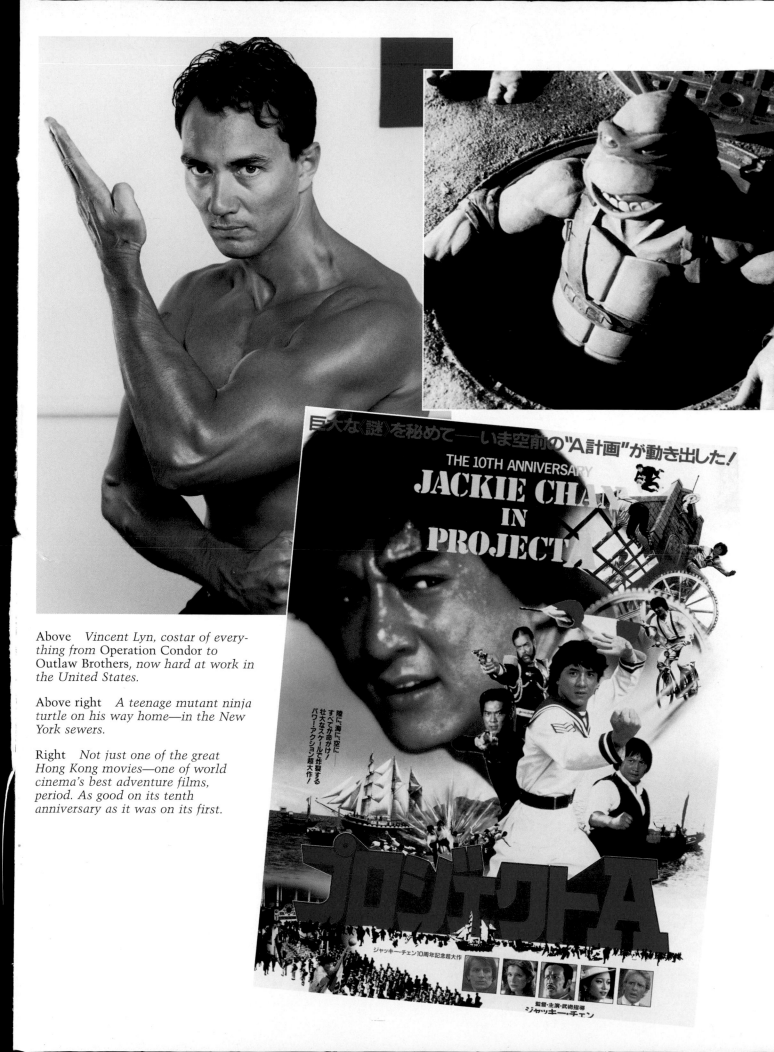

Above   Vincent Lyn, costar of everything from Operation Condor to Outlaw Brothers, now hard at work in the United States.

Above right   A teenage mutant ninja turtle on his way home—in the New York sewers.

Right   Not just one of the great Hong Kong movies—one of world cinema's best adventure films, period. As good on its tenth anniversary as it was on its first.

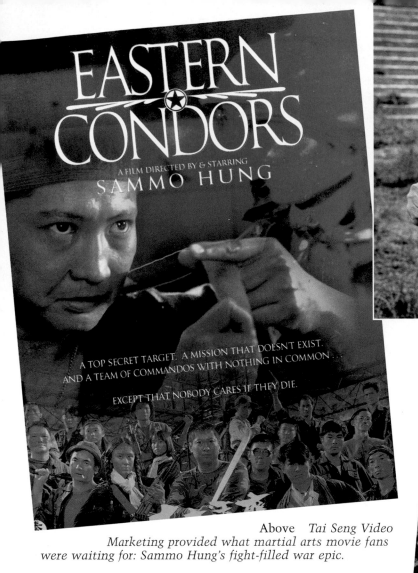

Above   Tai Seng Video
Marketing provided what martial arts movie fans were waiting for: Sammo Hung's fight-filled war epic.

Below   The big three from Twinkle, Twinkle Lucky Stars: Jackie Chan, Andy Lau, and Yuen Baio.

Top right   Yuen Baio at his best—starring in one of Sammo Hung's most brilliant and satisfying films, The Prodigal Son.

Above   Toshiro Mifune shines in Akira Kurasawa's legendary classic, Seven Samurai.